Dedication

To my amazing wife, Alisha. Your support, encouragement, and love have strengthened me in this new adventure of writing. I'm so grateful for your heart for the Lord, His Word, our family, and the ministry. It is the privilege of my life to serve the Lord with you. You make the ministry even more enjoyable and I'm excited for all the memories that we will share together serving our Saviour. Proverbs 19:14 says, *"...a prudent wife is from the LORD."* There is no doubt that God has graciously gifted me with the privilege to be your husband. I love you!

VOLUME 2

One Great Truth for Your Daily Walk

365 Bible truths for every day of the year

STEVEN BECKER

Table of Contents

A Word from the Author

Dear Friend,

Every Christian must develop a one-on-one walk with the Lord. However, most will struggle with the consistency of a daily walk. Partly, this inconsistency is due to how we view the Bible as we read it. We can view it more as a textbook, not a personal letter. The Bible was given to speak to our minds and also to our hearts so that we may apply its truths to our lives.

When I became a pastor, I asked another pastor I greatly respect about expository preaching (verse-by-verse study). Ashamedly, I thought this might be less exciting of an approach than a different style of teaching. I was convicted. This preacher told me, "I spend the first part of my message talking about the text. Then, as I near the final part of my message, I tell our people, 'here is one great truth that you can take away from this passage.'"

I believe every passage of the Bible has a truth that can be taken and applied to your life. This devotional is to show just some of those truths throughout your daily reading. This is not to tell you what truth God wants you to learn specifically. He may speak to you about something completely different, but my desire is that it will be a help in understanding various passages and to shine a light on some of the wonderful lessons in God's Word. I pray that this is a blessing to you and an aid in your walk with Him.

In His Service,
Pastor Steven Becker

The Battle Begins

Read Genesis 1–3

"READY. SET. GO." The race begins. You've decided to get in the race. You've probably even made a commitment that you will finish your race. That first decision is vital, because you cannot finish a race until you start the race. As you read your Bible and walk with the Lord, you are beginning not only your race, but also your battle.

As we read the book of Genesis, it doesn't take long for that serpent to appear. God doesn't give us books upon books, stories upon stories, and chapters upon chapters of bliss and joy in the perfection that God created. In fact, just as soon as everything was created and laid in store, Satan is introduced. Chapter 3 begins, *"Now the serpent...."*

Whatever you set out to do for God in your life—and I do hope that you have a desire to do something for God in this life—expect the serpent to show up. Did you know that 92 percent of people who make a commitment in the new year fail by February? Certainly, many reasons exist for this colossal drop off, but much can be attributed to the fact that they were not ready for the battle.

Those who expect a battle will prepare for battle. Soldiers prepare their weapons, their battle armor, their plan of attack, etc. Practical preparation is important, but we must also prepare mentally. So much of what we battle lies within the battle of the mind. Let me encourage you by saying that the battle is worth fighting. I'd rather be fighting in the battle than rotting on the bleachers.

—— Today's Truth ——

Are you prepared for the battle that lies before you? God has given us help in every area of life to assist us in our battles if we take the time and effort to go to Him for the help we need.

The Right Sacrifice

Read Genesis 4–6

THE FIRST ACT of sin, aside from the fall of man, is between two siblings. If you're a sibling, you can relate. Brother and sisters drive each other crazy. Human nature is selfish, and when you put young children in one room, some contention will undoubtedly arise. However, as heated as things might get, it is difficult to imagine killing your sibling.

Cain was so furious at Abel—not because Abel did anything wrong, but because Cain's sacrifice was rejected by God and Abel's was received. Instead of drawing focus on the sin, I'd like you to see what made Abel's sacrifice the one that the Lord accepted. In the end, God wants us all to sacrifice ourselves to Him, and we must be the right sacrifice He wants.

Little detail is given regarding Abel's sacrifice, though it does have significance, but the heart of the application is the fact that Abel gave God what pleased God, not Abel.

Too many "Christians" try to give God sacrifices that do not please Him. They throw the name of Jesus into their worldly lifestyles and tell people they are surrendered to Him when the Bible clearly teaches against that in which they are involved. Just because you give God something doesn't mean He is going to accept it. Have you ever given a child a carrot? If I gave my children what truly pleased them, they'd have desserts and junk food for dinner, because that's what pleases them. God is not looking for you to live your life how you want and give Him what you think He should have. Do you know what the Bible says the Lord wants you to give to Him?

—— Today's Truth ——

Give God what He wants, not what pleases you. You were not created for yourself, but for His pleasure; and you can please Him by giving Him what He has commanded in His Word.

All I Really Need to Know
I Learned from Noah's Ark

Read Genesis 7–9

A MAN NAMED Robert Fulghum wrote a book of essays on life called *All I Really Need to Know I Learned in Kindergarten.* Many created similar lists as spinoffs. This one is entitled, "All I Really Need to Know I Learned from Noah's Ark."

1. Don't miss the boat.
2. When you commit, don't turn back. God closed the door, and it stayed closed.
3. Remember that we are all in the same boat.
4. Plan ahead. It wasn't raining when Noah built the ark.
5. Stay fit. When you're 600 years old, someone may ask you to do something really big.
6. Don't listen to critics. Just finish the job that needs to get done.
7. Build your future on high ground.
8. For safety's sake, travel in pairs.
9. Speed isn't everything. The snails were on the same ark as the cheetahs.
10. When you're stressed, just float awhile.
11. Don't be too quick to judge. Noah got drunk afterward, but have you ever been on a boat with that many animals and fewer than ten people to clean up after them?
12. Remember the ark was built by amateurs, and the Titanic was built by professionals.
13. No matter the storm, when you're with God, there's always a rainbow waiting.

—— Today's Truth ——

Noah's ark is a timeless story that reminds us that God rewards faithfulness, hates sins, keeps His promises, and reminds us of His love for all mankind.

Making a Name for Yourself

Read Genesis 10–12

SOME NAMES REQUIRE no description or explanation. Names like Abraham Lincoln, Michael Jordan, Bill Gates, Christopher Columbus, and others throughout human history are so widely known that their name alone makes us think of what they accomplished or who they were, whether good or bad.

The people in Genesis 11 decided to build what we know as the Tower of Babel. What was the reason for this construction project? Genesis 11:4 gives their motive: *"And they said, Go to, let us build us a city and a tower, whose top may reach unto heaven; and let us make a name, lest we be scattered abroad upon the face of the whole earth."* Their reasoning for building this tower was driven by fear, but fear is a close relative to pride in our lives.

Are you concerned that your name will be recognized while you live or that it will be remembered after you die? The desire for recognition is something we may modestly tell people we don't enjoy, but it sure makes us feel good when our good deeds are noticed. As shy as I was, when I played basketball and my name was announced over the loud speakers in the gymnasium, it felt pretty good, even if it was just temporary. Whether you need to feel recognized for your accomplishments at your job or the hard work you do on a daily basis at home, ask yourself this: do you find more fulfillment in the actual work you do or only in the recognition for that work?

While we all should strive to leave a legacy for others to follow, is it the impact you'll leave behind that consumes you or simply the memory and praise of your name that motivates you? Living for your name will always provide the same results. Disappointment is inevitable because you were not created to be uplifted and praised, but to bring God glory.

—— Today's Truth ——

Point others to Jesus. Don't worry about your name being recognized or remembered. It's not about you. Only one name deserves praise.

Uncle Abraham to the Rescue

Read Genesis 13–15

AT SOME POINT in life, we are all in need of saving. Our greatest need, of course, is the need for our sin-sick soul to be saved by the blood of Jesus Christ; but in this life, you may drift away, lose purpose, or simply fall into sin. In this passage, Lot was that man. Having chosen to dwell in Sodom, Lot got in a heap of trouble he hadn't anticipated. A war was taking place, and Lot was taken captive.

Your first response when you read this story may be the same as mine: "Well, he got himself in this mess. He deserves every bit of what is happening." Truth be told, we think this about the people around us who reap the fruit of the seeds of sin they have sown.

While this all may be true, it is also true that every person will be in this place at some point in their life. You will find that you can hardly recall how you reached the place where you find yourself. Sin does work gradually, but in many ways, it also works so quickly.

Despite Lot's failures, Abraham still loved his nephew and came to the rescue. Genesis 14:14 says, *"And when Abram heard that his brother was taken captive, he armed his trained servants, born in his own house, three hundred and eighteen, and pursued them unto Dan."* Lot was still a "brother" to Abraham. He meant something to him, even though he fell. He was worth investing time into his life. He was worth sacrificing himself and those around him, even if it meant there was a possibility that Lot could be restored.

—— Today's Truth ——

All people mean something to God. If Jesus found us worth coming to this world and dying on a cross, we must do the same for others in the times when they need an Abraham to come to the rescue.

Secret Agent Christianity

Read Genesis 16–18

Perhaps you've played the group game "Mafia." The whole premise of the game is deception. The better you are at appearing to be something you're not, or the better you are at convincing people you really are something (whether it's true or a lie), the more likely you are to win. Some people are even paid millions of dollars for this kind of talent. However, there is no reward in the Christian life for this skill.

Genesis 18 ends with God declaring His judgment upon Sodom and Gomorrah. Abraham responded and pleaded with God to spare the city if fifty righteous people could be found. After some negotiation, God agreed to spare the cities if ten righteous people were found.

Remember, one family in Sodom was surely on Abraham's mind during this exchange. Lot and his family were living in sin, and while they deserved to be punished, Abraham still had a heart for his family. As we know, the cities were destroyed, and God's judgment came down upon the wickedness of those people. This means that while Lot and his family were there, they didn't have an impact on the city; but Sodom certainly made an impression on their family.

If Lot's family had reached only a few people, Abraham's prayer would have been heard, and those cities would have been spared. Instead, Lot's family became secret agent Christians and decided to blend in rather than to stand out for the gospel.

Do the people in your life know that you're a Christian? Do they hear you thank the Lord, witness to people, or even talk about the work of God that you're involved with? We should be ashamed if we are so politically correct and consumed with not hurting feelings or stepping on toes that we hide our faith. You have no idea what your light can accomplish if you'll let it shine, and you have no idea what damage you can do if you decide to hide it.

—— Today's Truth ——

Jesus calls Christians the "light of the world." Let your light shine. Don't deceive yourself into hiding your faith.

Remember Lot's Wife

Read Genesis 19–21

YOU WILL BE remembered for something. We remember Abraham Lincoln as "Honest Abe." We remember Hitler for the Holocaust. Many remember Peter for denying Christ. In Luke 17:32, Jesus tells us, *"Remember Lot's wife."* When teaching on the Second Coming, Jesus used this woman from Genesis 19 as an example to us.

First, remember her privilege. Some of the greatest heartache you will face is watching someone with potential, someone into whom you've invested, or someone who's been given a great opportunity throw it all away. She married into a family that had a special purpose from the Lord, yet she wasted it.

Next, remember her pause. This is how we remember this woman. When God told her not to turn back, she paused, instead of just moving forward. From this moment of hesitation, I believe her heart toward Sodom is revealed. She built a life there, and something in her mourned to leave that place, even though she knew it was sinful.

Lastly, remember her punishment. Sadly, many will hear the warning and have a chance to get saved or to make things right, but lose out on God's best for their life. She could've enjoyed the blessings of God's promises. She could've raised her family and watched them grow to serve the Lord. Instead, she serves as an example of the many that will follow the same path.

In the next verse (Luke 17:33), Jesus says, *"Whosoever shall seek to save his life shall lose it; and whosoever shall lose his life shall preserve it."*

—— Today's Truth ——

Will you trust the Lord and follow His will for your life? Allowing yourself to hold on to your old life, your own agenda, or your sinful pleasures will lead only to ruin.

True Worship

Read Genesis 22–24

Tʜᴇ ᴡᴏʀᴅ *ᴡᴏʀsʜɪᴘ* comes from the Anglo-Saxon word *wo-erthscipe*, meaning "worth ship." This means "to ascribe worth to a person or object." In Genesis 22:5, Abraham says, *"…I and the lad will go yonder and worship."*

We know worship services, songs of worship, and worship that is spoken. However, worship cannot be manufactured. It cannot be given that title if it is not the kind of worship described in God's Word. This chapter is one of the most genuine examples of real worship. Let me remind you that Genesis 22 is the chapter of Abraham offering Isaac upon the altar as one of the clearest examples of Jesus in the Old Testament.

The message of this chapter tells us about a man who was dedicated to following God's leading. Abraham wasn't living for himself, but for His heavenly Father. Genuine worship begins with a devotion to the ways of God. It's not about how it makes us feel, but if it pleases Him. Because they don't get the fulfillment they are seeking, too many will leave church, walk away from their Bibles, or exit their prayer closet either to look for something else or walk away forever.

Worship is not selfish, it is selfless. It's all about Him! It is something you offer to God, and although it is not a gift you can touch and feel, it is one of the greatest gifts you can give. When you are ready to sacrifice everything, surrender your future, and separate from whatever He may ask, it is then that you will find genuine worship. It shouldn't be just during a church service that God is worshipped, but with our lips and with our lives!

—— Today's Truth ——

Worship must be given because of who God is, because of all that God has done, and for all that He will do in the future.

Digging Wells

Read Genesis 25–27

MUCH OF ISAAC'S life is overshadowed by either his father, Abraham, or his son, Jacob. In Genesis 26, we get a glimpse into the life of Isaac and the wells that he dug.

Isaac's obedience to stay out of Egypt and remain in God's will, even in a time of famine, is an example of the kind of man he was and how he honored God. Isaac is known for digging wells, and we find great truths in this passage.

The Wells of the Past: In Genesis 26:18, Isaac re-dug some wells. Similarly, we will have to revisit some things in life. we'll have to fight some battle again or do some work again, and these will still have a purpose. Notice that Isaac didn't try to rebrand these wells of his father. He named them as his father did. He didn't try to invent a new way of doing things. The way his father taught him was good enough.

The Wells of the Present: Live in the present. Understand that if you are following God's leading in your life, then you can know that you are where you are for a reason. God has a purpose in your present. You may feel like certain seasons are pointless, or you may be counting down the days until you get through. Wherever God has you, just keeping digging the wells that God has placed in your past, and trust the purpose that He has set before you.

The Wells of Prosperity: Genesis 26:32 says, *"And it came to pass the same day, that Isaac's servants came, and told him concerning the well which they had digged, and said unto him, We have found water."* Stay faithful, and God will come through. Your labor is not in vain. God always honors those who honor Him.

—— Today's Truth ——

Be cautious about making life-changing decisions in the valley that you will regret in the future.

Do You Even Know?

Read Genesis 28–30

Y OU MAY BE familiar with the phrase "Ignorance is bliss." Sometimes, we'd rather be left in the dark on some things. We avoid the dentist because we don't want to be told of a cavity that needs to be filled. We avoid visits to the doctor so that we don't have to be told of high cholesterol, bad health habits, or even the thought of a possibly more serious diagnosis. We can agree that this is not a wise way of thinking, yet we find a man ignorant of something much more serious in this passage.

Genesis 28:16 says, *"And Jacob awaked out of his sleep, and he said, Surely the L*ORD *is in this place; and I knew it not."* Jacob was completely oblivious to the presence of God. God could have been on vacation or He could have been right in front of Him, and Jacob would not have known any different.

I fear too many of us go throughout each day completely unaware of God's presence in our life. Part of the problem is that we don't seek His presence. Every day must include a time when you enter into your prayer closet and seek the Lord for the day, and you should seek Him in your decisions throughout the day. Seek Him by thanking Him, seek Him by thinking about His Word, and seek Him by desiring fellowship with Him. Nothing good in the Christian life will come by accident. It must be sought.

In addition, the Lord's presence is clouded when sin is present. Our modern-day culture preaches "God is love" to a fault. God loves you even though you sin, but God will not abide with you while you continue to live in sin and feed your sinful desires. You have to choose between having the presence of sin or the presence of God, and you will decide this every day and all throughout the day.

—— Today's Truth ——

Do you even know if God is with you today? You may not always feel His presence, but you can be sure that God has promised and desires to dwell with you in every aspect of your life.

Get Even or Get Over It

Read Genesis 31–33

SIBLING RIVALRY IS a reality is many households. Siblings can be the best of friends and the worst of enemies all in the same day. I have a great relationship with my brother and sister now, but that was not always the case when we were growing up. Of course, it was never because of anything I did. After all, I was the youngest, so I was clearly always just the victim. We see sibling rivalry in the Bible in the first two brothers, Cain and Abel. Joseph and his brothers are another example. Also in Genesis, we read of Jacob and Esau, two brothers who got into quite the duel with each other.

After Jacob deceived his father into giving him Esau's blessing, Esau was furious, and Jacob fled. Time went by, and Genesis 33 documents the reunion of these brothers for the first time since Jacob stole the blessing. We can see clearly that Jacob was nervous. He wasn't sure what Esau was feeling, but he certainly was fearful that Esau still sought vengeance. Genesis 33:4 gives Esau's reaction when he saw his brother: "And Esau ran to meet him, and embraced him, and fell on his neck, and kissed him: and they wept." Instead of getting even, Esau decided to get over the hurt his brother had caused.

There is no question that you will experience hurt in life. You may be driven to get even with your accuser, and you may even believe that your wish is justifiable. Let me kindly suggest to you, get over it! Life is too short to allow one person, one hurt, or even a number of moments to cause you to live a life of bitterness and anger. When you choose to focus on revenge, you will live in that sorrow—but know that is completely your choice. Here's the good news: you don't have to live that way. Move forward, and choose to live your life with joy.

——Today's Truth——

Forgiveness doesn't mean that you are weak. It means that you are choosing not to live in the past, not to live in the hurt, and not to live in sorrow. Choose joy!

The Book of Esau

Read Genesis 34–36

WALKING THROUGH A cemetery is a strange feeling. Every time I have walked through the tombstones, I think very carefully where I step, but I also consider all the names and dates listed around me. In such a setting, I also wonder whether the people achieved their goals in life. I wonder whether they made an impact, whether they left behind people who miss them, or what would they do over if they had the chance?

In this passage, we see in some sense Esau's family given and the earthly success they achieved.

Success is relative—impossible to define. What you consider success could be totally different from my definition. Many would read Esau's lineage and think what a great success he was, but I don't believe that is what God is showing us here. Esau's decision to turn away from the true God and toward false gods may have produced earthly pleasures and power; but just as all those things are temporal, so too was Esau's legacy. It ends here.

Genesis 36 and 37 are a contrast of the lives and decisions of two brothers. Esau and his family's power and prestige is listed in chapter 36, while chapter 37 begins with the understatement, *"And Jacob dwelt in the land wherein his father was a stranger, in the land of Canaan."* The world defines success by what they can see as tangible achievements that equate to true results in life. God's path is rarely played out that way. The right path may not yield flashy results. You may not even notice what God is doing, but fast forward through the pages of Scripture, and the evidence is overwhelming for how God used Jacob once he surrendered himself to God.

—— Today's Truth ——

You will drift away from God at times. When you do, get back to Bethel and restore that relationship.

Dreams

Read Genesis 37–39

Most people dream while sleeping between three to as many as seven times every night. Most of those dreams are forgotten. During some dreams, we sometimes have a sense of paralysis, feeling stuck or as though we have no control.

We also dream in the sense that we picture how we want the future to be. Malcolm S. Forbes said of this type of dream, "When you cease to dream you cease to live."

The account of Joseph in the latter part of Genesis begins in 37:5, *"And Joseph dreamed a dream, and he told it his brethren...."* His brothers despised him for his dream about being a leader over his family. In verse 19 they describe him this way: *"Behold, this dreamer cometh."*

Let me clarify that because we have the complete Word of God and the Spirit of God indwelling those who are saved, I do not believe that God speaks through dreams today as He did in stories like this. However, it was through a dream that God revealed His plan for Joseph. That literal dream became a vision for Joseph for his life. Even after his brothers betrayed him, he thought about what the dream meant. After Potiphar's wife wrongly accused him of misconduct, he still knew that his life had a greater purpose. All those years in prison, Joseph held to that dream that God would use him for a purpose greater than his understanding.

Looking into the future and dreaming of what could be is not just something you do when you're bored at school or work. I've often dreamed about big days before they took place, my wedding day, and what my kids would look like before they were born. Dreaming of what God could do with your life is a way to remind yourself that God is limitless in what He can do with anyone who is surrendered to Him.

—— Today's Truth ——

Giving thought to what could be is not just a way of wishing for your future, but also a way to cuase you to work in the present to fulfill God's possibiities for your life.

Falsely Accused

Read Genesis 40–42

AMERICA WAS FOUNDED on certain standards that gave tribute to the uniqueness and power of this country. One of those is freedom of speech, religion, press, and assembly. Another is found in the 6th Amendment where our Constitution guarantees a speedy trial and a fair trial by the jury, among other things. It is this system that gives innocent people that have been wrongly accused a chance to clear their name. Thus, we have the term, "innocent until proven guilty."

Unfortunately, Joseph did not live in a place like America. When he was falsely accused of a crime that he did not commit, we do not see the opportunity for Joseph to stand up for himself. Without due process, an innocent man was treated as a guilty man.

You may find yourself in a situation one day where you are accused of a wrong that you did not do. People may believe you, or they may foam at the mouth while calling for your punishment, regardless of your defense. How do you respond when you are falsely accused?

Let God take care of the situation. When you're no longer in control, God has it covered. You may not win, and you may not clear your name; but you don't have to do God's job for Him.

Stay in the right. Don't allow the wrong of a false accusation to bring you to commit sin through bitterness, anger, resentment, or an action of vengeance.

Find favor in prison. Joseph didn't know this, but that prison was his path to get to the palace one day. He needed to be used in prison to interpret dreams in order to fulfill God's plan for his life.

——Today's Truth ——

First, no one is completely innocent. We have all have done wrong in our lives. While we may be attacked for a particular sin we didn't commit, God is still in control.

A Family Reunion

Read Genesis 43–45

EVERY YEAR OR at least every few years, many families get together for what some call "family reunions." We see family who don't live near us and use the event as a way to stay in touch. I believe that is what makes the holiday season so special. In a sense, we have family reunions during the holidays that bring a certain joy and laughter that we cherish.

Genesis 45:1 says, *"Then Joseph could not refrain himself before all them that stood by him: and he cried, Cause every man to go out from me. And there stood no man with him, while Joseph made himself known unto his brethren."* This meeting was Joseph's family reunion, and a very special time for his family.

Too often, we ruin family time with drama, fighting, politics, bitterness, or other meaningless distractions. The simple truth here is found in the heart of Joseph. He wasn't bitter because of what his brothers did to him. Instead, he had a yearning in his heart to be reunited with his family again. Many have lost touch or chosen to stay out of touch because of drama. All family has some drama, but in most cases, nothing should keep us from having a relationship with the people God specifically put into our lives.

We tend to learn when it's too late. Tell your family you love them today. Call that person you've been meaning to talk to. Pray for your family. Make the effort to spend time with one another. You don't need to do something expensive or lavish. Just make it happen, and enjoy the time that you have with them.

——Today's Truth ——

You get only one family. Family is a gift from God. Make the most of the time that you have with them, and whenever possible, cherish the memories of the past.

JANUARY 16

Visions of the Night

Read Genesis 46–48

Gᴏᴅ sᴘᴏᴋᴇ ᴛᴏ Jacob in a dream, more than forty years be-
fore the events in these chapters took place, when he was in
a similar situation. In Genesis 46, Jacob is again set to leave this land:
*"And God spake unto Israel in the visions of the night, and said, Jacob,
Jacob. And he said, Here am I."* (Genesis 46:2). In the next two verses,
God reminds Jacob of several lessons we can learn in the dark times.

"I am God" – When we forget who God is, we lose sight of our relationship with Him, our purpose, and every part that God has in our
lives. We must seek His face first.

"the God of thy father" – This isn't the Lord's first rodeo. We put
faith in companies that have a good track record. Seeing that a company
has been in business for multiple decades gives us assurance they know
what they're doing. God has been here before, even if this is new for you.

"fear not" – Over and over, this statement is repeated throughout
Scripture. Look up the different phobias people have. We fear everything, even if we don't admit it. Fear of man, fear of the unknown, fear
of failure—it all leads to a depletion of faith in God.

"I will there make of thee a great nation" – Jacob was surely hesi-
tant to go to Egypt, yet God used him there. God's promise to use you
will always be fulfilled when you follow His will, even in the most unlikely of places and scenarios.

"I will go down with thee into Egypt" – God promises not only to
use you, but also to go with you. Others may drift away, but God will
be with you every step of the way when you heed His calling.

"I will also surely bring thee up again" – You won't stay in Egypt
forever. You will have to learn to endure for a time while there, but
Egypt will end for you. God ends with the promise of a reunion with
his lost son, Joseph.

—— Today's Truth ——

*With the new life God has given, don't go back to the old miser-
able man you once were and could be again.*

A King That Knew Not Joseph

Genesis 49–Exodus 1

EVERY GENERATION HAS a responsibility to teach the next generation. At Regency Baptist Church, we have the Christian school, Sunday school, bus routes, youth group, kids' choir, teen choir, nursery, and more for the youth in our church. These ministries require workers, effort, and dedication. But they are also near the very heart of our church because they are ways that we are teaching and reaching the next generation.

The book of Exodus begins with God's people in bondage. How did we get from the end of Genesis, where God's people were saved and living in prosperity, to the next chapter of the next book, where they are now living in the same place as slaves? The reason is given in Exodus 1:8, which says, *"Now there arose up a new king over Egypt, which knew not Joseph."*

The early years of a life is the time to teach. We learn throughout our entire lives, but we learn the most in the first part. Young people need the generation before them to pass down godly teaching for that legacy to continue.

In our home, we have Bible Time. Our children are young, so we don't discuss in-depth doctrine (nor do I believe you need to become scholarly), but we sing godly songs together, I read the Bible, we help our children memorize verses, and then we all pray. We make an effort to do this because we want our children to have for themselves what was passed down to us.

—— Today's Truth ——

Every generation and every person of that generation must have a part in teaching the next generation about the Lord.

Addapting to a New Lens

Read Exodus 2–4

MOSES GREW UP in Pharaoh's home. He ate Egyptian food. He wore Egyptian clothing. He lived like the Egyptians. However, in his heart, he knew he didn't belong. When Moses killed the Egyptian in Exodus 2, I believe that Moses finally decided that he was not going to live like an Egyptian any longer. It may not have been the right way for Moses to go about this, but in his heart, he chose to look at life differently. He couldn't put blinders over his eyes to what God wanted for his life.

Have you ever been working in a room with the lights off when someone walks in, flips the switch, and says something like, "Do you like working in the dark?" If you grew up in a Christian home, you might flip the switch and proclaim with a booming voice, "Let there be light!"

Until you perform an honest evaluation and confess the faults in your life, you will never make the necessary changes to truly be used by God. Exodus 2 was the turning point in Moses' life, and what separates him from other Christians was his willingness to realize that he needed a change in his life because the path he was on was leading nowhere good.

After Moses decided who he was, he committed to it. God put him in the desert for forty years, and Moses waited patiently. He didn't make a "New Year's resolution" and give up because he didn't drop twenty pounds in the first two weeks. He stuck it out because he knew that he was where he was supposed to be.

—— Today's Truth ——

In every life, change is needed. This isn't a change for the sake of change, but a change for the right. Honestly consider your life, then confess your faults. Commit to God's path, and change what is necessary to keep yourself on that path.

No Contest

Read Exodus 5–7

HAVE YOU EVER found yourself staring at the sidewalk watching two snails "racing" in the same direction just to see who will win? Perhaps you've watched a lion chase down a gazelle on television just to see if the lion will catch his dinner or if the gazelle will get away. In Exodus 7, we see a contest between the serpent of Aaron's staff and the serpents of the wise men, sorcerers, and magicians. Exodus 2:12 gives the outcome of this contest: *"For they cast down every man his rod, and they became serpents: but Aaron's rod swallowed up their rods."* (I imagine Aaron had to work hard to keep from grinning too proudly before Pharaoh.)

I admit that I am not a good loser. I want to be good to others, but I do not enjoy losing. I'll turn off a game if my team is losing. I'll continue to watch with a smile on my face if my team is winning. I like living in the greatest country on the earth. And when it comes to the contest between God and the devil, the world, and anything else that will foolishly oppose Him, there is no contest.

I John 4:4 states, *"Ye are of God, little children, and have overcome them: because greater is he that is in you, than he that is in the world."* No matter what strength this world seems to possess, God will always win. Here's some good news—you don't have to be a good loser, you don't have to get used to losing, and you don't have to worry whether or not you'll win. If you're on God's side, there is no contest!

——— Today's Truth ———

God wins every time. No matter the opponent, God wins. No matter the situation, God wins. No matter what you are facing, God has already claimed victory, and you should live like that is true.

The Frog Fiasco

Read Exodus 8–10

T HE EGYPTIAN GODDESS Heqet was pictured with the head of a frog. From this, the Egyptians considered frogs sacred and something that could not be killed. The Lord told Moses to warn Pharaoh in Exodus 8:2, *"And if thou refuse to let them go, behold, I will smite all thy borders with frogs:"* Because they would not kill them, they would infiltrate their homes, their beds, their kitchens, and completely take over all places of living. This was bound to be a mess!

God taught Pharaoh and the Egyptians an important lesson here. The sin they allowed to become a god in their culture was soon used by God to show them how much of a disaster that decision would cause. When we think we have control over our sin, we are lying to ourselves and headed for sure disaster. Sin must be confessed and forsaken, or you might just have a bigger problem than you anticipated.

A man in Haiti wanted to sell his house for $2,000. Another man wanted to buy it, but could only pay $1,000. After some negotiation, the homeowner agreed to sell the home for $1,000, provided he was allowed to retain ownership of one single nail just over the front door. After some years, the original owner wanted to buy back the house. The new owner refused to sell, so, the original owner went out and found the carcass of a dead dog and hung it over the front door on the single nail that he still owned. It wasn't long until the house became unlivable, and the new owner and his family had to move out of the house.

—— Today's Truth ——

You cannot live in sin, give place to the devil, and expect anything but disaster in your future. Either confess and forsake your sin, or your sin will have a larger part of your life than you ever wanted.

The Hyssop Branch

Read Exodus 11–13

Times have changed since the days of Moses. While we enjoy our modern medicine, people in these times had to have a much different approach to sickness and injury. Hyssop, in particular, was an herb that was used in many different ways for cleansing, medicinal purposes, and even for flavor in food.

God instructed hyssop to be used this way in the last plague for those who wanted their firstborn to be spared: *"And ye shall take a bunch of hyssop, and dip it in the blood that is in the bason, and strike the lintel and the two side posts with the blood that is in the bason…"* (Exodus 12:22). The hyssop branch was the tool to be used to apply the blood on their doorpost and to bring their cleansing and salvation.

David prays in Psalm 51:7, *"Purge me with hyssop, and I shall be clean: wash me, and I shall be whiter than snow."* In Leviticus 14, lepers were to use hyssop to apply the blood for their cleansing. The same purification method was used for homes with mold. Most notably, however, hyssop was used during Jesus' death on the cross. John 19:28–30 says, *"After this, Jesus knowing that all things were now accomplished, that the scripture might be fulfilled, saith, I thirst. Now there was set a vessel full of vinegar: and they filled a spunge with vinegar, and put it upon hyssop, and put it to his mouth. When Jesus therefore had received the vinegar, he said, It is finished: and he bowed his head, and gave up the ghost."*

Hyssop was used in the Old Testament to apply the blood of the animal sacrifice to the doorpost during the Passover as a picture of the blood of Jesus being applied to bring us the cleansing we truly need. In the New Testament, as a reminder of the Passover, hyssop was used during the crucifixion. These small details point us to the big picture of Jesus!

—— Today's Truth ——

No work of our own can cleanse us of our sins. The blood is required if we are to be cleansed of our sins. We must receive it and daily seek it.

Go Forward

Read Exodus 14–16

LIKE MOSES, THERE will be days in your life where you feel trapped. The world is on your tail. Your old life is in the past, but you just can't get rid of it. The people that are supposed to be a help and a support to you aren't giving you what you want or need. You look for encouragement or strength in people, but more often than not, you find complaints, doubt, and frustration. Trying to look ahead, you see no clear direction. Instead of a wide-open road, you see only an ocean. You don't know where and how to step in the right direction. What do you do? Go forward!

As Moses stood before the Red Sea, God tells him in Exodus 14:15, *"And the LORD said unto Moses, Wherefore criest thou unto me? speak unto the children of Israel, that they go forward."* You may not understand even as you're taking your leap for God, but you can understand that He already has the "how" all figured out. Too often, we want to understand before we move. Seldom is that how God works. God requires faith, and then He reveals His plan as we move forward in His will.

Stop waiting for the perfect moment to start serving God. Abraham, Moses, David, Daniel, Joseph—none of these men began their journey in the timing that was perfect in their eyes. Instead, you move because although it may appear to be out of place for you, it is just how God intended.

The truth is that moving forward sometimes means you're standing still. It isn't implying a literal walk or run, but a spirit of continuing in the path that God has laid out and following His leading every step of the way. Standing still in faith leads to God's leading. There is no second or third option. What else will you do if you do not continue on and move forward?

—— Today's Truth ——

The past is written. The future is unknown. The present, however, is the daily walk of faith as we follow God in everything that we do. You may face those "quitting times," but just keep going anyway. Go forward, Christian!

Lightening the Load

Read Exodus 17–19

WHENEVER WE'D COMPLAIN that we were tired during school, our principal would often reply, "Tired people run the world." The truth is that we all get tired. This isn't a problem; it's a reality. I'm satisfied when I am weary at the end of the day, because it tells me that I did something with my life that day. If you are busy in the work of the Lord, you're going to grow weary. Sometimes, you may need some rest. Sometimes, you may just need someone to lighten the load.

Israel was in battle with Amalek. Moses told Joshua to lead an army against the enemy, and that he would be on a hill with the rod of God. Moses would raise that rod, and the Israelites would prevail. When his hands got weary, the enemy would prevail. Aaron and Hur came to help and stood on each side of Moses, lifting his arms until God's people had victory.

We find an important lesson in this example from these two godly men, but we probably don't see it the way we're supposed to. You may read this and think, "It sure would be nice if someone would help lighten my load for a change." We all undoubtedly have burdens, but that shouldn't be the focus. Because instead of looking for someone to lighten your load, you should be on the other end, seeking to be an Aaron and Hur for somebody else. It would have been impossible for Moses to do this on his own. He needed help. All throughout our lives, people need us to lighten their load during certain seasons. The weight has to be carried, but you can remove a lot of pressure by having a small part in someone else's life.

——Today's Truth ——

Look for ways to lighten the burden that others are carrying. It can be anything from a small gesture to a big sacrifice. Focus on others' needs, and find something you can do to be a blessing to someone today. You never know what victories God will give if you are willing to help.

What to Do?

Read Exodus 20–22

LIFE IS FULL of rules. It's humorous to think of rebellious teenagers who will turn eighteen, leave their parents' home, and join the military thinking that somehow will be the place of freedom from the rules that have taken the fun out of life.

When we think of rules, we tend to focus on the negative. I remember being in my first orientation in Bible college, thumbing through the rule book looking for all the things I was not allowed to do. What catches our attention is the restrictions, not the commands.

In Exodus 20, God gave the Ten Commandments to Moses to give to the people. Out of the Ten Commandments, all but two begin with *"Thou shalt not."* While there certainly are many sins we are commanded to avoid, God also wants us to keep certain commands.

First, God commanded the people to observe the Lord's day. As New Testament Christians, we observe the Lord's day on Sunday, the day that Jesus rose from the grave. Back in the beginning of Genesis, we again see the principle that God rested on the seventh day of creation. He didn't need the rest. God was setting an example for us. We need a day of refreshment, and what better refreshment than to be in church? Many look to the lake, television, or other activities for this day of rest, but we are commanded to be in church every time the doors are open.

Next, God commands us to honor our parents. Your parents deserve respect. At an early age, children must learn to respect, obey, and grow in their relationship with their mother and father. I believe this relationship prepares a child's heart for their relationship with the Lord.

—— Today's Truth ——

You need to keep yourself from plenty of things in this life, but that doesn't mean your purpose is to simply stay away. God has given clear and simple commands for what we shouldn't do, but also for what we should be doing.

Other "gods"

Read Exodus 23–25

THERE IS ONE God, plain and simple. Isaiah 44:6 states, *"Thus saith the Lord the King of Israel, and his redeemer the Lord of hosts; I am the first, and I am the last; and beside me there is no God."* James 2:19 tells us that the devils believe this: *"Thou believest that there is one God; thou doest well: the devils also believe, and tremble."* Jesus states in Mark 12:29, *"And Jesus answered him, The first of all the commandments is, Hear, O Israel; The Lord our God is one Lord."* Every other "god" is a false god, and the true God gives instructions concerning other so-called "gods."

Exodus 23:24 gives the following instructions:

1. ***"Thou shalt not bow down to their gods"*** – No one else deserves our worship. God tells us that He is jealous, and it is a complete disgrace to give anyone or anything but Him our worship.

2. ***"nor serve them"*** – What you live for shows where your heart is. If you love, God, you'll serve Him. If you love the world and the false gods it has to offer, you will serve just that.

3. ***"nor do after their works"*** – Keep your eyes fixed on Jesus, His Word, godly people, and by His Spirit, you must determine to follow the model He has given and abstain from all else.

4. ***"thou shalt utterly overthrow them, and quite break down their images"*** – We're very soft when it comes to false gods. We cannot be passive about the idols in our world that are consuming the lives of people. They must be destroyed!

—— Today's Truth ——

The God of the Bible is the true God, but you have to decide for Him to be your God. We can get entangled in sin and serve other gods, but none else can take the place of the one true God.

The Office of a Priest

Read Exodus 26–28

EVERY BELIEVER, AT the moment of salvation, becomes a priest (I Peter 2:5, 9; Revelation 1:6). In Exodus, the office of a priest was strictly designated for a particular group of people. Although we do not practice the same requirements of the priests in that time, we can learn what it means to be a priest and the picture here of God's purpose for this group of people.

To become a priest, you had to be a descendant of Aaron. You had to be a part of the family. Still today, to be a priest, you must receive Jesus Christ (the ultimate sacrifice). We are called *"children of God"* (John 1:12) after salvation.

Also, priests were privileged to be intercessors between God and the people. They went to God on behalf of the people. We, too, have that privilege at any time, to approach the throne of grace and come boldly to Him with any needs that we have or any confession that we must give.

Priests had a purpose. These men were servants of God and of the people. This was an important truth for them to learn. A position does not make you important. It means that you have been given grace for a task that can bring glory to God through your service.

Many will notice the great attention to detail given regarding the priests' attire. They had to look the part. Much like a ball player puts on a jersey, we must look the part as Christians. The priests' attire made them noticeably different. You don't have to be strange to be different, but we should appear different than the world nonetheless. Your appearance is your testimony of what's different about you on the inside.

——Today's Truth——

We have a great responsibility and opportunity as priests. Recognize this office that you hold and ask yourself if you have been meeting the requirements. We must live up to the task that we have been graciously given.

Are You "There"?

Read Exodus 29–31

TRYING TO REACH somebody by phone while in an area with bad reception can be frustrating. We find ourselves asking that question over and over: "Are you there?" Children ask their parents on a long trip, "Are we there yet?" They do so in a very gentle, quiet, and polite way of course. We meet people in busy places and when the meeting time comes, we think, "Are you here?"

God wants to meet with you. We receive many blessings from meeting with God, and we meet with Him for many reasons. Through fellowship with Him, we gain peace, comfort, knowledge, wisdom, and much else from time with Him. We also receive direction in life, answers to prayer, and strength. The blessings are endless, but the possibility of these blessings is made possible by getting to our meeting place with God.

Exodus 29:43 says, *"And there will I meet with the children of Israel, and the tabernacle shall be sanctified by my glory."* God specified that there was a meeting place for the children of Israel to be with Him. If they wanted a relationship, they knew where to be. They knew that their meeting was not in whatever fashion they wanted, but that God told them in clear terms, "This is where you need to be if you want to meet with me."

Are you in the place in life that you can meet with God daily? We use grace as an excuse, and we lie to ourselves until we think that God will meet us in our rebellion just because He loves us. He does love us, but we have to get ourselves to the place in our heart and in our lifestyle that we can fellowship with Him. We must determine to come daily to the place where we can have a closeness in our walk with the Lord.

—— Today's Truth ——

Get to the place where you can meet with God. You have to leave something behind, but nothing is worth missing the time that you can spend with Him.

How to Corrupt Yourself

Read Exodus 32–34

S IN MOVES GRADUALLY, but it also moves quickly. It won't take over your life in one day, but it won't take long before you find yourself in the wrong place, wondering what went wrong and how that downward spiral took place. God told Moses in Exodus 32:7–8, after just forty days of being away from the people, *"Go, get thee down; for thy people, which thou broughtest out of the land of Egypt, have corrupted themselves: They have turned aside quickly out of the way which I commanded them."*

Corruption will always be brought on by yourself. "The devil made me do it" doesn't fly. The people made their own choices, and those choices led them to a place where God was ready to carry out His wrath upon the people (v. 10).

They had a corrupt worship. In verse 4, Aaron states after they made the molten calf, *"These be thy gods, O Israel, which brought thee up out of the land of Egypt."* Now, I know some do struggle with memory problems, but I'm not betting on that excuse working. No one, absolutely no one, deserves the credit for the good done in your life besides the God of Heaven!

Their worship carried over into their music. Verse 17–18 shows that the noise Moses and Joshua were hearing was the sound of their wicked music. Music is a way that we express our heart. God wants to be glorified through music. Giving yourself to the wrong music is giving your heart to the wrong worship.

They had a corrupt wardrobe (v. 25). When your heart for God changes, your appearance changes. Any time people backslide, you'll notice their appearance sliding too. Clothing becomes more revealing, more form-fitting, and modesty goes out the window.

—— Today's Truth ——

The solution for corruption is consecration (v. 29). Clean up the corruption in your life. Don't wait until sin runs its full course to turn back.

God Enlists and God Equips

Read Exodus 35–37

APASTOR TRAVELED with his wife to a conference where he was to preach. As the host introduced him before the sermon, he said, "We are so thankful to have such a great preacher here tonight." Surprised and pleased, those words stayed in the preacher's mind. While driving back home, the preacher asked his wife, "How many great preachers do you think there are?" His wife gently replied, "One less than you think there are."

We are all pretty ordinary. Although I'd like to think that I have areas of my life that are extraordinary, the truth is that I am not special. I am unique and special because I am God's creation, but on my own and by my flesh, I am nothing. The good news is that God uses ordinary people, and He does extraordinary work through us.

When we understand that God has a plan for our life, the common response is fear. "What does God want from me?" "How will I do what He wants me to do?" "Will I fail?" We have these thoughts because God's plans are too big for us. We can't do the extraordinary on our own. We need His help.

I wrote down this statement in Bible college: "God doesn't call the equipped. He equips the called." I remember feeling that same inadequacy, knowing that whatever big plans God had drawn up for my life, my talents were not enough. God will use us, not because of what we have to offer, but despite what we possess.

Exodus 36:1 speaks of how God equipped men to do His work: *"Then wrought Bezaleel and Aholiab, and every wise hearted man, in whom the LORD put wisdom and understanding to know how to work all manner of work for the service of the sanctuary, according to all that the LORD had commanded."*

—— Today's Truth ——

When we lack the skills needed to perform our duty, we realize that we must rely on the Lord to fulfill our purpose. Never forget where the help comes from. We can only do so much on our own.

Finish the Work

Read Exodus 38–39

THINGS CHANGE AS we get older. I often frustrated my parents at the dinner table. I have no problem finishing my food now, but when I was younger, I made a habit of leaving food on the table. The funny part is that it was usually just a bite or two left over. Sometimes, I'd catch myself eating a burger, and putting it down with barely one bite left and thinking, "Why didn't I just finish it?"

Finishing isn't always easy. We fight the process to reach the end of the task at hand. It may be a struggle in the process that causes us to quit. Maybe it's just a lack of heart or passion. Whatever the struggle may be, we have a responsibility to finish the work that God has commanded in Scripture and personally called us to do. Exodus 39:32 says, *"Thus was all the work of the tabernacle of the tent of the congregation finished: and the children of Israel did according to all that the LORD commanded Moses, so did they."*

Life is full of stops and starts. We begin things, and then we stop them. We decide to start soul winning again. Time goes by, and we can't remember the last time we witnessed to someone. God's commandments are not to be partially obeyed. Partial obedience is still disobedience. We don't get partial credit because we gave Him a partial effort.

This kind of mindset could be accurately described as the "lukewarm Christian." We may feel like quitting. We may not be as excited as we were when we made the decision. Perhaps we're just discouraged because we can't see an end in sight. We need to just keep on serving God anyway. If we've made some progress, we shouldn't throw it all away. Let's finish the work!

—— Today's Truth ——

The finish line is our homecoming with the Lord, and we are not done as long as God gives us life on this earth. Determine to finish!

"As the Lord Commanded"

Read Exodus 40

W HENEVER I HAVE to fill out a form, I look for the lines that show the word "optional." You may be an over achiever, but if I don't have to take the time to tell some stranger what my first dog's name was, then I'm going to save the time. However, if someone offers to pay for my meal at a restaurant, I like that option of getting a free meal. "Optional" can be great. We get the freedom without the restrictions.

Little in the Bible is optional. With the small amount that God has given to us in His Word, He purposefully tells us what He expects from our lives. These are not options, they are commands. This phrase is repeated eight times in similar ways in this chapter: *"...as the LORD commanded Moses."* Moses didn't do anything special; He just did what the Lord commanded Him to do.

To mature as a child of God, you must come to the place where you obey the Lord, merely because He commands it. Disregard your feelings and your personal agenda. Do what it right because it is right. God has clearly laid out in Scripture what is right and wrong, written in black and white.

Do you do what is commanded only when you want to do it? Doing right just because it is right requires character. I have heard character defined as "doing what you're supposed to do, even when you don't feel like doing it." If you're reading your Bible, you will see what God commands of you. Don't think about it. Decide in your heart that whatever commands God has given, you will obey.

—— Today's Truth ——

God's commands are not optional. Fulfilling His commands is obedience, and disregarding His commands is disobedience. Obey His Word today.

Introduction to Leviticus

Read Leviticus 1–3

THE BOOK OF Leviticus can be the most overlooked book in the Pentateuch by most readers. When you begin in Genesis, you begin by reading the book of the Bible that covers more history than any other book. The majority of Exodus is captivating as you read of Moses and how God led His people out of Egypt and into the wilderness on their journey to the Promised Land. Unfortunately, many lose their excitement in the latter part of Exodus and Leviticus. However, Leviticus is inspired and kept by God just like every other book in the canon of Scripture, and it contains great truths to be found and applied.

Leviticus is the shortest book in the Pentateuch, consisting of twenty-seven chapters. The time frame it covers is also short. While Genesis covers about 2,000 years of history, Exodus records less than 100. Leviticus covers only about 50 days. The book begins by saying, *"And the Lord called unto Moses…."* This shows that this book is a continuation of what has already been presented. Exodus closes, but the story continues. The purpose of this book can be found in the name of the book. It was written relating to the tribe of Levi.

The first part of the book deals with the sacrificial system. This system was necessary, and it is exciting to see the connection with Jesus Christ, the perfect Lamb sacrificed on our behalf. The later part of the book covers the sanctification of the people. After salvation, we are to draw nearer to Jesus in our hearts and lives. If you will take the time to read, study, and ponder the beauty of this book, you will see the incredible truths it contains.

——Today's Truth ——

All of God's Word has a purpose. We must realize that there are always great truths on every page of Scripture.

Guilty

Read Leviticus 4–6

WHILE NOBODY READILY accepts this fact, the truth remains the same for everyone: All are guilty due to their sin nature. In this passage, the term guilty is found nine times, but not once in the first three chapters. The first three chapters deal more with the process of the offerings while this passage deals with the product of the offerings.

I can probably count on one hand the number of times I've been soul winning when somebody has told me that they truly believe they are sinless. While we may think we are decent and good for the most part, most people will honestly admit that they have committed sin in their lifetime. We are usually much more modest than what the truth would show, but nonetheless, we understand that there is a guilt.

It is because of this guilt that Jesus came to this world. It is because of this guilt that God has given us a Bible. It is because of this guilt that we can pray, and there is much we could list that God has done because of our sin. Sin does have a consequence, but there is also a remedy. As you read of these offerings, recognize that God has instituted a remedy for every sin that we have committed. He has the solution, and the remedy is Jesus Christ. To be redeemed, you must recognize your guilt, accept the punishment, receive the payment that Jesus made on the cross, and praise Him for the path to redemption that He has given.

In the midst of our guilt, God has been merciful to give us a way out. It is by His grace that we are made whole again. We are guilty, and it is this that draws us to the Saviour.

——Today's Truth ——

All men are guilty. God reminds us of this, not to condemn us, but to draw us to Him. He wants us to see that He has the solution, and we can have the remedy through His sacrifice.

The Original Thanksgiving

Read Leviticus 7–8

THANKSGIVING IS ONE of my favorite holidays. A day of quality time with family, giving thanks to God for His goodness, and some of the most delicious food you will taste all year. Giving thanks should not be just a seasonal practice, but a trait that we possess all year long.

The sacrifice of thanksgiving found in Leviticus 7:11–15 was linked with the peace offering. While giving thanks gives the proper praise to the person that is worthy to be praised, it also gives a peace in the one who gives it. Philippians 4:6–7 says, *"Be careful for nothing; but in every thing by prayer and supplication with thanksgiving let your requests be made known unto God. And the peace of God, which passeth all understanding, shall keep your hearts and minds through Christ Jesus."* When we give thanks, the outcome is peace in our hearts.

Also, notice that the sacrifice had other parts. Verse 12 shows a variety of items that were to be included in this offering. While we are easily inclined to praise God for a few things, we must give Him thanks for all things that He has done. Don't pick and choose what to thank Him for. Thank Him for the hard times that taught you to have faith. Thank Him for the answered prayers, and also for the times that He made you wait when your character was put to the test and made stronger.

Verse 15 says, *"And the flesh of the sacrifice of his peace offerings for thanksgiving shall be eaten the same day that it is offered; he shall not leave any of it until the morning."* In other words, the thanks that you gave God yesterday must be offered again today. Your commitments in the past don't count for the present. Your offering of thanks must be renewed every day.

———Today's Truth———

You will never be more thankful than you decide to be. Give God an offering of thanks. Thank Him for everything!

You First

Read Leviticus 9–10

THIS MAY APPEAR to be selfish, but I when I pray, I almost never pray for others first. I have determined that every time I come to throne of grace, I will praise and thank God before I ask for anything. After that, the first person I pray for is myself.

We see this example as Aaron offered the sin offering in Leviticus 9. Verse 8 reads, "Aaron therefore went unto the altar, and slew the calf of the sin offering, which was for himself." Before Aaron gave an offering for the people, he gave it for himself.

As a preacher, I am reminded regularly that the sermons I preach for others are most effective when they have first rooted into my heart and life. This is like the "do what I say, not what I do" mentality. We cannot help others until we have helped ourselves.

Some struggle with this, because they feel guilty taking care of themselves before taking care of others. They will serve others, pray for the needs of others, and help anyone they can, even if it means they suffer. Please note that sacrifice is a part of living for others, but the clear command is also given to pray for your life, take ownership of your responsibilities, and fulfill your God-given obligations to your family.

If you're still not persuaded, look to Jesus' example as He prayed in John 17. He first prayed for Himself, then for the saved, and lastly for the lost. You are not being selfish by praying for yourself first. In fact, you are strengthening your influence by setting the example before you lend a hand to those in need.

—— Today's Truth ——

Only you can live your life. You can help others, but your life is your responsibility. Keep yourself right, and use your example, as well as your help for others, to make a difference.

No Explanation Needed

Read Leviticus 11–13

THE CHRISTIAN LIFE will not always make sense. Does it make sense to be better off living from 90% of your income instead of 100%? God's way will not always add up to you, nor should you always need an explanation in order to obey.

God gave the Israelites some strict dietary laws. Throughout this passage, notice the rules God gave concerning the animals the Jews could eat. Remember, God gave animals for us to have dominion over. I can't think of a better way than to enjoy a juice double cheeseburger with bacon, extra cheese, and grilled onions. Unless your health requires you to not eat meat, I will never understand those who will not eat meat. To each his own, I suppose.

Ask yourself this question: "What if God asked me to take something out of my life that I enjoy, even if I didn't understand why?" It could be certain foods, coffee, desserts, or anything that you enjoy. Would you still obey? We joke that we can eat bacon because we live in a different dispensation, but what if you had lived during Moses' day?

The mark of your devotion will often lead you to choosing God over anything else, especially the things that mean the most to you. Too many Christians give God part of their lives, but hold back in areas that they are not ready or simply not willing to give up. God doesn't need you to agree, He just expects you to obey.

—— Today's Truth ——

The test of your heart for God is shown by what you will and what you will not give up for Him. Could God ask you to give up anything, with no explanation needed?

Bald as a Baby

Read Leviticus 14–15

Youth pastors will do anything to motivate teenagers. After all, teens may be the most difficult people to get excited about something. My youth pastor told our basketball team if we won a particular tournament that he would shave his head completely. We lost, and then a couple years later, he shaved his head all on his own. In the end, it still felt like a win.

Leviticus 14 deals with the cleansing of a leper. Part of that process was to shave their head, beard and eyebrows. Leviticus 14:9 shows, *"But it shall be on the seventh day, that he shall shave all his hair off his head and his beard and his eyebrows, even all his hair he shall shave off: and he shall wash his clothes, also he shall wash his flesh in water, and he shall be clean."*

Leprosy is a picture of sin in the Bible. Thus, there is much comparison to salvation when we look at the cleansing of a leper. To be shaven can be a comparison to a baby being born. This is the symbol of a new birth and being born again in Jesus. Also, this shaving was a way to be completely cleansed and made new.

When you got saved, you didn't just get partly saved. You were completely cleaned and fully born again. Titus 3:5 states, *"Not by works of righteousness which we have done, but according to his mercy he saved us, by the washing of regeneration, and renewing of the Holy Ghost;"* This washing is not referring to baptism (as some false religions may claim), but the internal cleansing that takes place by the blood of the perfect Lamb of God, Jesus Christ. Spurgeon said it this way, "You are a great sinner, but He is a great Saviour."

——Today's Truth——

God cleanses us from our sins the moment we are saved, and one day we will be cleansed in our heavenly bodies forever in eternity.

The Abomination of the LGBTQ Movement

Read Leviticus 16–18

SOME ISSUES ARE not up for debate. As our culture continues to accept more sinful and wicked lifestyles, God's Word appears to be more "out of date" to the world. In 2009, only 37% in America supported marriage between sodomites. In 2019, that number grew to 61%. Still, this issue of the LGBTQ lifestyle is not up for debate. God's Word says in Leviticus 18:22, *"Thou shalt not lie with mankind, as with womankind: it is abomination."* The Bible is very clear concerning this lifestyle:

• Sodomy is sinful. We cannot deny that God never condones, but only condemns this kind of conduct.

• Sodomy is unnatural. (Romans 1:23–27) It doesn't matter if people say they're born that way. Aside from the fact that we are born with a sin nature, God creates us to have an attraction for the opposite gender. My pastor always told us in school, "If you kiss a girl, we'll kick you out. If you don't want to kiss a girl, we'll kick you out."

• Sodomy is idolatry. Putting your heart, desires, and feelings above God's is stripping God of His proper role in your life.

• Sodomy is an abomination. (Leviticus 18:22) Study the word abomination. This is not a light description that God attaches to this sin and others.

• Sodomy contradicts God's design for the home. (Matthew 19:4–6) God created the home with a perfect order. We do not need to try to reinvent what God designed.

• Sodomy makes it impossible to obey God's first command to spouses to replenish and multiply (Genesis 1:27–28). It's not rocket science.

• A desire to sin does not excuse the act of sin. Your fleshly lusts do not give you the freedom to do as you please.

—— Today's Truth ——

What the world glorifies will often contradict God's Word. The home is being attacked. God's design for the home is perfect, and this kind of lifestyle ruins what God created.

Sealed with a Handshake

Read Leviticus 19–21

FOUR COLLEGE BUDDIES decided, rather than study for a final exam, they would take a road trip and party. Afterward, they all slept late and missed the exam, so they decided to concoct a story to see if their professor would let them take the final late. They said they were traveling back to the school and had a flat tire, didn't have a spare, and couldn't find the help necessary to make it to campus in time for the test. The professor graciously agreed they could take the exam. They studied hard and arrived at the professor's office. He placed them in separate rooms and gave them the exam. The problem on the first page seemed easy and was worth five points. They were relieved they had gotten away with their lie. Then they turned to the second page and saw the second question: (For 95 points): Which tire?

Spam emails, false advertisements, online hackers, crooked charity cases looking for money—we are all too familiar with the dishonesty around us. Quite frankly, it makes it more difficult for honest people to prove their integrity with all the skepticism we've created.

Leviticus 19:11–13 says, *"Ye shall not steal, neither deal falsely, neither lie one to another. And ye shall not swear by my name falsely, neither shalt thou profane the name of thy God: I am the Lord. Thou shalt not defraud thy neighbour, neither rob him: the wages of him that is hired shall not abide with thee all night until the morning."* Keep your word. Don't lie, even if the truth is hard to say. Treat people fairly. Respect others.

—— Today's Truth ——

Men used to make deals and seal with them with a handshake. Lawyers and contracts weren't necessary. Have the integrity to deal honestly with others in every aspect of your life.

A New Day

Read Leviticus 22–23

N O ONE CAN keep all of the commandments of the Bible. I don't want to discourage you from trying, but it is impossible to do so. This is not an excuse to sin, but it is a reality. While we may try to do our best, and we absolutely should, we will fall. What then? Are we in need of salvation again? Are we cast aside, unworthy to be in the service of the Lord? Is God done with us? Absolutely not!

As God gives instructions to the priests, we see a restoration process if a priest becomes unclean. Leviticus 22:6–7 says, *"The soul which hath touched any such shall be unclean until even, and shall not eat of the holy things, unless he wash his flesh with water. And when the sun is down, he shall be clean, and shall afterward eat of the holy things; because it is his food."* At the start of the new day, he is cleaned and able to continue his duty to the Lord.

You may have committed sins in your past that have gotten the best of you. You're reminded of them often, and feel that somehow you are unfit to be used in any way for God's purpose. I will readily admit that none of us are worthy of anything, but God's mercy and forgiveness is available to all who are willing to go to Him for cleansing.

God gives us new years, new months, and new days. These can be a reminder of a new day and a fresh start. You may have failed God yesterday, but your failures in the past do not have to be repeated today or in your future. Learn from your past, but don't repeat it, and certainly don't let it keep you from moving forward in life. If God hasn't given up on you, then why should you choose any different?

—— Today's Truth ——

Past sins do not have to dictate your future service. Today is a new day, and you can make the most of the gift of the present that God has given you.

The Oil in the Lampstand

Read Leviticus 24–25

THE TABERNACLE WAS completely enclosed, and the lampstand served as the light within the tabernacle. In the details all throughout the tabernacle are beautiful pictures of the Lord Jesus. For example, the oil that gave light to the lampstand has certain attributes that attest to a divine design. Leviticus 24:1–4 gives the command for the light in the holy place.

It was a particular oil. Verse 2 begins, *"Command the children of Israel…."* God's will should always to be done God's way. We can take liberties in the Christian life that were never permitted. If you realize anything from these passages concerning the Law and the tabernacle, understand that God has a detailed, specific purpose for everything He does.

It was a pure oil. The purity of this oil that spread light to the tabernacle is a picture of the Holy Spirit. The power of God's Spirit has a purity. God doesn't use junk. If we are to be the "light of the world" (Matthew 5:14) that we are commanded to be, we must be pure in our lives in order to shine the brightest. The slightest imperfection can hinder our light and our influence. Think of a dinner plate that hasn't been washed since your last meal. Will you use it for that beautifully prepared dinner, or will you clean it so that it is ready to be used?

It was a perpetual oil. This oil was to burn continually. Three times in these four verses, the Lord repeats that word "continually." Too many lives are filled with Christians who turn their lights off and on. They shine brightly at church, but their light is dimmed at work or with certain crowds. The place you are at or the people you are with should never determine whether or not you let your light shine for the Lord.

——Today's Truth——

The impact of your light will be determined by the oil (the presence of and relationship with the Holy Spirit) in your life. Fill yourself with His power, and your influence will extend wherever you go.

The Tithe Is the Lord's

Read Leviticus 26–27

A FATHER GAVE his little girl two dollars and told her, "You can do anything with one of your dollars, but the other dollar belongs to God." Excited to spend her dollar, she ran to the candy store. On the way, she tripped and dropped one of her dollars, and it fell into the storm drain. She got up and said, "Well, Lord, there goes *Your* dollar."

Tithing has become a doctrine filled with controversy. Some will argue that tithing is an Old Testament law and that we are not bound by a specific amount to give, but we are to practice grace giving as New Testament believers. While I do believe in grace giving, I also believe that tithing is a Bible command that goes beyond the law.

Leviticus 27:30 says, *"And all the tithe of the land, whether of the seed of the land, or of the fruit of the tree, is the LORD's: it is holy unto the LORD."* Remember, tithing was practiced by Abraham long before the Law was given to the Israelites in the wilderness. Tithing is a not a dispensational command; it is a Bible command.

The word *tithe* means "one-tenth." This means that ten percent of everything you receive belongs to God. While this may sound like quite a sacrifice, don't forget that God has given you one hundred percent of everything you have been given in life, and He requires only one-tenth in return. When you view money as your possession, it sounds like a rip-off. When you recognize what God has given to you, your view transforms into the grace giving model where God deserves not just a fraction, but all that we possess.

God doesn't need your money, but coming to the place where you are willing to obey any command, regardless of the sacrifice, is evidence of a surrendered and obedient will. Giving proves to God that He has control of everything that is closest to you.

—— Today's Truth ——

Nothing you possess should reign supreme over God's standing in your heart. While finances can be a touchy subject for most, finances can also be a telling indicator of the spiritual state of believers..

Declare Your Pedigree

Read Numbers 1–2

I F YOU ARE going to be used by God, you must know what you are and where you're from. In Numbers 1, God ordered Moses to number the people who were ready to go to war. Moses organized over 600,000 men, 20 years of age and older, besides women and children. Verse 18 reads, *"And they assembled all the congregation together on the first day of the second month, and they declared their pedigrees after their families."*

A pedigree refers to a lineage or an ancestry. You may or may not know much about your family and those who have lived before you, but if you're saved, you must know your pedigree. I John 3:2 says, "Now are we the sons of God." Your family name might not have any significance, but being a part of God's family and holding His name as your pedigree gives you reason and power for any battle that lies ahead. Romans 8:17 also states, *"And if children, then heirs; heirs of God, and joint-heirs with Christ; if so be that we suffer with him, that we may be also glorified together."*

Fanny Crosby penned these words:

> *Blessed assurance, Jesus is mine!*
> *Oh, what a foretaste of glory divine!*
> *Heir of salvation, purchase of God,*
> *Born of His Spirit, washed in His blood.*

—— Today's Truth ——

Everything good in life is possible because you are a child of God. This pedigree gives you access to help that we will never fully comprehend in this lifetime.

FEBRUARY 13

Sin Has No Respect of Persons

Read Numbers 3–4

I T HAS BEEN said before that God has no grandchildren. Just because you know someone or you're related to someone that is saved, surrendered, and sanctified, that does not mean that you hold any of those things personally. While I am thankful that my parents are saved, it is not their salvation that saved me. I was saved when I called upon the Lord as an eight-year-old boy in my mother's bedroom on a Sunday night after church.

Numbers 3 opens with the record of Aaron's family. Unfortunately, it is not a happy story, but a record of the consequences of sin. Nadab and Abihu offered strange fire before the Lord and died as a result of their sin. This home was wrecked and brought disgrace to Aaron's family as his sons died.

Sin has no limit to the damage it can cause. It will ruin lives, and nothing will hinder it from unleashing its devastating blows. These boys were from a good home, but that good home couldn't keep them from the destruction of sin. It makes no difference where you grew up, what your last name is, or what position your parents hold. Judgment will come to anyone who spits in the face of God and arrogantly defies His name.

I believe in forgiveness, mercy, and longsuffering. However, we should not count on God to always bail us out as an excuse to sin. Every day, I ask God for forgiveness, but His willingness to restore me does not give me a license to live according to my lusts. Sin is a dangerous fire waiting to destroy the lives of its victims.

——Today's Truth ——

No person is exempt from the consequences that sin will bring. Many will foolishly indulge in sin, somehow thinking that they will be the exception. Heed this warning. Don't be another casualty!

Happy Valentine's Day

Read Numbers 5–6

AMERICANS SPENT APPROXIMATELY $20 billion on Valentine's Day in 2019. The average consumer spent around $150. One hundred forty-four million cards were given, and $4.7 billion was spent on jewelry. Fifteen percent bought gift cards, and seventy-five percent of candy sales were chocolates. It's no secret that people will spend money on this day of love. However, the climate of marriages today does not reflect the healthy, God-given relationship that should resemble happiness, selflessness, and unity as the Bible describes marriage should be.

The Lord gives instructions for the law of jealousy and what to do when a spouse has been unfaithful. It is sad that we even have to address this subject, but many marriages will have to navigate through moments like this.

Marriage is designed to be awesome! It is a gift from God, plainly laid out in Genesis 2:18–24. That passage is mentioned four times in the New Testament because there is so much truth in those verses on marriage. If you're married, take a moment to realize that God created and designed your spouse specifically for you, and the same is true about you for your spouse. This relationship should be the closest, most fulfilling part of our lives.

When you got married, surely you repeated vows to your loved one. Were those vows just an emotional declaration of your love or a spiritual, lifelong commitment to that person through every season of life? Don't allow a moment of temptation or a valley of frustration to blur your vision of the gift that you have been given!

—— Today's Truth ——

Give up on your marriage, and you may have to navigate through the heartache of a situation described in this passage. Marriage is a perfect journey travelled by imperfect people. It's worth the work!

The Gift List

Read Numbers 7

THE BULK OF this lengthy chapter is the gifts that were offered by the leaders of the twelve tribes. On a side note, this chapter is the second longest chapter in the Bible next to Psalm 119. God chose to give us the details of this offering, and we can glean several truths from this list.

After Abraham Lincoln became president, before the days of civil service, office seekers besieged him everywhere trying to get appointments to various jobs throughout the country. Once, confined to bed with typhoid fever, exasperated, Lincoln declared to his secretary, "Bring on the office seekers; I now have something I can give to everybody."

The honest truth is that we do not give the Lord what He deserves. C. S. Lewis said, "I do not believe one can settle how much we ought to give. I am afraid the only safe rule is to give more than we can spare." We allow others to suffer while we watch our bank accounts grow. We watch churches suffer while boat sales continue to flourish.

What if God listed every gift you gave Him and listed it in detail like this chapter describes? I doubt these people knew that their gifts would be in the Bible for thousands of years, and I doubt any of us really understand the fact that God sees and remembers all that we do for Him.

——Today's Truth ——

Giving should be a natural outflow of the life of a child of God. We must continually offer ourselves and our possessions to God and to others after all the blessings He has given to us.

Red Light, Green Light

Read Numbers 8–9

Among a myriad of childhood memories, one game I can still clearly remember is "red light, green light." The winner of the game would be the one who ran as fast as they could when the instructor said, "green light," and reached the finish line first. But as soon as that instructor said, "red light," if you did not stop dead in your tracks, you would be eliminated. It may be the only time that a seven-year-old is straightly focused on the command of an adult to run or be still immediately.

In the final nine verses of Numbers 9, we see how God directed His people by a cloud in the day and a pillar of fire by night. When the cloud was taken up, they moved. When the cloud settled, they stopped. If they were to be in motion, they must keep on moving until it was clear to do otherwise. Once the cloud came down, the people stopped and were to wait patiently, only to begin on their journey when they were commanded to move.

God is the world's best navigator. Unlike those people who seem to know every shortcut and the best times to drive through the mountains to see the beautiful view but avoid the dangerous weather, God has your life all mapped out. He will send you on a journey you are not expecting, but if He says it's time to move, then it's time to move, not debate. God will tell you when it's time to sit tight and wait. You can complain and question, but taking matters into your own hands isn't the answer.

—— Today's Truth ——

Focus in on the instructor. Watch His calls. Listen to His commands without hesitation or delay. Allow God to guide you.

No Whining Allowed

Read Numbers 10–11

CERTAIN PEOPLE HAVE an infectious personality. At a party, people are drawn to them because of their laughter and passion, or just for pure entertainment. A group of people better compared to mosquito repellant to those around them would be the complainers.

It wasn't until I became a parent that I understood the humor and popularity of the signs beloved by parents that say "no whining allowed." Kids are cute, but whining is never cute. My little girls can stick out their bottom lip and look up at me with hope in their eyes, and it is very likely that daddy will grant their wish. Throwing themselves on the ground, throwing a pity party, or screaming because they didn't get their way will get them a different kind of a gift that every parent has to give more often then they'd like to admit.

As much as the complaining of others makes you cringe like you do when hearing nails on a chalkboard, Numbers 11:1–3 shows us clearly that God has the same view toward complaining. Maybe you do well to be grateful for the big things, but what about the weather, traffic, food that isn't prepared the way you like, or something at church that you think should be done another way? To the people, it may have just been food they were complaining about, but to God is was what His grace had given them to keep them alive.

——— Today's Truth ———

The antidote for a grumbling attitude is a grateful spirit. Instead of complaining about what's wrong, thank God today for the blessings He's given you!

Two Kinds of People

Read Numbers 12–13

Y OU'VE HEARD THIS statement prelude many different comparisons: "There are two kinds of people in the world." For example, there are the saved and the lost. There are Jews and Gentiles. There are those who check every app with the little icon at the top corner to get that number to go away, and then there are those who have little red notifications on so many apps, it looks like ketchup got splattered on their phone. Numbers 13 also shows two classes of people. They were from the same place, they served the same God, they spied out the same land, but their attitude separated them.

In this familiar story, it's easy to condemn the ten spies that feared the land because of the opposition in front of them. The two men who had faith greater than their fear were clearly the minority, and the same is true today not just among the population in general, but among believers.

D. L. Moody once said, "Faith looks not at the mountains, but over them. There is nothing that pleases the Son of God so much as faith." As you are presented with God's leading, you will usually notice the opposition first. It will scare you to death. If you have faith, however, it can scare you to life. Opposition, enemies, hazards, and potential failures are all very real. But remember that if you are following God's will, failure is not an option. Valleys aren't failures; they are divine detours that lead us to the same destination, even if it brings us along a different path than we expected.

—— Today's Truth ——

You will be identified with the group with which you choose to identify. Living by fear or living by faith will dictate what God can do through you and what kind of person you choose to be.

Ignorant Sin

Read Numbers 14–15

IN A POSITION of leadership or authority, you'll eventually hear this excuse, "I didn't know what I did was wrong." Children too will play the "dumb card," hoping that their ignorance will get them off with a warning instead of having to face their punishment. As we grow, we may not express it the same way, but we hope that God will show mercy for our ignorance in sins that we commit. Yes, God is merciful, but ignorance is never an excuse to do wrong.

Numbers 15 deals with sin that is done in ignorance and how to make it right. Atonement had to be made for the wrong that was done, because sin was still committed. Sin is still sin, whether you realize what you did or not. If ignorance was a valid excuse, I believe we would be motivated to close our Bibles, then avoid church and any teaching from God's Word so that we could enjoy our sin in ignorance.

Instead, mercy is given by our loving God to make right the wrongs that we have done, whether intentional or not. Jesus taught in Matthew 6 by the "Model Prayer" that asking forgiveness is to be a daily habit. You may not always remember all your sins, so ask forgiveness for the sins you have committed ignorantly and offer your confession as an atonement by the blood of Jesus to restore your relationship with God. Numbers 15:25 states that forgiveness is given to those who offer the proper sacrifice. Offer your confession to God, not your excuses.

—— Today's Truth ——

Every sin can bring hurt to your life, but God has provided a remedy for the obvious crimes we've committed as well as the ones we've committed in ignorance.

The Day the Earth Ate Korah

Read Numbers 16–18

WITH LEADERSHIP WILL always come a rebellion. It will be masked as a spiritual cause justified by its leader and deceived followers. Numbers 16 gives the account of the rebellion led by Korah against Moses.

The Kohathites had an esteemed duty in the temple as they were the ones to carry the holy things. Korah attacked Moses for taking too much for himself. The root of this attack was clearly discontentment. Korah forgot how good they had it. He forgot the privilege to do anything for the Lord, much less the important tasks given to them. This flaw is always found in bitter Christians.

In verse 3, this group gathered together and said, *"Ye take too much upon you, seeing all the congregation are holy, every one of them, and the LORD is among them."* This kind of people will use the name of Jesus to make their cause sound justified. They made it sound like the cause was for "the people." It amazes me how people jump on the bandwagon of a group like this just because it sounds noble. People want to be a part of something, but be careful what you insert yourself into.

We also can see that this accusation was made publicly. It's amazing how bold people can be in their defiance, and they want and audience. Many use social media to scold and crucify people to make a point. A point is being made, but it's not the one that they're trying to get across. Instead of looking for someone to attack, someone to accuse, or someone to overthrow, take a step back and see if the situation is really what it is alleged to be.

—— Today's Truth ——

Every rebellion has a leader, but you must choose if you will follow. The wrath of God came not just to Korah, but to the foolish followers that hopped on board his parade.

Adding to the Problem

Read Numbers 19–20

PEOPLE PRODUCE PROBLEMS. It's the sad and ugly fact of life. You are either the cause of the problem, being affected by the ones causing the problem, or being blamed for the problem. Drama, drama, drama! Even a godly leader like Moses had reached his tipping point with the wilderness wanderers. In a righteous fit, Moses struck the rock twice that God told him would produce water. The rock did just that, but God told Moses to speak to the rock, not smite it.

In a tense moment, Moses acted out in his emotional rage and made a bad situation worse. The people were complaining, and this wasn't the first time. Moses and Aaron did right in going to God, and God was right there to hear their cry and meet their need. God gave the instructions, and Moses obliterated them. The miracle was all set, but Moses added to the problem as opposed to taking advantage of the solution.

When you allow your emotions to take over, problems become worse. What started as a minor disagreement turns into a vicious fight because one reacted emotionally. Going back and forth like this will make a problem larger and more severe, until someone reaches the point of explosion.

Speak with grace. Work toward a Biblical resolution. Cry out to God to express your struggle. Ask Him for wisdom and help in dealing with the situation. God has the solution. The miracle is all set to make things right. You can either add to the problem and join others in the complaint and bitterness, or you can be in the best seat in the house as God turns the tide and works it all together for good.

—— Today's Truth ——

Frustration comes from many different scenarios. Don't give in to temptation and make matters worse. Follow God's solution to work it all out.

Snakebite

Read Numbers 21–22

ABOUT ONE-THIRD OF humans are afraid of snakes. This is known as ophidiophobia, and is the most common phobia. My ophidiophobia goes back to when I was pretty young and my friend had a pet snake at his house. I don't know the type or size of snake, but for a seven-year-old, it might as well have been as big as the ones on *National Geographic* or horror movies involving snakes. Watching that snake out of its cage triggered every sense in my body to do one thing—survive.

If the Hebrew people didn't have this phobia yet, they certainly developed it after this passage. God sent serpents to bite the people; this claimed many lives. Again, the people complained, looked back, doubted, and turned their back on God. You would think they would have learned by this point.

Truth be told, the same could be said about us if others could read of our lives the way that we are able to read about the Jews.

All of mankind has been bitten by the snake of sin, beginning with the first humans and the first snake in the first book of the Bible. We cannot save ourselves, but we have been given a Saviour, lifted for all to see and look to for salvation. Just as the requirement for healing was the faith to accept the simple, yet powerful truth, so is the solution today. We must accept Jesus, lifted up on the cross to save us from the penalty of sin's bite.

The result? No more snake biting! Sin has no power over our souls anymore. Too many are looking for help or living on borrowed time when the answer is right in front of them. The bite of sin is deadly, but Jesus is the cure. The prescription is to accept Him, trust Him, and then follow Him after He's given your life back.

—— Today's Truth ——

You don't have to suffer. Living in the misery that sin brings doesn't have to be your life after salvation. Jesus is the answer if you'll look right in front of you to the cross. He's waiting!

Zealous for God's Sake

Read Numbers 23–25

To truly want God's favor, you must be vigilant in stopping sin as it presents itself. You may feel that you're spending more time killing weeds than planting flowers, but a beautiful garden is possible only when we remove that which can take away from the beauty. This cannot be done in a halfhearted or lackluster fashion. This can only be successful through zealous effort.

Perverse sin was taking place in the camp in Numbers 25, and God was not playing games with their wickedness and ungodly worship. Again, the Lord had to bring to the Jews' attention that serious sin had taken place, and the consequences were devastating. Then, out of the shadows came Phineas with his javelin. God commended him in verse 11, *"Phineas…hath turned my wrath away from the children of Israel, while he was zealous for my sake…."* It was the zeal of one man who acted when evil was destroying the chance of blessing upon his people.

Zeal is defined by *Webster's 1828 Dictionary* as "an eagerness of desire to accomplish or obtain some object, and it may be manifested either in favor of any person or thing, or in opposition to it, and in a good or bad cause." In this scenario, zeal is having a tenacity toward keeping sin out of your home, away from your children's eyes, out of your heart toward another person, and out of your life. Halford Lucock was quoted in *Progressive Magazine* for saying, "I was impressed several years ago when I read that Eugene Ormandy dislocated a shoulder while directing the Philadelphia Orchestra. I do not know what they were playing, but he was giving all of himself to it! And I have asked myself sadly, 'Did I ever dislocate anything, even a necktie?'"

—— Today's Truth ——

Exercise strong caution. Call it paranoia if you want. Do all that you can to keep the devil out and God in, and you will be thankful you were zealous and on guard, instead of being vulnerable and destroyed.

Left Out

Read Numbers 26–27

A GREAT EFFORT of preparation is often put into parties, cele-brations, and special events. Food is carefully planned, making sure to count every head and account for the portion each person will consume. Decorations fill the room to create an atmosphere to complement the event. Perhaps presents are purchased, games are planned, and a guest list is made. The only problem is that your name isn't on the list. Doesn't feel good, right? Nobody likes to be left out, but it happens. Sometimes, it's an honest mistake. Other times, when you're the one hosting the event, you just hope those who weren't invited for whatever reason don't get their feelings hurt.

This lengthy chapter of Numbers 26 may seem like just another list to you. The book of Numbers began with a similar list some thirty-eight years prior at Mount Sinai. God commanded them to take a census that was probably for strategic purposes as they prepared for battle for when they would embark on their quest to claim the Promised Land.

A lot has happened since then. No longer will this generation ever see that land. Now, another census is taken totaling over 600,000 people. During these intervening years, five tribes lost men (Simeon lost approximately 63%) and seven gained men (Manasseh gained 64%). These losses and gains aren't the glaring differences though. The most obvious difference is the people who were left out of the numbering. The original people numbered in chapter one were not numbered here. They could've been standing by watching this great counting take place knowing that they would never be a part of what this group was to experience. This is what happens when you serve the flesh and forget God's way. You, too, will be left out, standing on the sidelines watching while others enjoy the blessings of God.

—— Today's Truth ——

This doesn't have to be you. You can be on the right side of receiving God's blessings if you decide today to surrender to God and follow His instructions. He wants you to join the group!

The Middle Man

Read Numbers 28–29

THIS PASSAGE GIVES the order and timing of the sacrifices that the Israelites were to offer throughout the year. This was surely enough to keep the priests and Levites busy. God made it clear how He wanted it all to be done, and He gave the commandment to Moses, who then gave it to the people. Numbers 29 closes, *"And Moses told the children of Israel according to all that the Lord commanded Moses."* Moses was the middleman.

This is all God wants you to be as you witness for Him. Be willing to be a middleman, speaking the truth in its entirety and exactly how it was given. There's nothing glamorous about being the middleman. In fact, companies are eager to cut out the middleman and procure their product directly from the source. They don't need the middleman if they can get it themselves.

God has chosen to use people like you and me, His children, to tell others about the truth of the gospel and what the Bible teaches about the Christian life. Middlemen don't dictate or create; they are just messengers. Connecting people to Jesus is what we have been commissioned to do. When you go soul winning, you cannot save the lost souls of men, and you cannot answer their prayers; but you can connect them with the One who can. That's what you can do, and that what Moses did so well. John the Baptist understood this as we read of his response to those questioning him in John 1:22–23, *"Then said they unto him, Who art thou? that we may give an answer to them that sent us. What sayest thou of thyself? He said, I am the voice of one crying in the wilderness, Make straight the way of the Lord, as said the prophet Esaias."* May we be a middleman like John the Baptist today!

—— Today's Truth ——

Allow God's Word into your heart and then let it flow through you as a messenger for the truth.

God Settles the Score

Read Numbers 30–31

Getting even after you have or someone you care about has been hurt or mistreated is a mindset that will never satisfy. God never commands us to settle the score. It's not our job to make sure that evildoers pay, but to leave it in God's hands and let Him do what needs to be done in the way that He chooses and in the timing that He sees fit. Numbers 31:1–2 gives the order from God to avenge His people, *"And the Lord spake unto Moses, saying, Avenge the children of Israel of the Midianites: afterward shalt thou be gathered unto thy people."*

Perhaps you have a score with someone that you feel needs to be settled. You may be tempted to act or bring justice in a way that you believe is right, but only evil can come from that. God gives those in authority the right to take care of matters in a proper way, but not every person has been instituted to be judge, jury, and executioner. This command will undoubtedly leave us helpless, and maybe that's exactly what we need. It is in our helplessness that we will let go of bitterness and turn our hearts to God and trust that He will make things right.

Here's the honest truth: not every situation—in fact, not many situations—will work out how you'd like them to. You will go crazy focusing on all the injustice that you see in the world around you. Let it go, and allow God to do His job as only He can. Romans 12:19 states, *"Dearly beloved, avenge not yourselves, but rather give place unto wrath: for it is written, Vengeance is mine; I will repay, saith the Lord."*

——— Today's Truth ———

When you are tempted to act, get even, or settle the score, instead have faith that God will take care of the situation. God's way and timing is always the right way. Ours is often the opposite.

Settling Down

Read Numbers 32–33

Now that the children of Israel had conquered Midian and Moab, the tribes of Reuben and Gad looked around at the land before them and said unto Moses, *"...if we have found grace in thy sight, let this land be given unto thy servants for a possession, and bring us not over Jordan"* (Numbers 32:5). They decided that after the battles they had faced, it was time and probably appropriate to settle down for a while. Notice the last phrase of that verse though: *"...and bring us not over Jordan."*

In their weariness, they allowed fatigue to cause them to be content to stay where they were, instead of resting, recuperating, and pressing forward across the river to the land that God had prepared for them. The verse to follow shows Moses scolding them for this way of thinking, knowing what it meant for them and for the other tribes that would see this.

Too many Christians see God give a few victories and settle down instead of pressing forward. Someone said it this way: "Some people dream of great accomplishments while others stay awake and do them." Basically, it's usually the minority that is willing to press forward into the Promised Land, seeing victory after victory. People will see one person get saved out soul winning and then quit after that door. Some will make a special sacrifice to give, then check that deed off their bucket list to never repeat it again. Others will read their Bible through then leave it on the shelf since it's already finished. Don't quit while you're ahead. Don't settle down when God still wants to give you more miraculous victories that you'll recite to your children and grandchildren. Keep pressing forward!

—— Today's Truth ——

Contentment has two parts. We should be content with what God has given us, but never content with what we've done for Him. Strive to do more. You still have something left in the tank to do something for God!

Near Jericho

Read Numbers 34–36

THE BOOK OF Numbers begins in the wilderness then, fast forwarding some forty years, ends in the wilderness. But where they end is much closer to the Promised Land than where they began. Numbers 36:13 closes, *"These are the commandments and the judgments, which the Lord commanded by the hand of Moses unto the children of Israel in the plains of Moab by Jordan near Jericho."* They were still in the wilderness, but now they were so close they could almost taste what it was like to finally be in that land. The people had to leave Egypt and cross the Red Sea. They had to experience the wilderness (a test that generation failed miserably). An unbelieving generation had to die off. They had to wander. Now, they were ready, but not there yet.

Excitement is found in seeing people getting saved, growing in their walk, and living like Jesus. However, that is not the end. Having the Jordan River separating the Israelites from the Promised Land was better than where they were before, but they were still in the wilderness. You see, being close to where God wants you isn't enough. Giving most of your life to God isn't the plan. Going ninety percent of the way just doesn't cut it. Eventually, you have to cross over.

Isn't it exciting to look forward in life and just imagine what God is going to do? The wilderness is absolutely necessary, but it is not the end, even when there is excitement. God wants to you step forward by faith and claim what He has prepared for you, but you have to cross the river to do it. You have to let go of the sin that's holding you back. Move on from past mistakes. Then have faith in the great, big God that we serve and watch Him do what you can only dream. "Near Jericho" isn't where you want to be. It's a checkpoint, not a finish line.

—— Today's Truth ——

Close to the will of God won't give you peace, power, or, most important of all, the presence of God that you need. Cross over. The water's just fine!

A Final Task

Read Deuteronomy 1–2

DEUTERONOMY, THE LAST book of the Pentateuch and the last book Moses' wrote, is a repetition of the Law. It is known as "the second Law." It needed to be repeated because repetition is the key to learning. In order to keep the Law, the people had to be familiar with the Law. It's difficult to forget something you've heard, read, or written multiple times. Moreover, I believe a clearer and greater reason for the second giving of the Law exists: A new generation had been born who were not around the first time it was given.

This new generation was camped on the east bank of the Jordan River, and they were about one month away from entering the Promised Land. Before they could move forward, Moses had one more job to do. He needed to give the Law to this new generation—the Law that the former generation had failed to keep.

The world is constantly changing around us. When I was a teenager, smart phones were introduced. Camera phones were the rage. Looking back, those cameras were a joke compared to the technology and ability of phones in 2020. Times have changed. One thing that will never change is the law and commands that God has given. Just because the old generation failed to obey it didn't change the purpose of the Law. Now, the responsibility lay with this new generation.

The generation following you needs you to pass along the law of God to them. You may have failed it a time or two. You may have even disagreed with it in part. Nevertheless, it is up to you to encourage this group to hold fast to the commands of God, to not repeat the same mistakes that you made, and to trust that God will give His favor to those who follow His leading.

—— Today's Truth ——

Moses' final purpose was to pass down what he'd been given. This purpose is the same for every individual. You will have people following behind you, and it is your duty to teach them and to repeat the law that you've been given.

You've Seen It Before

Read Deuteronomy 3–4

JOSHUA WAS FACED with a huge task. He had to unify the people and lead them into enemy territory where they would face battles unlike anything they had seen before. Joshua was only human, so I imagine a part of him questioned, "Can I really do this? Moses couldn't even get the people to follow God. How am I supposed to do it? I'm not sure we're strong enough to win these battles." Moses gives this charge to Joshua in Deuteronomy 3:21–22: *"And I commanded Joshua at that time, saying, Thine eyes have seen all that the Lord your God hath done unto these two kings: so shall the Lord do unto all the kingdoms whither thou passest. Ye shall not fear them: for the Lord your God he shall fight for you."*

Fear isn't always sinful. After all, we are human. However, it's laughable what we allow to scare us. While the human side of Joshua was undoubtedly afraid, Moses directs his eyes to the past. He reminded Joshua that the God of Israel that gave them victory in the past was the same God who would fight for them in their future battles.

Past victories increase our faith for future battles. Your faith will feel empty when you forget what God has done in the past. A good memory of the past gives us fuel in our spiritual tanks for the testing that lies ahead. Don't forget what God has done for you. Don't overlook the victories God has given others. In other words, He's done it before, and He's done it more than once. You have no reason to be afraid, even if it feels just as scary as the first battle you faced.

—— Today's Truth ——

The great tragedy for Christians is our forgetfulness of God's faithfulness throughout our lives. Your list of the blessings that God has given you will never end, and that should open your eyes to see that God is still able to give you victory. You won't doubt Him if you won't forget Him!

Listen Up

Read Deuteronomy 5–7

WERE YOU EVER told this as a child: "God gave you two ears and one mouth." This statement is more than an anatomy lesson. Deuteronomy 5:1 begins this way as Moses instructs the people, *"And Moses called all Israel, and said unto them, Hear, O Israel, the statutes and judgments which I speak in your ears this day, that ye may learn them, and keep, and do them."*

Here's what he wanted them to do with the message he was giving:

Hear. It is very frustrating to try to talk to somebody who won't stop talking, won't focus on what you're saying, or appears to be listening until you realize that you have to repeat yourself because what you said went in one ear and out the other.

Learn. Knowledge isn't the most important thing, but you can't follow what you don't know. In order to teach others, you have to learn for yourself. Pick up your Bible and study it. We live in an era with a massive amount of information at our fingertips. It's a shame we know more about the newest movies in Hollywood and the current events in the sports world than we do about Bible examples of baptism by immersion without searching the Internet.

Keep. Learning something in your head is not the same as keeping it in your heart. You can learn something without accepting it and holding it in your heart and life. God's Word should not be something that you learn for the moment like you would cram for a test or a job in the near future. The instruction He gives is what you need for your entire life.

Do. All of this is worthless if you don't follow what's been given to you. I'll never understand those who will attend church faithfully and never change their lives to follow what God commands. As Nike so eloquently puts it, "Just do it."

—— Today's Truth ——

God has a message that He wants you to hear, and this is the process that needs to take place in order for you to follow and receive the blessings God wants to give you—hear, learn, keep, and do.

Don't Forget to Remember

Read Deuteronomy 8–10

To me, one of the saddest things to happen to people at the end of life, aside from physical pain and suffering, is the drifting of the mind. I've visited with family and church members who are present physically, but they are no longer the person I remember them to be from the past. The look in their eyes is different. The way they talk is different. If you ask whether they remember something from the past, they just offer a blank stare that reveals no recollection of the memory.

Forgetfulness is sometimes caused by illness due to disease, but it is also an illness caused when Christians forget the God of their past. In Deuteronomy 8:11, God warns the people, *"Beware that thou forget not the LORD thy God, in not keeping his commandments, and his judgments, and his statutes, which I command thee this day:"* God knew that the key to a successful future was to keep a good memory of the past.

The truth is that we can forget who God is while we're in the midst of a battle or down in the valley. We believe He is real, but we've forgotten how real He is. It seems silly to think that God had to tell the people not to forget Him. I don't think He really thought they wouldn't remember who He was. This command was given to teach them to keep God and the commands that He had given at the front of their minds.

Every day, as you open your Bible, you bring the presence of God back into your mind. This can happen when we pray, attend church, heed the Holy Spirit, and do any spiritual work. Forgetting is easy when you don't purpose to remember. You may not literally forget who God is, but if you don't think of Him as you go into the battlefield of life, is there really a difference?

—— Today's Truth ——

Keep God in the memory banks of your mind all the time. When you think of Him, you'll obey Him, you'll have more faith, and you'll not end up like those who missed out on God's blessings.

Be Careful Up There

Read Deuteronomy 11–13

Our nation is full of beautiful God-made and man-made structures that rise high into the air. Some love to stand right at the edge of a building or cliff and look down. As spectacular as these views from great heights are, the Grand Canyon average two to three deaths per year because people fall over the edge. The vast majority of these deaths occur in men. Some are posing for pictures or pretending to fall. No wonder women statistically live longer!

Just as we can enjoy the beautiful view from heights here on earth, God also brings us to spiritual heights as we journey through life. However, even these spiritual heights have a danger, and God warns the Jews about it as they prepare to enter the Promised Land in Deuteronomy 11:16–17, *"Take heed to yourselves, that your heart be not deceived, and ye turn aside, and serve other gods, and worship them; And then the Lord's wrath be kindled against you, and he shut up the heaven, that there be no rain, and that the land yield not her fruit; and lest ye perish quickly from off the good land which the Lord giveth you."* In other words, "Don't fall when I bring you to the top of the mountain of spiritual blessings"!

The valley requires a certain focus. Getting through a trying season makes you dig deep down to push through. It's on the mountaintop that we tend to pull out the recliner, grab an iced tea, and enjoy the scenery. We're not as sharp or motivated on the mountain. And the result can be deadly. You may not be able to be as fervent in prayer as when you desperately needed God to do that miracle, but losing your fervency in prayer or any other part of the Christian life is like standing at the edge of the cliff, posing for a funny photo. You're at risk of falling, and your focus makes all the difference. Verse 16 begins, *"Take heed…."* Don't fall off the edge. You may not like the climb back up the second time.

—— Today's Truth ——

Because blessings are so enjoyable, the fall becomes easy. Take heed to keep yourself in the position that got you to the mountaintop.

Ye Are the Children of the LORD

Read Deuteronomy 14–16

Y OU'VE LIKELY BEEN asked by someone, "Tell me about yourself." We tend to start with our career: "I own my own business," "I work in retail," "I work construction," etc. Maybe we go into detail about our family life, and then personality traits. While there are many facts about you that can describe who you are, none is greater than, "I am a child of God." Your work may describe what you're passionate about or what you do to provide for your family. Your hobbies may describe your interests. Your family may give insight into your personal life. Being a part of the family of God encompasses so much more. This truth doesn't just flow into some parts of your life. It is the very reason for your existence. To live outside of the family of God is scattered, pointless, and a sad waste.

Following Deuteronomy 14:1, which says, *"Ye are the children of the LORD your God,"* are a series of laws and precedents for the people of Israel to follow. What is the reason for this? Doesn't salvation give us freedom? Verse 2 states, *"For thou art an holy people unto the Lord thy God, and the Lord hath chosen thee to be a peculiar people unto himself, above all the nations that are upon the earth."* Because you are His, you are special. God chose you to be a part of the family, even long before you chose to accept Him. With this new title, you are different now.

All the commands, the standards and convictions we hold to are what separate us from the lost in the world. Being a part of God's family is so special and so incredible, but a certain way of living comes with this new life. God doesn't want you to be in the family by name only, but also by the way you live.

—— Today's Truth ——

Live in a way that represents the family of which you are a part. Don't be ashamed of it. Broadcast it. Enjoy it. And learn to heed the instruction God gives with this special privilege.

Phony Preachers

Read Deuteronomy 17–20

DON'T KID YOURSELF. God won't tolerate His name being associated with wickedness or watered down with man's teaching. In all parts of the world and at all times, there always have been and continue to be people who claim to be messengers of God who do more harm than good to the name of Christ. Famous speakers such as Joel Osteen, T.D. Jakes, Beth Moore and others have been widely accepted by Christians. Their book deals continue to fund their lavish lifestyles, and their watered down, twisted doctrine that proclaims everyone to be good with no real flaws other than a need to overcome their fears of whatever obstacle they are facing is consumed by millions of people.

While the punishment for the false prophet of Moses' day may not be applicable to us today, we can understand God's seriousness regarding those who misrepresent His name.

The final word given about these false teachers in Deuteronomy 18:21 is this, "…thou shalt not be afraid of him." The power of God is not behind the "wolf in sheep's clothing," but in the child of God who is rightly following and representing Him. Be careful not to be deceived by some who claim to serve in "the name of the Lord." But don't be so consumed by false teachers or prophets that you take your focus off the true God that you serve. Enemies, wolves, and deceivers come in a variety pack of all shapes and colors, but false teachers come and go. Stick with the One who started it all, sustains it all, and is supreme above them all.

—— Today's Truth ——

Deceit is one of Satan's dirtiest and most effective tricks. You don't have to wonder what or who is of God when we have the Word of God. The standard for truth will always be clear with those who follow His ways above their own.

Back and Forth

Read Deuteronomy 21–23

I WONDER HOW many times God has heard, "Lord, I promise I'll never do it again if You…." We promise God the moon and stars if He does what we request. Decisions are made at the altar on a regular basis. "I give You my life, I'll do what You ask, I surrender to Your will"—we make bold proclamations of our commitment to God. We've all been there. We commit in our sincerity, only to find ourselves at the altar, on our knees, begging God to give us another chance for going back on our commitment.

I'm all for decisions. I believe the altar call at the close of a service is an important time as it urges people to respond to God's Spirit. But what we do after the decision is made is what God is really interested in. Once you've given God your heart, you must follow through with your actions.

Deuteronomy 23:21–22 states, *"When thou shalt vow a vow unto the LORD thy God, thou shalt not slack to pay it: for the LORD thy God will surely require it of thee; and it would be sin in thee. But if thou shalt forbear to vow, it shall be no sin in thee."* God expects you to keep your word to Him. I'll never forget hearing my grandfather tell the story at my grandmother's funeral of their decision to empty their home of alcohol. The pastor had preached, and they fell under conviction. They had been growing in the Lord, and they went home and gathered all the alcohol in the house, dumped it out, and never touched another drop for the rest of their lives.

Thank God for decisions and good intentions, but they're of little worth unless we follow through. This passage tells us that God expects us to keep our vows. He believes us when we tell Him that we'll do better and that we'll do what we said we would do. This shouldn't scare us away from making decisions. However, it should keep us from breaking our vows.

—— Today's Truth ——

Follow through with the vows you've made to God. Don't make them lightly. God expects us to follow through when we make a vow to Him.

Every Good Thing

Read Deuteronomy 24–27

R.A. Torrey said this: "If you want the deepest, purest, sweetest, most overflowing joy there is to be known on earth, come to Jesus Christ." There is more joy in Jesus in the smallest ways than the biggest and best this world has to offer. God has been so good to us, and we are to rejoice in what He has done. Deuteronomy 26:11 says, *"And thou shalt rejoice in every good thing which the Lord thy God hath given unto thee, and unto thine house, thou, and the Levite, and the stranger that is among you."*

You will never be more joyful than you decide to be. The Israelites had all the reason in the world to be joyful, yet they complained over and over and missed out on the good things the Lord had planned for them. Every good thing they received happened because of Him. Nothing good that has taken place comes without the hand of God pulling the strings. Those good things are a gift from God.

Athletes, politicians, CEOs, celebrities, and a variety of men and women are praised every day by man. But what have any of those people done for us? Their admirers will wait in line for hours, sometimes days. They will pay unthinkable amounts of money. They will sacrifice time away from family and work. And they will do all of this to praise people who have not done a single good thing for them. What they've done, they've largely done for themselves, yet people rejoice in that. They don't deserve the praise, God does! Have you forgotten what Egypt was like? Have you forgotten the miracles that He performed not long ago? Have you forgotten the Spirit that guided you through that wilderness? Rejoice in the Lord today, and in all of the good things He has done for you!

—— Today's Truth ——

Good things happen every day. When you notice them, give God the glory. He is the giver of every good thing in this life and the next!

The Business of Blessing

Read Deuteronomy 28

GOD IS IN the blessings business, and He is interested in blessing you. We all have already received blessings from God, no matter what point we're at in life. Regardless of the hard times we've faced, God has still blessed us.

A young boy went to a local store with his mother. The owner passed him a large jar of suckers and told him to help himself to a handful. But the boy held back. The mother nudged him to take the candy this kind man was offering, but he didn't budge. Finally, the man reached in and gave the boy a handful of suckers. When they got outside, the mother asked her son why he did this. He replied, "Because his hand is much bigger than mine!"

Friend, God can bless you in ways no other human can give. This is why I believe it is not wrong to give children incentives. God uses blessings to motivate us to live for Him, and the thought of what the mighty hand of God can bring should give you an abundance of reasons to serve Him.

Just because God wants to bless you, and just because He can bless you, doesn't mean that He will. He requires something of you. Deuteronomy 28:1 says, *"And it shall come to pass, if thou shalt hearken diligently unto the voice of the LORD thy God, to observe and to do all his commandments which I command thee this day, that the LORD thy God will set thee on high above all nations of the earth."* What God requires is that we diligently listen and do what He's commanded. No wonder God isn't blessing those who are skipping church, neglecting soul winning, and holding back their tithe. Our obedience is the requirement to receive God's blessing.

—— Today's Truth ——

Everyone wants to be blessed, but not everyone looks to the right source or listens to the right voice. Look no further. Serve no one else. Come to God's business of blessing. There's nothing like it!

Blinded to See

Read Deuteronomy 29–31

FANNY CROSBY WROTE thousands of hymns. In fact, she wrote so many hymns that she used other names so that hymnbooks would not be filled with just her name. This godly lady, through a heartbreaking event, lost her sight shortly after her birth. A man who claimed to be a doctor prescribed a treatment to her parents of applying hot mustard poultices on her eyes when she was ill. She was blinded, and the man fled, never to be seen again. A few months later, her father died. Consequently, her mother was forced to work to provide for the family, and Fanny was raised primarily by her grandmother. Her grandmother was the reason she developed a love for poetry. She wrote her first poem at the age of eight:

Oh, what a happy soul I am,
although I cannot see,
I am resolved that in this world,
Contented I will be!
How many blessings I enjoy
That other people don't,
To weep and sigh because I'm blind,
I cannot, and I won't!

A preacher once told Fanny how he felt pity that the Lord did not give her sight when He had blessed her with so many gifts. She replied, "Do you know that if at birth I had been able to make one petition, it would have been that I was born blind?" She continued, "Because when I get to Heaven, the first face that shall ever gladden my sight will be that of my Saviour!"

—— Today's Truth ——

In Deuteronomy 28:4, we see that though the Israelites saw the wonders of God with their eyes, they were blinded and missed what was right before them. Don't miss what God is doing right in front of you!

A Front Row Seat

Read Deuteronomy 32–34

THIS MOMENT WAS bittersweet. Moses knew what God was about to do. The Israelites were about to enter the land that he had dreamed about for so many years. This is the land that made leaving Egypt, crossing the Red Sea, and enduring the wilderness all worthwhile. However, Moses knew he wouldn't get to experience the joy of this land with the people.

God's final command given to Moses was to go up on the mount and die there (Deuteronomy 32:28–30). Moses couldn't enter, but God let him see the land that He had originally promised him. Deuteronomy 34:7 makes it clear that Moses didn't die due to illness or lack of strength. Moses died because of his disobedience and God's chastisement. Verse 10 summarizes Moses' life with this conclusion: *"And there arose not a prophet since in Israel like unto Moses."* God used this great man, but I'm sure Moses undoubtedly felt pain as he saw the Promised Land yet failed to have the chance to experience it for himself.

Moses had a front row seat to the Promised Land, but the front row seat was still the bench. Are you tired of watching God answer the prayers of others, use others to see souls saved, and give blessings to the people around you? Surely you ought to rejoice in this, but you don't have to just watch the work of God in the lives of others. You can see God work in your life too if you'll get in the game. Too many are living on the sidelines, watching God's hand move on the lives of His church and fellow Christians. Too many can't remember the last time God answered a specific prayer because they can't remember the last time they prayed for anything other than a meal or in a church service. I don't want to belittle Moses, because God used him mightily, yet his life ended in a different way than he probably ever pictured that it would. Let this story and the end of the life of a great man of God move you to be a part of the group that God uses, not just a spectator.

—— Today's Truth ——

Some watch. Some do. In which group are you?

The Scarlet Line

Read Joshua 1–3

As the spies were sent to gather intelligence about Jericho, a harlot named Rahab was used to protect God's people. She saw them as ambassadors of something greater than a nation; she saw them as representatives of the God of their nation. She helped them escape by placing a scarlet cord in her window. Through this deed, she saved herself and her family and trusted in God's people for their protection.

It may appear that it was because of the spies that Rahab was saved. It may appear that it is because of the soul winner that a sinner is saved, but salvation comes by none other than Jesus Christ! By her simple act of faith, Rahab saved herself and her family. The scarlet cord in her story symbolizes the blood of Christ. I Peter 1:18–19 tells us, *"Forasmuch as ye know that ye were not redeemed with corruptible things, as silver and gold, from your vain conversation received by tradition from your fathers; But with the precious blood of Christ, as of a lamb without blemish and without spot."*

Sin separates us from God. It brings a need for reconciliation. Our relationship with the Father cannot be reconciled by our own merit. Here's a harlot, living a wicked lifestyle. She lived in the world, but she wasn't satisfied with the life that the world had to offer. Salvation came not because of what she did, but because of her faith. Hebrews 11, the "hall of faith," even recites her story. Works will never be enough. So many place their hope in their good deeds and their good intentions. None of that will matter. When the walls of Jericho fell and Rahab's house was the only one unmoved, she knew it wasn't because of anything she had done. The security of salvation is solely by the scarlet cord—the precious blood of Christ.

——Today's Truth——

Just like Rahab, your house will stand when judgment comes; but this "house" isn't the place where you sleep. It is your life. The scarlet cord reminds us of the One behind this miracle and the only One who deserves to be praised.

Kaboom!

Read Joshua 4–6

T HIS HAD TO have seemed like a terrible plan. No military expert would advise you to walk around the fortress of your enemy every day and multiple times on the seventh consecutive day. Yet that is exactly what Joshua and the Israelites did. It made no sense, but God's will doesn't have to make sense to be of God. For numerology enthusiasts, the number seven is very predominant in Joshua 6, as it is shown eleven times. This numbers symbolizes a perfection or completion. Since Jericho was the first "battle" the Israelites would face as they entered the land promised to them so long ago, this seems very fitting.

The people followed the plan. As crazy as it seemed to risk their lives to go on a stroll around this city, they obeyed. The result is given in Joshua 6:20: *"So the people shouted when the priests blew with the trumpets: and it came to pass, when the people heard the sound of the trumpet, and the people shouted with a great shout, that the wall fell down flat, so that the people went up into the city, every man straight before him, and they took the city."*

Kaboom! The walls fell. What an amazing spectacle this was for the people to see!

God is capable of doing the impossible, no matter how daunting the opposition may seem. Whether it's reaching the whole world or reaching that one person you've been praying for, God can do it if you follow Him and obey in faith. We tell this story to children in Sunday school classes, because children need to know how big and mighty God is. If it is His will and if we obey in faith, every wall of opposition before us will fall.

—— Today's Truth ——

Whatever wall stands before you, God can tear it down. With faith in His plan and obedience to His will, He is able.

The Second Half

Read Joshua 7–8

URING HALFTIME OF the first game of the 2018 NFL season, Vontae Davis announced his retirement. It should be noted that his team was losing 28-6 at halftime. If you've played sports, you know halftime to be an opportunity to regroup. It is a chance to slow down, get your mind right, and get ready for the second half.

In a sense, Joshua 8 was the second half of the showdown with Ai. Like Mr. Davis, some of the Israelites probably wanted to throw in the towel after suffering loss at the hands of an underdog like Ai. After some spiritual cleansing, however, they were ready for battle.

This is one of my favorite battles in the book of Joshua. It was strategically an ingenious plan to lure the enemy out while a second group went in and took over. Once the army began to retreat, they were surrounded on both sides and Israel was easily victorious. This had to have been one of those "feel good" moments for the army of God.

Halftime is just that—the halfway point. Halftime doesn't mean "game over," even though sometimes we feel this way. We give up in our heart, wave the white flag, and coast in defeat until the finish line. This may be your chosen path, but it doesn't have to be.

In 2001, Erik Weihenmayer reached the top of Mount Everest. About 150 people do this every year. This was special considering that Eric was blind. This man was born with a disease and was completely blind by the time he was thirteen. He was the first blind person to achieve this feat. He was victorious because of his determination to win, despite feeling the sensation of defeat. Instead of giving up because of hardship, he achieved something that seems impossible to most. But Eric refused to concede defeat. Don't treat halftime like it's the end of the game.

—— Today's Truth ——

Quitting should never be on your option list. God does His greatest work at times when we least expect it. After all, victory wouldn't require faith if you knew it was coming.

The Day That Wouldn't End

Read Joshua 9–10

Some days just feel like they'll never end. DMV lines, ER waiting rooms, stop lights in the middle of nowhere that don't turn green as soon as you pull up—these situations throughout our lives are times that feel extended. However, we know that sixty minutes is still sixty minutes, whether we're staring aimlessly at the clock or working diligently on a project we're passionate about. Time is the same. It is our perception of time that changes due to our activity.

There is, however, one exception. The day that God made the sun stand still will forever be an antagonist to scoffers. The truth remains that God is God, and He is not constricted to time or space like man. He is free to do what He wants, when He wants, and He will do it in the way He wants it done. Joshua 10:13–14 tells us about this day, *"And the sun stood still, and the moon stayed, until the people had avenged themselves upon their enemies…And there was no day like that before it or after it, that the Lord hearkened unto the voice of a man: for the Lord fought for Israel."*

While it was God that performed the supernatural act, it was the prayer of Joshua that started the process. Notice that the Bible said there was no day like this day, not only because the sun stood still, but also because the Lord answered the request of Joshua. We need men and women like Joshua who are willing to pray big, impossible prayers that make no sense to man, but prayers that are possible because the One to whom they pray is the God of the impossible and bigger than any request we could make. Don't you see that God does not share our limitations? Pray for the impossible. It may be to see revival in the world, or it may be for a miracle that affects just one person. Whatever the case, God can make the exception in time and space if He chooses to answer your prayer in that fashion.

—— Today's Truth ——

God is not limited like man. Our big God can answer our big prayers in bigger ways than we can imagine!

Nothing Undone

Read Joshua 11–13

THIS PASSAGE CONCLUDES the battles that Joshua will face. The rest of the book of Joshua deals with dividing the land and Joshua's final charge to the people. The first eleven chapters of this book are some of my favorite in all of the Bible. They contain so much truth to be learned about how God gives victory, how He fights for us, how we must follow instruction and trust His game plan, and much more. To sum up all that has taken place, Joshua 11:15 states, "*As the LORD commanded Moses his servant, so did Moses command Joshua, and so did Joshua; he left nothing undone of all that the LORD commanded Moses.*"

I had a bad habit growing up. I would eat ninety-five percent of my meal and leave a small portion untouched. My parents corrected me for wasting, but I think part of it had to be just annoying to see one bite of a burger leftover. That's enough to drive any perfectionist mad. This temptation to leave some leftovers is how many Christians treat the Word of God. Many are content to think of all that they are doing for God, forgetting what they are leaving on the table.

I am happy for anything that anyone does for the Lord that is right. However, our perspective needs to change. This verse focuses on what Joshua left undone, not what he did for God. Instead of running down the list of what you've done for God, ask yourself this question: "What have I left on the table?"

God has given His Word to mankind in its perfect form, not so we could do most of it, but so that we will leave nothing undone as Joshua did. It is often one sin or one command left unfinished that has the potential to drastically impact a life. We can't be nonchalant about what remains undone. Even if we feel pretty good about what we've done, the fact is that we need to give attention to what we're leaving on the table rather than feeling good about that we've accomplished.

—— Today's Truth ——

Finish the commands that God has given you and spoken to you about recently. Don't leave anything on the table!

Give Me This Mountain

Read Joshua 14–16

I N THE TWILIGHT of life, many look to retirement and a life free of the stress, worry, and duties of a day-to-day working schedule. Not Caleb. As an eighty-five-year-old man, Caleb had his eyes set on the mountain. Joshua 14:11 reads, *"As yet I am as strong this day as I was in the day that Moses sent me: as my strength was then, even so is my strength now, for war, both to go out, and to come in."* Caleb wasn't ready to exchange his sword for a pair of slippers. He was ready for another battle.

We've all seen that middle-aged man who was an athlete in his youth get onto the court only to find that his body can't keep up with what his mind thought he could do, so perhaps you laugh at Caleb for his zeal; but as long as Caleb had breath in his lungs, he was ready to fight for another victory in the army of the Lord.

Let me clarify that I am not against retirement. However, there is a difference between retiring from a day job and retiring from God's army. As long as we are alive, there are battles to fight. I know many men and women who have retired from their careers and, in turn, dedicated several hours every week to serving in their local church. They may not be able to work a full-time job in their field anymore, but they see the value they can have in the Lord's work.

Many will look at the mountain and think to themselves, "I'm too weak," "I'm too old," "I'm too young," or "It's too big for me." Would you have the zeal of Caleb and say to God and to yourself, "Give me this mountain!" Caleb was anxious to win another victory for the Lord. Have you "hung it up" in your spiritual life, or do you see that mountain that you can fight to win for the Lord?

—— Today's Truth ——

Mountains all around us need to be won. If God's people throw in the towel while they're still living, who will win the victories?

Can't or Won't?

Read Joshua 17–19

So many parents share striking similarities regarding the phrases they say to their children and in their homes. We've all heard the one, "Back in my day...." When you are a child, this can be irritating, even as you try to respectfully obey your authority. The humor in this is that when those children become parents, they often find themselves saying those same phrases to their children and think to themselves, "I sound like my father/mother." I use a phrase with my children that I remember hearing my mom and dad say to me after I'd given some excuse about why I couldn't do something. I'd hear, "You can't or you won't?" This was their challenge to me not to give up.

God gave clear instructions to the Israelites as He does throughout His Word through both example and direct commands that apply to us. Joshua 17 continues the description of the inheritance given to each tribe. In verse 12, the Lord tells us of Manasseh, *"Yet the children of Manasseh could not drive out the inhabitants of those cities; but the Canaanites would dwell in that land."* The Canaanites became a thorn in their side because of Manasseh's partial obedience. It's more likely that their failure to drive out the Canaanites was a lack of true effort and determination. It wasn't that they couldn't drive them out, but that they wouldn't. Whenever God gives you a command, don't fulfill it just halfway. Follow through and finish the direction God gives, or you too will have a thorn in your side due to your lack of determination to finish.

—— Today's Truth ——

All that God has commanded is all that He expects you to obey. Doing just most of it isn't enough. Determine to finish what you start for God.

Failed Not

Read Joshua 20–21

F AILURE IS A common experience for all people. We live and talk like we are immune to failure, because there is shame when you think about the ways that you have fallen in the past. Failure can be minor, but in some cases, everybody has many regrets that they probably wish they could wipe from their memory and their past. Because we know this about ourselves, we ought to have a greater appreciation for the fact that God never fails.

When the land was divided, the people received what God promised them. For forty years, they wandered because of their disobedience and unbelief, but God was still willing to give them the land. Joshua 21:43 says, *"And the LORD gave unto Israel all the land which he sware to give unto their fathers; and they possessed it, and dwelt therein."* What He promised to give, He gave. This is what God does because this is who God is. He is sinless and perfect. Whatever He promises to do, He will always fulfill. Verse 45 continues, *"There failed not ought of any good thing which the LORD had spoken unto the house of Israel; all came to pass."* As the people looked around at what they now possessed, they realized how God kept His promises to them.

Alan Redpath said, "In the light of the Cross, is it not true that the enemy has no right to dwell in the land? Is it not true that Satan's claim to your life was taken from him at Calvary? Is it not true that sin has no right to a foothold in the life of the child of God? Is it not true that Satan has no power in the presence of Omnipotence? Is it not true that by virtue of His blood and His resurrection, Jesus Christ is pledged to destroy the enemy utterly? Is it not true that in the indwelling power of the Holy Spirit there is strength for every temptation, grace for every trial, power to overcome every difficulty?"

—— Today's Truth ——

If God has never failed you, then your desire should be to return the same tribute back to Him.

They Stayed

Read Joshua 22–24

BABE RUTH WAS one of baseball's greatest players, and still remains as one of the icons that made the sport what it became. Our Daily Bread gives the following story about one of his final games: "One of the all-time greats in baseball was Babe Ruth. His bat had the power of a cannon, and his record of 714 home runs remained unbroken until Hank Aaron came along. 'The Babe' was the idol of sports fans, but in time age took its toll, and his popularity began to wane. Finally, the Yankees traded him to the Braves. In one of his last games in Cincinnati, Babe Ruth began to falter. He struck out and made several misplays that allowed the Reds to score five runs in one inning. As 'the Babe' walked toward the dugout, chin down and dejected, there rose from the stands an enormous storm of boos and catcalls. Then a wonderful thing happened. A little boy jumped over the railing, and with tears streaming down his cheeks he ran out to the great athlete. Unashamedly, he flung his arms around 'the Babe's' legs and held on tightly. Babe Ruth scooped him up, hugged him, took his hand and the two of them walked off the field together."

Loyalty is proven when the crowd is against you. Bandwagon fans are some of the most irritating in all of sports. That's not loyalty, but sports also isn't life or death. Joshua commends the people at the end of their journey in Joshua 22:3, "*Ye have not left your brethren these many days unto this day, but have kept the charge of the commandment of the LORD your God.*" In other words, "You stayed loyal through every battle." Because they stayed and didn't waver in their allegiance, their loyalty was rewarded. God notices the ones who remain loyal regardless of the circumstances.

—— Today's Truth ——

The reward after the battle is for those who stayed until it was finished. Life has its battles, and we must determine to remain loyal to the end.

Gone

Read Judges 1–2

ONE OF THE truly difficult parts of life is having to cope with the truth that there are people who will die and are gone from this world forever. Heaven gives an incredible comfort to the believer, but until Jesus returns, there is still work to be done in this world. It is especially hard when a truly remarkable Christian dies who was used of God in a tremendous way. This is where Israel is in the beginning of the book of Judges. Judges 1:1 says, *"Now after the death of Joshua it came to pass, that the children of Israel asked the LORD, saying, Who shall go up for us against the Canaanites first, to fight against them?"*

The book of Judges describes a time in Israel's history when they had no president, prime minister, or king. The judges mentioned in this book were not judges like we think of today, but rather leaders that rose to the occasion that God could use. Some were successful. Some failed to do what they could. Israel had to learn to seek the Lord and trust Him during this time. We also see that when this was done, it was the best way to follow God. Although God uses leaders, He doesn't need a king to lead His people if they will follow Him wholly.

Joshua was gone, but Israel still had work to do. They couldn't quit because the Lord took Him home. Although you may have lost someone who guided you in life, your faith should ultimately be in the Lord. God will never die, because He has always existed and will always exist for all eternity. Those who put their allegiance in man will fall when man falls or when they pass off the scene.

—— Today's Truth ——

Thank the Lord for the leaders God has used to shape your life, but remember that God is your leader no matter who sits on the earthly throne.

Prove It

Read Judges 3–5

HITLER IMPRISONED A German pastor, Martin Niemoeller, for eight years. He spent some time in prisons and concentration camps, including Dachau. Hitler realized that if Niemoeller, a First World War hero, could be persuaded to join his cause then much opposition would collapse, so he sent a former friend of Niemoeller to visit him, a friend who now supported the Nazis. Seeing Niemoeller in his cell, the one-time friend is reported to have said, "Martin, Martin! Why are you here?" To which he received from Niemoeller the response, "My friend! Why are you not here?"

God has a purpose in everything He does and in everything He allows. There was a purpose for the Israelites' time in Egypt. The wilderness had a purpose, along with every experience they faced during their years of wandering. Judges 3:1 states, *"Now these are the nations which the LORD left, to prove Israel by them…."* God's purpose is clearly stated. Enemies were left because God was looking for Israel to prove itself. They had claimed the land, they had followed the Lord up to this point, but all along the way, God gave them tests to see if they were sincere and real in their quest.

Talk is cheap, some will say. While we are certainly good to speak about what we believe, what we stand for, and what we're willing to do, it's still just talk. Until the action is taken, the words we speak have little weight. If we talk about soul winning and never witness to anybody, then we have proven ourselves to be hypocrites. The Lord wants to see action. If you tell Him you'll serve Him, then prove it with a faithful life. God is looking for proof of your dedication to Him.

—— Today's Truth ——

What you do and how you respond is the proof that God is looking for and what He notices. If you want to live for Him, then prove it by doing just that.

God's Specialty

Read Judges 6–7

GOD RARELY CHOOSES the obvious person. Even the man of God thought Jesse's eldest son was the obvious choice for the next king, but God looked beyond their appearance and saw a ruddy shepherd boy that was fit for the task. This is where God specializes. He uses unlikely people to do unlikely work. He used Jacob, a liar and deceiver, to be the father of the future nation of Israel. He used Joseph, a forgotten slave, to save the world. He used Moses, a murderer, to save His people. He used Jephthah, son of a prostitute, to deliver Israel. He used an unnamed servant girl to tell Naaman about Elisha and the Lord. He used Esther, a captive, to save His people from genocide. He used Saul of Tarsus, a former murderer of Christians, to write much of the New Testament. This is God's specialty.

When God called Gideon to be the one who would lead Israel into battle against Midian, Gideon had his concerns. By the way, any Christian worth their salt will realize that they don't have what it takes to do the task. If you're honest, you know that the work is too big for you. The one who thinks that he has it all handled is the one who will surely fall. Gideon told the Lord in Judges 6:15, *"And he said unto him, Oh my Lord, wherewith shall I save Israel? behold, my family is poor in Manasseh, and I am the least in my father's house."* Gideon felt inadequate, which was true, but He neglected to remember that God was calling Him. And when God calls, God will give you the help you need. You don't have to be somebody special to serve God, because just having God with you makes you special.

—— Today's Truth ——

God specializes in using nobodies. You don't have what it takes, but God can work in you to get the job done.

Not Suitable for Children

Read Judges 8–9

MUCH OF THE Old Testament is filled with stories that most of us wouldn't read to a five-year-old before bedtime. Nevertheless, God's Word is filled with colorful stories and vivid lessons that are filled with truth. Judges 9 is one of those passages. Although it might not be a passage you read from in your next children's Sunday school class, God put it in His Word for our benefit.

Abimelech ruthlessly murdered sixty-nine of his seventy brothers in order to be king. This is a common story that we find throughout history and in the Bible when looking at regions ruled through a family line. His brother that survived, Jotham, warned Abimelech that one day he would be punished for his atrocities; and Jotham turned out to be right. Fast forward a few years, and Abimelech has a rebellion on his hands. He escaped the first uprising by burning several hundred alive in a tower, but the second time, an anonymous woman drops a millstone on his head. This didn't kill him completely, and because he didn't want the people to have the opportunity to lay hands on him, he had his armorbearer finish him off with a sword. Just like that, his bloody reign was ended.

Sometimes it seems like God is unaware of the evil that is around us, but whether we notice it or not, God is always aware and always in control. God hadn't missed the wickedness of Abimelech, and He had not forgotten his awful sins. While it may appear like the wicked men of the day are getting off easy with the crimes that they've committed, God will always bring justice. It may be in this life or it may be in eternity, but He will bring it to pass.

——Today's Truth ——

Sin is messy, atrocious, and vile. Sin will not be tolerated by the Lord. Don't mistake His delay for His inaction.

From Reject to Ruler

Read Judges 10–11

THE book of Judges can be a discouraging study. Over and over again, we read about judges who didn't follow the Lord and brought evil upon their nation. However, we also see a few bright lights in the darkness of this era. One of those is Jephthah. He was far from a model ruler, but God used him as Israel's leader.

Jephthah was rejected by his family. He was the son of his father's harlot. When he and his siblings were grown, he was kicked out of the house. He was probably a daily reminder of their father's sins, and he was paying the price for his father's lack of integrity. However, the time came where the people came to Jephthah to be the ruler ,and he accepted the job and led the people to victory.

This is the unfortunate reality of the way many treat their leaders. They reject them when they feel no pressing need, but when a problem arises, they look to them for help. Only in their desperation did the people turn to Jephthah.

Rejection is hurtful. I hate being told "no." When your heart is set on something, rejection can cause a lot of pain. The more you want something, the more the rejection hurts. Being rejected by his family could have ruined Jephthah's hope of ever being anything more than a reject, but the time came where he was ready to be used.

Underdog stories like this fill the pages of Scripture. God pulls a man out of the shadows and sets him up in a way that was unthinkable for that person. But their life is changed because God says, "It's time now to lift you up." Surely, you've faced some kind of rejection in your life, but that rejection doesn't mean that God has put you on the shelf. It may not be the time that God wants to bring you into the light, but God has a plan for you, even if it seems like you've faced only closed doors to this point.

—— Today's Truth ——

God can use any person. Others might reject you, but God will not reject you if you draw close to Him.

Destined for Greatness

Read Judges 12–14

THE NAMES OF many throughout history have had great meaning and impact at the time of their death. Names like Albert Einstein, George Washington, Billy Sunday, and others will be remembered for generations to come. Their accomplishments echo in the classrooms, books, and legacies that they left behind. When they died, they were remembered for what they did; but when they were born, they were just a name. Their parents were clueless of the impact they'd have. When a child is born, their potential lies before them. The canvas of their life is blank, and God has given them the opportunity to make of their life what they choose for it to become.

When God told Manoah and his wife that they were going to have a baby, He told them what He wanted to accomplish with that child's life. Judges 12:5 says, *"For, lo, thou shalt conceive, and bear a son; and no razor shall come on his head: for the child shall be a Nazarite unto God from the womb: and he shall begin to deliver Israel out of the hand of the Philistines."* Every parent wants to see their children succeed, but there was no way that Samson's parent had any idea of what the Lord had in store for his future.

Your life has the same opportunity as those about whom you have read, watched on television, or been influenced by though they lived hundreds of years before you. God doesn't have the same plan for you that He had for Samson, but He does have a plan for how He wants to use you. Whatever the plan, you can be confident that there is greatness in it. You might not be in a college textbook, but you can be used to make a difference. Follow God's plan and trust that He will make something beautiful out of the blank canvas that He's given when He gave you your life.

—— Today's Truth ——

God has a great plan in store for every person. Follow His plan, trust His leading, and watch to see the great things He will use you to accomplish for His glory.

Too Late

Read Judges 15–17

H OW MANY TIMES have you prayed a prayer like this, "Lord, if you answer this prayer, I promise that I will serve You wherever You lead me, I'll give up whatever You want, and I'll do anything to please You. Just do this one thing for me!" This is a prayer of emergency. Perhaps it's at a time when a bill must be paid or consequences will follow. Maybe health is failing and every hour is precious. Whatever the case, you may find yourself in this time of desperation, ready to give God anything in the world just so He will intervene.

What if your prayer is only an emergency because you put yourself in that position? Our former school principal used to tell us, "A lack of preparation on your part does not constitute an emergency on my part." In other words, "You're only in an emergency because you failed to prepare or you made a bad decision to put yourself there." This is the story of Samson. Judges 16 records the dreadful prayer of this man while bound to pillars in the colosseum of his enemies. His eyes had been plucked out, and he had been humiliated because he had failed to make the right decisions while he had the opportunity to get his life right. It wasn't just one decision that led Samson to this painful scene, but a series of poor choices that drove him to his demise.

There's no perfect way to calculate how long it takes to get to such a point or to know how many chances the Lord will give you. In fact, we shouldn't take this for granted at all. God gives second chances, but He won't be treated like a priest in a confessional booth, forgiving the same blatant sins day after day when there is no remorse or repentance. This time of desperation can be used to draw you back to God, but you don't have to wait until you're at a dead end to get right with Him.

—— Today's Truth ——

God is more than merciful and longsuffering to His children, but His mercy can wear out if you continue to deny His opportunity to truly be restored to Him.

Idol Worship

Read Judges 18–19

GOD DOESN'T HAVE any competition. He is the authority over everything, and no false god, human, nation, or spiritual enemy can even come close to His power and strength. All false gods are manmade. Because they're made by man, it's easy to realize that their abilities can be compared to man. They are limited, if they have any life in them at all.

The city of Dan became a center for idol worship for generations to come, and Micah established this shrine of false gods in Judges 18. Dan became one of the most prominent cities of the north, but their apostasy would lead them down a dark path. Worshipping a god that is dead and one that is limited is a kind of oxymoron. It's like the reporter who came across three looters leaving a store during the Los Angeles riots in the 1990's. He asked them what they took, and one replied, "I got some gospel music. I love Jesus!" The idiocy makes you scratch your head in amazement. People praying to gods of stone or worshipping men they refer to as gods is about as foolish as it sounds.

Idol worship isn't dead in our modern society. People may not bow down to a statue (though some certainly do), but many will have a better relationship with a device they hold in their hands than they do with their heavenly Father. The Japanese people are an example of a modern society that is still consumed with idol and spirit worship. There is no competition when you stack up the false gods against the true God, yet many will treat their deities as if they have the power to do what they pray for.

—— Today's Truth ——

God is the only true God. He requires no competition, and we must not try to give any person or creation His rightful place in our world and in our lives.

Fight On!

Read Judges 20–21

I SRAEL SOUGHT JUDGMENT for the murder of one of their women by the tribe of Benjamin. Matters escalated quickly, and the two armies rose up for war. Israel united mightily in their cause, but their efforts failed them for two days of battle. It appears that they did the right thing at the start. They sought the Lord before the battle began, yet they lost thousands. This happened again on the second day. Finally, after two bloody days of defeat, the Lord told the Israelites in Judges 20:28, *"Go up; for to morrow I will deliver them into thine hand."*

Abraham Lincoln said in his second inaugural address with regard to the dreadful Civil War, "Fondly do we hope, fervently do we pray, that this mighty scourge of war may speedily pass away. Yet, if God wills that it continue until all the wealth piled by the bondsman's two hundred and fifty years of unrequited toil shall be sunk, and until every drop of blood drawn with the lash shall be paid by another drawn with the sword, as was said three thousand years ago, so still it must be said 'the judgments of the Lord are true and righteous altogether.'" Lincoln realized that the fight had to continue because God wasn't done with America yet.

You may be tempted to quit after days of defeat. Not all battles are won by the first wave of your efforts. Just keep fighting for His cause and seek His guidance for every battle that you face. Now isn't the time to quit and waste the sacrifice you've made to this point. It baffles me to see aged men and women finish their race by quitting just before it's over. Couples get divorced in their late years of life. People leave church and the will of God as aged Christians with just a few years left. Don't quit until the battle is over. Fight on, Christian!

—— Today's Truth ——

As long as there is still a battle to fight, there is a call for God's army to rise to the occasion. One day or even a season of defeat doesn't mean that it's over. It's over only when God says your time is up. Keep fighting for Him!

Now What?

Read Ruth 1–4

As a 14-year-old boy in the Revolutionary War, Andrew Jackson and his brother were captured and held captive by the British. After we won the war, the prisoners were released. His mother came to get him, and they made a forty-mile hike back home. His brother was very sick and died shortly after. His father died while he was held captive, and his mother volunteered to help the wounded, contracted cholera, and died. In one summer, Jackson lost two brothers, his mom and his dad.

Have you faced a time in life when your feet were knocked out from under you and you wanted to ask the Lord, "Now what?" Ruth 1 presents a similar situation. The men in the lives of Naomi, Ruth, and Orpah had all died, and these widows found themselves in a "now what" predicament.

What do you do when you don't know what to do? When Naomi decided to go back to Bethlehem, she tried to convince her daughters-in-law to stay in Moab, but Ruth was persistent that she would go with Naomi. Some people would rather suffer alone than have a friend by their side along the way. Your pride may convince you that you don't need help or that the problem can't be fixed, but you should not refuse people in your life who are trying to reach out to you.

After they arrived in Bethlehem, Ruth put herself to work. She got busy doing something, and the rest is history. Instead of wallowing in her misery, she put herself in a place where God could use her. You might think your purpose is over when life gets turned upside down, but God still has a plan if you'll continue to see it through. Ruth could have never written or even imagined her own story, but she did something about her situation, and God blessed her for it.

—— Today's Truth ——

Some roads you travel are less clear regarding what lies ahead. Move forward, accept help along the way, continue in God's will, and watch as His plan unfolds right before you.

Can You Hear Me Now?

Read I Samuel 1–3

AN ELDERLY GENTLEMAN had serious hearing problems for a number of years. He went to the doctor and the doctor was able to have him fitted for a set of hearing aids that allowed the gentleman to hear perfectly. When he went back to the doctor a month later, the doctor said, "Your hearing is perfect. Your family must be really pleased that you can hear again." The man replied, "Oh, I haven't told my family yet. I just sit around and listen to their conversations. I've changed my will three times!"

Three times, Samuel went to Eli in the middle of the night until Eli realized that the Lord was speaking to the boy. Samuel answered the third time in I Samuel 3:10, *"Speak; for thy servant heareth."* The Holy Spirit is continually at work, speaking to the hearts of men. He wants to speak to you about salvation, He wants to speak to you about your sin, He wants to speak to you about your decisions for the future and every decision you will make in this life. It's God's job to speak; it's our job to listen.

If you're like me, you think of what you're going to say while other people are talking. We are taught at a young age that God gave us two ears and one mouth because He wants us to do twice as much listening as we do speaking, but we usually do the opposite. Do you hear the voice of God speaking to you? I Kings 19:12 describes the voice of God as a *"still small voice."* Think of a whisper. You can't hear a whisper if you're talking. You have to intentionally listen. God is constantly speaking to you if you will intentionally listen to Him. The busyness of life can distract you from hearing His voice if you're not careful. He has something to say to you today, and it is definitely worth listening to.

—— Today's Truth ——

God's voice is at work. He speaks, and we listen. Lift your heart and your ears to the voice of God daily as He speaks to you throughout the day.

A Hard Lesson

Read I Samuel 4–7

People can be stubborn, it sometimes requires a drastic consequence to get somebody's attention. If the Lord gave us a casual slap on the wrist when we played around with sin, we might never get the hint. We read some passages in the Bible and think, "Wow, that was harsh!" I Samuel 6 is one of those passages for me. The Philistines moved the ark of God using a cart, but they were not punished for it, likely due to their ignorance. Yet, God dealt more strictly with His people. Once the ark was returned, 670 were slain by the Lord for looking into the ark. They broke God's law and were severely punished.

God's commands are not given lightly. He does not care less about some commands than others (although some are certainly emphasized in Scripture). We should view His commandments all the same and realize that when God gives instruction, He means for us to keep it. This is serious business to Him, and it should be serious to us. God instructed Israel regarding who was to move the ark and how it was to be moved (Numbers 4:15). Specific guidelines were given regarding who could handle it and move it.

Churches change Bibles, lower dress standards, welcome the world's style of music, and embrace modern theology while arguing that there are more important things to fuss about. I believe that we cannot make too big of a deal about what is right and what is wrong. Instead of downplaying sin and compromise, we have to be diligent to obey the Lord in every command and principle that He has given. You don't know what your casual view of God's commands will do. It may just take a hard lesson to get your attention if you don't take it seriously.

—— Today's Truth ——

God's instruction should be carefully and diligently followed. Good intentions and sincerity don't excuse disobedience.

Who Do You Want to Be Like?

Read I Samuel 8–11

WHEN SOMEONE IS better than you at something, you are wise to copy their patterns so that you can learn to excel like they have. Wisdom comes from watching other wise people. However, we can also pick up on bad habits and poor examples from some whom we attempt to emulate. When I was in elementary school, I wanted to be fast like the high school boys. So, I copied how the fastest boy in school ran. I watched his style and tried to copy it for myself. One day, my dad took me to a small lake to run laps with him. As I ran, he said, "Steven, what are you doing? You're running like a girl." I thought I was pretty cool because I was running like the fastest kid in school, but I picked up a goofy style because I was just copying somebody else.

Israel played the comparison game. They looked at the world and saw that other nations had something they didn't have; then they convinced themselves that their lives would surely be better if they had a king as well. So they asked God for a king. Their comparison and envy of other nations led down a quick path to spiritual apostasy. The majority of kings that Israel and Judah had did evil and brought future judgment from the Lord. But Israel looked at the world and said, "We want to be like them."

Young people graduate from a Christian high school and leave church with this mindset. They think the world has something for them that they're missing out on, but their new lifestyle and new truth will bring new battles, new judgment, and new heartache that they can't imagine. What Jesus gives is all that we need and more than we could ever wish for. The world offers nothing that we need.

—— Today's Truth ——

Apostasy comes from embracing the ideas of the world and turning from what God has. Seek what God can give and keep your eyes and heart away from the deceptions of the world.

Warning Signs

Read I Samuel 12–14:23

THE TRANSITION OF leadership was in full swing from Samuel to Saul in the hearts of the people. After Saul's victory over Ammon, Samuel gave a challenge to the people concerning their new king. In a dramatic fashion, Samuel asked the Lord for a sign to display the judgment God would bring if the people did not obey the voice of the Lord. God sent thunder and rain during the wheat harvest. This was rare, and it could have destroyed their crops. Samuel wanted to make it clear that they were entering new territory and dangerous grounds with their new king. The people responded with a renewed fear of the Lord.

One Arkansas farmer discourages trespassers with this admonition: "Please do not trample the poison ivy or feed the bull." We are wise to heed warning signs. Argentinean race driver Juan Manuel Fangio discovered that after the opening lap of the 1950 Monaco Grand Prix. As he approached a dangerous bend for the second time, Fangio noticed that something was wrong. The faces of the spectators, which he usually saw as a whitish blur as he drove by, were all turned away from him. "If they are not looking at me," Fangio thought, "they must be looking at something more interesting around the corner." So, he braked hard and carefully rounded the bend, where he saw that his split-second assessment had been accurate. The road was blocked by a massive pileup.

You don't have to experience the consequences of poor choices. You can avoid judgment by heeding the warning signs. God's Word is filled with stories and instruction that gives us admonition to listen so that we do not harm ourselves by ignorance. You have no excuse for not listening. Open your eyes and heed the signs before you.

—— Today's Truth ——

You can be spared if you will listen. A sign should make you more diligent, more aware, and more careful of the possible danger ahead.

A Universal Language

Read I Samuel 14:24–16

MUSIC HAS BEEN called the "language of emotions." You don't have to understand the lyrics to understand the emotion conveyed with soft, instrumental music or with loud, heavy metal music. Music has an effect on people; and in I Samuel 16:23, we see the effect that it had on Saul: *"David took an harp, and played with his hand: so Saul was refreshed, and was well, and the evil spirit departed from him."*

Physical Effect. The Hebrew word for *refreshed* suggests a physical relief. Dancing is a physical response to specific types of music. I'll often tap my toes or tap my hand in time with music during church. Music has a way of making the body respond. The message of the music (not the lyrics, but the sound) will produce a physical response. People say as long as the lyrics talk about Jesus, the music is good; but music is much more powerful than just the lyrics.

Emotional Effect. Saul was "well" after David played for him. He was uplifted by this music. Godly music should be encouraging. The world's music is filled with sin, violence, lust, greed, and depression. This message has an effect on the listeners. You can't listen to hard rock and be the happy camper in the office. Also, it's difficult to listen to and sing godly music and remain depressed.

Spiritual Effect. Realize that there were no lyrics in this personal concert. It was just sound. Yet, the Bible states, *"...and the evil spirit departed from him."* Saul's spiritual state was affected because of the music David played. Music isn't for entertainment. It is given to draw us closer to the Lord. For many, music is Satan's snare; but it can have a positive effect in your spiritual walk if you give your ear to the right music.

—— Today's Truth ——

Music speaks to all people and is a gift from God that can affect us in a negative or positive way depending on what we listen to.

All In

Read I Samuel 17–18

A WOMAN VISITING a farm noticed a limping pig with a wooden leg in the backyard. She asked the farmer, "What happened to the pig?" The farmer said, "Oh, Betsy is a wonderful pig. One night the house caught fire, and she oinked so loudly she woke us; we got the fire truck here in time to save the house." The woman remarked in astonishment, "That's really something!" The farmer continued, "That's not all. One day my youngest daughter fell into the pond, and Betsy oinked so loudly that she got our attention; and we were able to pull my daughter out of the pond before she drowned." The woman exclaimed, "That's really amazing! But I still don't understand why the pig has a wooden leg." The farmer replied, "Well, when you have a pig that special, you don't want to eat her all at once!"

The famed story of David and Goliath is recorded in I Samuel 17. This young boy probably seemed pretty ignorant to Goliath and the Philistine army. In fact, his own people doubted his ability to defeat, much less even make a mark on, the mighty giant. However, we know how the story ends. David stands over Goliath's body, draws the giant's sword, cuts off his head, and reigns victorious.

David had no time for second guessing as he approached his enemy. He had every reason to be afraid. He was not properly trained for battle. He had no real defense. His weapon of choice was far inferior to Goliath's. But when you hear him speak before he threw that stone, he was as confident as anyone could be in battle. Christians needs this kind of dedication on the battlefield. Marriages need this kind of commitment. Soul winners need this kind of zeal. The "all in" mentality is one of confidence because of the God who stands beside you.

—— Today's Truth ——

You can be confident with God by your side in the battle. There's no need to doubt or question. Move forward fully and by faith.

Stuck in the Crosshairs

Read I Samuel 19–21

ONE OF THE worst things that children of divorced parents have to endure is being caught in between their parents. I'll jokingly ask our kids sometimes who they like more between Mommy or Daddy. Then, before they can answer (because I know they'll probably say mommy!), I explain that we're not supposed to have favorites. Mom and Dad love them all unconditionally, and we never would want them to have to choose between us two. As Saul sought after David to take his life, Saul's son, Jonathan, who was also David's best friend, was caught in the middle. What can we learn from Jonathan's example in this situation?

Stay loyal to what is right. People can be loyal to a fault. You shouldn't be loyal to a friend if that friend is deep into sin, lest they pull you down in the process. Jonathan could have remained loyal to his family to a fault if he had mirrored his father's actions or aided in them. People should retain a heart for their family, but letting your family be your excuse to be in sin is inexcusable.

Don't play favorites. Jonathan tried everything he could to protect David, but he also didn't disown or revolt against his father in the process. He continued to respect his father while also being a true friend to David.

Put out the fire instead of adding to it. Middlemen can make matters worse if they try to play both sides or use their position as some ploy to control the situation themselves. You can insert yourself into a situation that you're not meant to be a part of.

Leave the matter in God's hands. Middlemen sometimes feel a responsibility to fix the problem. They try to work it all out in their own power because of their connections to both sides. Let God take care of the matter. Don't play God in the situation.

——Today's Truth ——

Your involvement in the lives of others will include you in their problems. Exercise godly wisdom to be used of God to be a help.

The Adullam Recruitment Agency

Read I Samuel 22–24

W E READ HERE of a low point in David's life. Here he is, the one chosen by God to be the king, and he is in a cave, running for his life. The cave of Adullam was not far from where David had defeated Goliath. I'm sure after that great victory, David did not expect that his life would lead to this point. He was tested and discouraged, but a group of four hundred men had gathered together and united under the future king in that cave. This wasn't the kind of crowd that David would have assembled himself, but they were the group of men that God used to encourage and support him.

The Bible describes these men being distressed, in debt, and discontented. They were distressed, tired, and weary from the pressure that came from their wicked king. They were in debt, not able to fend for themselves. They were discontented, not willing to continue in the life they were living. God would use these men to become mighty men in David's kingdom in the days to come, and they came to his side just when he needed it.

Every ministry needs people like this. People come into church beat down by the world, but we need to lay aside our baggage and unite under the Lord in the body of Christ and become a mighty army for His cause. You wouldn't think much of David's men at first, and I'm sure you wouldn't think much of most of the people that fill churches all around the world. We might not look like much to the world, but God can use people like us, just as He has time and time again.

—— Today's Truth ——

God can use those who are willing, even with baggage, to be mighty in His army in the time of battle. Your burdens should draw you to unite under His cause, not to flee in defeat.

Dumb Smart People

Read I Samuel 25–27

THERE IS A clear difference between those who are book smart and those who are street smart. Common sense is not always that common in our world. Even the spiritually mature or the godly and wise make foolish decisions at times. I Corinthians 10:12 says, *"Wherefore let him that thinketh he standeth take heed lest he fall."* David had made the right decisions up to this point, but somewhere along the journey, in a moment of weakness, he had forgotten to do things God's way. He consulted with himself and ran to the Philistines (the enemy) for help. This would turn out to be a hurt to David and to his people.

There is no telling what people will do in times of weakness. And just like a lion looks for the perfect opportunity to attack weakened prey, Satan will attack when you are vulnerable. When people make foolish life decision, it is often in a season of weakness. Think of Esau. In a moment of weakness, fearing for his life because he was so hungry, he traded away his birthright. He undoubtedly regretted this decision the rest of his life. Esau was not a dumb person, but he made a dumb decision in a moment of weakness.

To avoid a similar mistake, we cannot let down our spiritual guard. Why would you need church if you have already reached spiritual perfection? You need your Bible, prayer time, church, godly influences, and all the other aids that God provides as a safeguard against foolish decisions. Be careful not to make a life-changing decision in a moment of weakness. Like David, you can fall and end up with regrets due to your vulnerability.

—— Today's Truth ——

You are not exempt from following in the footsteps of Esau or David. Good men and women make foolish decisions, too. Be on guard and stay close to the Lord so that you won't make this same mistake.

Answering Your Critics

Read I Samuel 28–31

COLONEL GEORGE WASHINGTON Goethals was the primary supervisor responsible for constructing the Panama Canal. This feat of engineering called for the Pacific Ocean and the Gulf of Mexico to be linked by a canal dug across the country of Panama. Since its completion, ships have saved millions of combined miles by being able to go through the canal and avoid the trip around the tip of South America. While the work was being done, Colonel Goethals had to endure severe criticism from back home which predicted that he would never be able to finish what his critics called an "impossible task." This man refused to listen to his critics and pressed ahead with his work.

One day a subordinate asked, "Aren't you going to answer your critics?"

"In time," the colonel replied.

"How?" the man asked.

The colonel smiled and said, "With the canal!" His answer came loud and clear on August 15, 1914, when the Panama Canal opened to traffic for the first time.

David was not a novice at dealing with opposition; he faced it from the beginning. David was criticized throughout his reign. The hard part about criticism isn't necessarily the criticism itself, but who the criticism comes from. When it's a random Internet troll, you can brush it off and continue with life.

After the criticism came, David didn't take the time to respond to every critic. Instead, he pressed forward. He turned to God, not his critics. You may be tempted to answer every criticism that comes your way, but you will exhaust yourself by doing so. Also, there is not always a perfect answer to critics. They can't always be appeased. They might be wrong, but they may also be right at times. Continue anyway, and turn to God when you have a need.

—— Today's Truth ——

Expect criticism to land on your doorstep and decide now how you will respond when it arrives.

A House Divided

Read II Samuel 1–2

ONE OF THE important examples that we can learn from the local church in the book of Acts is that the people were described as being in *"one accord."* Abraham Lincoln quoted that verse often, *"And if a house be divided against itself, that house cannot stand"* (Mark 3:25). It is nearly impossible to move forward when there is fighting on the inside. After Saul's death, Israel divided itself from Judah when they made Saul's son their king. They fought the will of God for their nation as a whole and divided themselves.

Parents have to be on the same page. Children must know that if dad gives an answer, then mom is going to give the same answer. Some know how to work the system and will go to the other parent after one has given an answer, hoping they'll get the answer they want the second time around. This can divide a home. A home must have unity in order to move forward.

The ministry is no different. Churches are described as Christ's body. The body is to be united. Churches split, create separate groups, and develop a spirit of brokenness instead of one of unity. People won't always agree on everything, but they have to come to a place where they realize that bickering can hinder God's blessing on the work at hand. I bring substantial financial decisions to the church to provide unity. I used to think it was me against the church during business meetings; but over time I realized that the purpose of a business meeting is to put us on the same page so we can move forward in a unified manner. When people feel involved, they are more likely to get on board and be supportive. If I move secretly, then I'm dividing the people from the work. We need to have harmony with one another in order to see God work.

—— Today's Truth ——

Unity is vital for progress in any group, business, family, or ministry. Many things that can divide us, and we must determine to stay together in one accord.

Start a Journey; Start a Battle

Read II Samuel 3–5

WHENEVER OUR YOUTH group would go to a conference, revival, or a camp, we'd all get on fire for the Lord. Life-altering decisions were made by many of us. However, a pattern developed in our youth group that has been the story of many Christians. A decision is made, you move forward with that decision, then after some time, you go back on that decision. Why is this so? Leaders can become frustrated watching this with those into whom they're investing.

It is guaranteed that whenever you set out to do something for the Lord, you will not be welcomed with a red carpet, but with a battle. II Samuel 3:1 says, *"Now there was long war between the house of Saul and the house of David: but David waxed stronger and stronger, and the house of Saul waxed weaker and weaker."* The beginning of the journey for David as king didn't mean that his battles were over. In fact, it probably meant that his battles would grow even greater.

Satan isn't too worried about the Christians sitting on the sidelines. They require little effort for his minions. It is those who are busy that he must figure out how to get out of the fight. When you get in the fight, you can be certain that a target will be on your back. Making the decision is the easy part. Keeping that decision requires enduring the battle that will surely come as a result of that decision. People decide it's not what they expected, so they quit on the will of God. Expect the opposition and be ready to fight when it comes. Nobody that God has used was exempt from this. All of God's servants have been battle tested. Prove that you are sincere and genuine and press on when the battle comes.

——Today's Truth ——

The battle begins when you get in the fight. You have an enemy, but you have a greater ally.

Request Denied

Read II Samuel 6–9

BEING DENIED IS not an enjoyable experience. You can probably relate to a time in your life when you experienced this. It may have been after trying out for a sports team, applying for a job, applying for a college, or even after pursuing someone in whom you were interested. Denial hurts the flesh, but you can't always help or control those who do it. Sometimes, even the Lord will deny your request. A part of praying for God's will is praying for God's best, whether it's what you asked for or the exact opposite.

David wanted to build a temple for the Lord. His heart was sincere. This wasn't a selfish wish, but a genuine desire to do something special for God's glory. However, his request was denied. It wasn't that David couldn't do the job, but it just wasn't what God had planned for David's life.

It is moments like this that can birth a spirit of bitterness in the heart of Christians. We tend to take matters like this personally. Somehow, we twist rejection into a bigger statement of worthlessness and uselessness in this life. This may seem extreme, but it is how many feel after a good intention turns into a closed door.

The response that David gave to the Lord in II Samuel 7:18–29 is a testament to his faith in God's best for his life. David didn't understand why his dream was rejected, but he worshipped God anyway. Just because God shuts the door to a dream that you have longed to fulfill doesn't mean that God has put you on the shelf or closed the door of your life completely. One door closed doesn't mean all doors are closed. God's best may not come the way we believe it should, but it will come to those who follow the Lord with a heart surrendered to His perfect will.

—— Today's Truth ——

God's best may come in a different fashion that you expected. Your dream might be denied, but it isn't better than what God has planned.

The Other Giant David Faced

Read II Samuel 10–12

I F A VIDEO of your life was shown for the whole world to see, you would probably want to remove a few clips. It seems that every person has a chapter or two in their life that they would do anything to remove from their past. King David was no exception. If II Samuel 11 was removed from David's life, his life would warrant little criticism. However, this event wasn't just a small mishap. This was a giant error that almost ruined his life.

Sin is never about just one event. There are always small steps that lead to that moment of failure. For David, a number of little decisions opened the door for his fall. First, he neglected his duty to lead his people into battle. This led to an idle season, which is a danger for anyone. Also, his pride over his success had gone to his head, and he let down his guard. When David saw the woman in a way that no man should see any woman other than his wife, David allowed the thoughts to permeate and linger in his heart and mind. He didn't turn and repent immediately, but instead he connived an evil plan to have the woman he desired. This act led David down a slippery path to destruction that put her husband's blood on his hands and led to the loss of a baby.

This giant felled David fell, but it didn't kill him. After he was confronted, he accepted the consequences and was restored. You must be careful to keep yourself close to God and your spirit right. You can put yourself in front of temptation by drifting away from the Lord. David could have avoided this altogether if he had done what he was supposed to do. After temptation comes, get away from it immediately. Temptation that lingers only becomes more difficult to resist. David slew some giants, but this one almost got the best of him.

——Today's Truth ——

Temptation is inevitable, but you can prevent it by staying close to God and fulfilling your duty. In the face of temptation, you must be diligent to reject sin before it grows.

The Road to Restoration

Read II Samuel 13–14

T HE PARABLE OF the prodigal son is a beautiful picture of restoration after someone is scarred by their time in the world. When he finally came to his senses, he realized how he had ruined his life. He came home broken, but his brokenness opened his heart to his father again. Absalom's reunion with his father after his banishment could not have be more different than this parable.

Absalom felt justified for avenging his sister after she was violated. After being refused by his father for two years, he comes to David at the close of II Samuel 14. He was frustrated that his father wouldn't see him. To get his attention, he set Joab's field on fire. He responded to this dramatic stunt and said, *"…now therefore let me see the king's face; and if there be any iniquity in me, let him kill me"* (II Samuel 14:32). It was evident at this point that Absalom's heart was not right, and his actions only made matters worse.

Offering forgiveness when people fall so that they can be restored is a Biblical pattern. However, forgiveness is not an approval of the person's sin, especially when there is no repentance or remorse. David was gracious to a fault with Absalom. This was his son, but he also had a duty as a king. Absalom was acting out and came with no brokenness or repentance, yet David welcomed him with open arms. Instead of a kiss, Absalom deserved some kind of retribution.

Forgiveness doesn't return everything to normal. Forgiveness is just as much for the victim as it is for the perpetrator. David could forgive, but until Absalom showed real repentance, he should have been welcomed with caution. People need a chance to be restored, but you can't restore somebody who doesn't have remorse over the sin they've committed.

—— Today's Truth ——

You can forgive without excusing sin. You can also forgive without becoming a punching bag for your enemies.

Playing Politics

Read II Samuel 15–16

As soon as Absalom was welcomed to return to Jerusalem by his father, he soon began his political campaign to deceitfully win over the kingdom. People grow weary of political figures because the story is always the same. Many politicians will promise the world and smear their opponent in the same breath. They are smooth talkers, but slow with results. They tell you what you want to hear so they can get your vote, but in the end, they will do what they want when they are in power. They will compromise everything to win over the masses, even if it goes against everything they stood for in the past. II Samuel 15:6 says, *"And on this manner did Absalom to all Israel that came to the king for judgment: so Absalom stole the hearts of the men of Israel."* Absalom did what was necessary to win over the people.

Playing political games is all about the game, and generally all about selfishness. Churches, homes, business, friendships, and in every group setting in life, you can see people who play the political game. In the end, it's about getting what they want and getting ahead. Ministry should never be about what you want. Serving your family shouldn't be about who is more important or more powerful. Businesses shouldn't operate with workers constantly comparing themselves and working against each other. Friendships shouldn't be centered around who is considered the "best" friend or about deceitfulness. Don't be the one to turn your opportunity into a quest for personal gain at any price. There is no peace, purpose, unity, or joy at the end of it all.

—— Today's Truth ——

Absalom missed potential opportunities because he was consumed with his selfish desires. His future was ruined because he sacrificed and compromised everything to get what he wanted.

A Turning Point

Read II Samuel 17–18

Miracles happen when people pray. What seemed like a sure victory for Absalom turned into devastating defeat, though not because of David. Hushai wasn't to glory for his bravery. God was always in control, and this story played out exactly the way God intended.

Ahithophel committed suicide after his counsel was rejected, but I don't believe the rejection of his counsel caused him to take his own life. I believe he knew that Absalom was going to be defeated. Ahithophel betrayed the king, and he could see the writing on the wall when David took the reins again. His counsel meant something in the kingdom. His reputation was known abroad. When Absalom took the counsel of Hushai, David's spy, over Ahithophel, it was nothing short of a miracle orchestrated by the Lord. II Samuel 17:14 says, *"And Absalom and all the men of Israel said, The counsel of Hushai the Archite is better than the counsel of Ahithophel...."* This was the first time that anybody had said this.

This change of events can be traced back to I Samuel 15:31, *"And one told David, saying, Ahithophel is among the conspirators with Absalom. And David said, O Lord, I pray thee, turn the counsel of Ahithophel into foolishness."* Because David prayed and turned to God for help, God performed the unthinkable. This was the turning point in Absalom's scheme to steal the kingdom from his father. The difference maker was the prayer that David offered that defeated Absalom's pride-filled, vengeance-based plot. Through the power of prayer, God can turn the circumstances if He chooses.

—— Today's Truth ——

You will never see what God can do if you never go to Him for help in the battle. Prayer is one of your most powerful resources, no matter how much the odds are against you.

APRIL 18

Help Wanted

Read II Samuel 19–20

PEOPLE HAVE TROUBLE asking for help. In fact, some are so bent on not asking for help that they will work to the point of collapse before reaching out for a helping hand. At the close of II Samuel 20, we find the list of David's "cabinet." Even David couldn't do everything by himself. Every leader has followers who fill a role so that the workload is distributed in a way that tasks are completed efficiently.

The ironic part about this predicament is that those who don't ask for help usually want help and need help, but have a difficult time asking. Some feel it is selfish to ask for help. After all, if you have been given a task, you should be responsible to complete it, right? Surely there are areas of life that you alone should accomplish, but needing help makes only one thing clear—you are human.

Leaders don't ask for help so they can do less, but so they can better accomplish their primary tasks. Take the calling of deacons in Acts 6 as exhibit A. Pastors have a primary task to be students of the Word of God and men of prayer. Deacons were called to serve in daily, miscellaneous tasks and to help serve the widows of the church.

For the first four years that I was a pastor, my wife and I cleaned the church before services. After Saturday soul winning, I would mow the lawn, edge, blow, and straighten up for Sunday. My wife would clean the interior. After we had our first and second children, I sometimes did everything because my wife was far along in her pregnancy or taking care of our infant children. I loved doing this, because I loved our church, but it was very tiring. I was running a business on the side, and it came to the place where I needed help. One day, a man in the church approached me about making this his ministry, and now, I can't remember the last time I cut the grass at the church.

—— Today's Truth ——

Accepting help has its challenges, but as more people get involved, greater work can be accomplished.

Titles

Read II Samuel 21–22

THE PSALM THAT David gives in II Samuel 22 correlates with Psalm 18. As David looked back on his life, he offered this song of praise for all that God had done in his life. Singing to the Lord is a form of worship. To bow the knee, both physically and in your heart, is to give reverence to God for who He is and what He has done. In verses 2 and 3, David lists several titles that describe God's goodness to Him; from these titles, we can recall the various ways that God can work in our lives, too.

I am proud of some titles in life, because of what the title means. The title "dad" is one that I cherish. I love coming home from work to have our kids run up and yell "Daddy" as they come wrap their arms around my legs. The term "Christian" has great meaning, but our world has polluted it. I'm not demeaning the term, because I am proud to be called a Christian just like the early Christians at Antioch. However, I love the title "Baptist." When you study the heritage of Baptists, you understand and appreciate what the name stands for. Baptists weren't people of denominations, but rather were known for being Bible-first believers.

I could go on and on with important titles in my life like "husband," "pastor," "son," "brother," etc., but the point is that titles carry meaning. With all of the titles given to God throughout Scripture, we can learn more about Him by studying and picturing Him through these titles. We will spend eternity exhausting the glory of God and who He is. No human terms can fully describe Him. So, through descriptive titles like David gave, it helps us understand more about our heavenly Father.

—— Today's Truth ——

God is too grand to be described perfectly, but the Bible gives various titles that paint a beautiful picture of His glory.

APRIL 20

The Crime of a Census

Read II Samuel 23–24

Of David's great sins that the Bible records, only the sin of numbering the people is repeated in the Chronicles (1 Chronicles 21:1). It was not the sin with Bathsheba, but taking a census of the nation that was emphasized by the Lord. Why was a census taken so seriously by the Lord as a sin that David committed?

The NKJV wrongly attributes the "he" in II Samuel 24 to the Lord, thus capitalizing this supposed reference to meaning that God moved David to number the people. However, the KJV proves to be correct yet again. I Chronicles 21:1 says, *"And Satan stood up against Israel, and provoked David to number Israel."* Still, why was this such a serious sin in the Lord's eyes?

A census was to be taken only under certain circumstances. In Exodus 30:12, a principle is given that a man had the right to number only what he owned. David was the king of Israel, but he did not have ownership over Israel. The nation belonged to God, and David knew it based on his reaction after he was confronted (II Samuel 24:8).

After David sinned, God gave David a chance to choose his punishment. The first two options would put David at the mercy of other men. A famine would have caused them to turn to foreign aid for help. Fleeing from his enemies would make him a sitting duck before his bloodthirsty enemies. David chose the pestilence because he would be dealing directly with the Lord. He knew he had sinned, and he accepted the consequences for his actions.

No sin is a small matter in the Lord's eyes. With a little study, we see the severity in this sin. However, even if we don't understand why God's response to some sins seems more severe than with others, we should determine that if God views a particular sin a certain way, then we should as well.

—— Today's Truth ——

David sinned, confessed, and accepted the consequence. This process is how we overcome our failures, no matter the sin.

King in Your Own Eyes

Read I Kings 1–2:25

GERALD GARDNER TELLS this story in *Reader's Digest*: "Ronald Reagan, recalling an occasion when he was governor of California and made a speech in Mexico City: 'After I had finished speaking, I sat down to rather unenthusiastic applause, and I was a little embarrassed. The speaker who followed me spoke in Spanish—which I didn't understand—and he was being applauded about every paragraph. To hide my embarrassment, I started clapping before everyone else and longer than anyone else until our ambassador leaned over and said, 'I wouldn't do that if I were you. He's interpreting your speech.'"

A great principle to always remember is that God doesn't use those who exalt themselves. Rather, God exalts those who humble themselves (James 4:10). Adonijah is a fine example of how quickly people fall when they seek power and fame. While David was on his deathbed, Adonijah began to make his claim for the throne. He set up a kind of campaign for himself. He had chariots go before him and probably thought that if he portrayed himself as a king that he would be received as one. However, this didn't align with David's plan, much less with God's.

After Adonijah's bold and tasteless challenge, he was executed for his stunt. It's easy to fall off a throne that you build for yourself. He might have considered himself to be the rightful king, but he was not the one God had chosen to take David's place. Likewise, we must be mindful to not usurp ourselves over the Lord and exalt ourselves to positions and duties that are not a part of His will. Regardless of the title you hold, your desire should be to humble yourself to God's perfect will, so that He can exalt you to whatever position He wants you to hold and will give you the ability to fulfill.

—— Today's Truth ——

To be king in your own eyes and to be king in God's eyes are two very different positions. Humble yourself so God can exalt you, or God will humble you if you attempt to exalt yourself.

Except...

Read I Kings 2:26–4

I CAN SAY with great confidence that everybody has parts of their life that they wish they could erase. They would be happy to forget that one mistake, that one season, that one flaw they never conquered. Solomon could have been a great king. He had an amazing father. Can you imagine him arguing with his friends using the infamous line, "My dad can…." Solomon would have won that argument every time. He had so much going for him and so much potential for his future. Still, he ruined what he was given due to a few noteworthy flaws that are remembered far beyond the good that he did.

I Kings 3:3 says, *"And Solomon loved the LORD, walking in the statutes of David his father: only he sacrificed and burnt incense in high places."* This verse begins by complimenting Solomon, but it ends with a turn on his glaring sin in sacrificing at the high places. You could say of Solomon, "He was a great king, except for one or two areas." That one word "except" changes everything though.

Your Christian walk is limited to what you're willing to leave on the table. When Jesus compelled His disciples to take up their cross, it signified a total and complete surrender. The Lord isn't interested in "weekend" or part-time disciples. Solomon could have been used if he had understood this. Samson could have been used, except for his pride and lust. Judas could have been used, except for his greed and heart of rejection. Absalom could have been used, except for his bitterness. We can't even imagine what God is capable of doing with the life of a completely surrendered Christian.

—— Today's Truth ——

Dedicate yourself wholly to the Lord as you live for Him. When you leave a sin lingering, you open the door for that sin to destroy your future.

Building Projects

Read I Kings 5–7

Building projects can be exciting, expensive, stressful, and a lot of other adjectives that I could list. Our first major building project was a complete renovation of our church building in 2020 during much of the coronavirus lockdown. I learned a lot during that period that I could have learned only by experiencing it. As we read of the erection of the temple, I want you to think of areas of your life that God has put you in charge of building. It may be your home, your ministry, or even a physical project at the church. In this passage, we find several components to a successful building project.

Peace – One of the reasons David couldn't build is because he was a man of war. War prohibits progress. Battles have to be fought, but there is no room for building during this time.

Purpose – The purpose of this building should be the purpose for all that we build. We build for God's glory.

Promise – When God is in it, God will take care of the details. He'll give you the abilities you need and the resources required to get the job done.

Preparations – Projects need preparations made. Being diligent to prepare for the task will ensure that you do it right.

Prerequisites – God has a blueprint for everything we do. Stick to His plan, and you can be sure that it'll turn out for good.

Progress – Projects mean work. You can't make progress toward finishing a task if you don't work the task you've been given.

Praise – Whatever you accomplish in life, God deserves the glory. There is joy when you see results, but don't let your joy distract you from giving Him the praise.

—— Today's Truth ——

Everyone has a role to fill and work to do with what you've been given. Follow the Lord's leading and blueprints. Success comes at the end of doing the job His way.

Dedication Service

Read I Kings 8

Upon the completion of the temple, I Kings 8 describes the grand dedication that was given as the Ark was brought to the temple and the people praised the Lord for the work that was accomplished. Churches often have dedication services that follow this pattern. At the end of a great work, it is good and right to stop and look up and dedicate the work to the Lord.

Most people remember their "firsts" very vividly. First car, first house, first child and other significant firsts bring an experience that is so new that it is etched so explicitly in your mind for your entire life. When my wife and I rented our first apartment, I remember how overwhelmed I was that we had a place of our own. We weren't living at home anymore, nor were we dependent upon others at this point. When we arrived after our honeymoon, we prayed together and dedicated our home and our family to the Lord. This was our heart's way of saying, "Lord, we recognize that this was given to us from You. We want to please You by how we live in this house and what we use it to accomplish. We are Your vessels, and we dedicate all that we have for Your glory."

After the remodel of our church auditorium in 2020, we had a dedication service for our church. Nearly one hundred seats were added, every square inch on the inside was completely remodeled, much of the infrastructure was remodeled, and it was a beautiful completion to a year-long project. We covered the doors and windows so that no one could see inside beforehand. Minutes before the service, we opened the doors. I'll never forget seeing the faces as people walked in. While many were in awe of the material beauty, we took time in this service to direct our praise where it was rightly deserved. I preached from this passage, and we dedicated our building, ourselves, and our ministry to the Lord.

—— Today's Truth ——

A dedication is a purposeful action that shows the Lord that you recognize that He deserves the credit and He is the One that you seek to please with what He's given you as a steward.

The Half Was Not Told

Read I Kings 9–11

The story of the Queen of Sheba has been attacked by critics of the Bible. Solomon's wealth and wisdom gained a reputation around the world, and this queen came to see with her own eyes what the fuss was about. She wanted to see it with her eyes and hear from Solomon herself. After exhausting all of Solomon's wisdom and observing all of the beauty of his kingdom and the temple, *"And she said to the king, It was a true report that I heard in mine own land of thy acts and of thy wisdom. Howbeit I believed not the words, until I came, and mine eyes had seen it: and, behold, the half was not told me: thy wisdom and prosperity exceedeth the fame which I heard"* (I Kings 10:7–8).

This queen made a powerful statement: *"the half was not told me."* I believe that statement really sums up the Christian life after you realize how good it can be when you are in the center of God's will and following Him with your whole heart. Have you ever had someone try to describe something to you, only to finally say in frustration, "You just had to be there." Some things are beyond description. You have to see it to know. You have to experience it to understand. You have to feel it to realize how good it is.

The Christian life that is blessed by God is something we simply cannot begin to describe with words. When Jesus called His disciples, He told them to *"Come and see"* (John 1:39). I'm glad that I serve a God who is beyond description, even after using every compliment and adjective available in the English language. We can't describe His goodness even half as good as He really is. The world can easily be put into a box in man's understanding, but something so indescribably good as our God is surely someone worth living for.

—— Today's Truth ——

A life that is blessed by God is totally indescribable. Words can't do it justice, pictures can't describe it, and you won't be able to comprehend it until you experience it yourself.

Deception that Leads to Destruction

Read I Kings 12–13

W E SHOULD NOT be shy to preach and teach against the false religions and false teachers who are opposing the truth. We should also not be ignorant of the fact that the people that fill these churches, mosques and synagogues of these false religions are full of sincere people. However, their sincerity does not excuse the falsehood of the institutions of which they are a part. Good people can be deceived. Kind people can be deceived. Even godly Christians can be deceived. This is the case of the man of God that you'll read about in I Kings 13.

People will try to defend others by saying, "They have a good heart," "They love the Lord, too," or "They say they the Lord told them this." We need to be more spiritually mature than this. Just like children are taught not to believe everything people tell them or to understand that everything they watch on their cartoon shows is fake, so should believers have the same understanding. Not every place that has the name "church" on it is a real, Biblical church. Not everyone that calls themselves Christian is born again or Christ-like. Not every song that has Jesus' name in it is bringing honor to His name. Not every person that has a Bible verse tattooed on their body is dedicated to the life of a true disciple.

This realization shouldn't bring people to have a pessimistic view of others and of life. It should, however, open your eyes to have spiritual discernment. Take a step back and seek the Lord's wisdom before jumping in with both feet. You don't have to be negative to be wise, just like you don't have to be gullible about every so-called "prophet" to be a kind, compassionate, and gentle person. Many have been deceived, and their life is the casualty.

——Today's Truth ——

Not everything is what it appears to be on the surface. God gives us His Spirit and His guidance to avoid deception and also destruction.

Heart Problems

Read I Kings 14–15

H EART DISEASE IS the leading cause of death in the U.S., accounting for one out of every four deaths. One person dies every 36 seconds from cardiovascular disease, which amounts to over 650,000 deaths annually in the U.S. Heart complications can be frightening. Whenever you hear someone speak of heart surgery, it's always a little frightening. The heart is a vital organ of the body, and unless your heart is working and doing its duty, the rest of your body will be useless.

When the Bible speaks about the heart, it doesn't speak about the vital organ inside of our bodies. The heart refers to the inner man. This is what we feel and think, what fuels us on the inside. We judge people based upon their actions, but actions are just a product of what is in the heart. The spiritual heart of man is just as important as the vital organ. In I Samuel 16:7, the Bible says, *"But the LORD said unto Samuel, Look not on his countenance, or on the height of his stature; because I have refused him: for the LORD seeth not as man seeth; for man looketh on the outward appearance, but the LORD looketh on the heart."* Thus, we know that the heart is important to the Lord.

After Rehoboam died, Abijam took his place as king of Judah. I Kings 15:3 says of his reign, *"And he walked in all the sins of his father, which he had done before him: and his heart was not perfect with the LORD his God, as the heart of David his father."* He was not judged because of his lack of knowledge or skills, but because his heart was not right before the Lord. Just as there are signs that you might be having heart problems and need to address an issue, there are signs that make it clear when someone is having heart problems with the Lord. Be sure that you get your daily heart check up with the Lord.

—— Today's Truth ——

Your heart is a vital part of your spiritual health that needs to be checked daily. The Lord looks on the inside and wants to see that your actions are in order, but also that your heart is how it should be as well.

APRIL 28

God Will Take Care of You

Read I Kings 16–18

DALE CARNEGIE WROTE in *How to Stop Worrying and Start Living*: "James Cash Penney (who started J. C. Penney stores) made some unwise commitments and became very depressed. He worried so much that he developed shingles. He went to see his doctor who admitted him to the hospital, but his condition became worse. One night he was prescribed a sedative that quickly wore off, and he awoke believing that he would die that night. He wrote letters to his family and fell asleep. He woke up the next morning and was surprised that he was still alive. He heard people singing 'God Will Take Care of You' in the chapel and went in. He listened to the singing and message with a heavy heart, but then something happened. He later said, 'I realized then that I alone was responsible for my troubles. I knew that God with His love was there to help me.' He said that from that day forward his life was free of worry, and it was all because he realized that God would take care of him."

God has many ways to grow you and shape you into what He wants you to be. To do this, He will surely put you through difficult seasons where you must learn to live by faith and trust Him. I Kings 17 is the chapter where we see Elijah grow. In verse 1, he is *"Elijah the Tishbite,"* but in verse 24, he is *"Elijah…a man of God."* After delivering a message of judgment to the king, God told Elijah to hide himself. In the midst of his lonely and dark hour, God provided for Elijah just as He promised He would. Because Elijah followed the Lord, God fed him and gave him water. God provided for his needs because Elijah was obedient and faithful.

——Today's Truth ——

Elijah was cared for as a result of his obedience to the Lord. In return, God grew Elijah through these circumstances for the battles he would face in the future. Elijah knew he could trust the Lord no matter the trial.

What Are You Doing Here?

Read I Kings 19–20

I F YOU'RE SUPPOSED to be at work and you're at home, your spouse might ask, "What are you doing here?" If you're supposed to be at church and you're on the lake, a spiritual friend might ask, "What are you doing there?" If you're alone with a woman or a man who is not your spouse, you might be asked, "What are you doing with that person?" The question is asked when you are where you're not supposed to be and when you are not where you are supposed to be.

After the not-even-close showdown between the Lord and the prophets of Baal, Elijah almost immediately goes into a deep state of depression. I Kings 19:9 reads, *"And he came thither unto a cave, and lodged there; and, behold, the word of the LORD came to him, and he said unto him, What doest thou here, Elijah?"* Elijah wasn't in the place, both physically and spiritually, that he should have been. Elijah fixed his eyes on the opposition around him instead of the God above him. He sought the wrong thing when he asked for his life to be taken instead of seeking the Lord for the help that he needed. He even allowed himself to speak in a way that is so opposite of the story we read in the previous chapter, it's hard to believe that these stories reflect the same person.

When God came to Elijah, He showed him grace and called him out of that cave by the still, small voice. You might experience moments in life where you feel like you're not in the right place. If you'll listen, God will call upon you and speak to you in your time of need. You don't have to stay in your season of depression. You don't have to remain backslidden. You don't have to live outside of His will. He is graciously, gently, and generously calling you out of where you are to bring you to where you ought to be.

—— Today's Truth ——

Your flesh can drive you to places where you shouldn't be. God is calling you out by His still, small voice. This isn't a voice of condemnation, but a voice that is calling you out so that you don't have to stay any longer where you should not dwell.

Deal or No Deal

Read I Kings 21–22

Pastor R. G. Lee preached a sermon from I Kings 21 over 1,200 times entitled, "Payday Someday." After Ahab tried to buy Naboth's vineyard and was refused, then he pouted about it, his wife Jezebel came to his rescue and took care of his problem. She stole Naboth's vineyard, and Ahab and Jezebel were dealt with justly by the Lord. Most messages you'll hear from this passage focus on the wickedness of this duo, but I'd like you to focus today on Naboth's part in this story.

Ahab gave Naboth a deal. In fact, it was a very fair deal. Ahab wasn't trying to steal this land in the beginning. He seems to have made a real offer that he thought Naboth would have gladly accepted. This offer would have changed Naboth's life dramatically. Still, Naboth declined. Who would decline an offer from the king? You might wonder what caused Naboth to make this decision. We are told that he refused to give up his inheritance, no matter how beneficial the offer seemed.

Temptation works the same way. The devil presents his offer to you so that you might think it's a win-win scenario, or just too good of an opportunity to pass up. Truth be told, the world can offer you nothing that can give you what the Lord can give you. You should have no second thoughts when Satan makes his offers. Don't review the details. Don't "pray about it." Don't talk it over. Don't even ponder the idea. Salesmen believe that everybody has a price, and they will stop at nothing to find out what you're willing to say yes to. However good the offer and temptation might seem, don't sell and give away what you have.

——Today's Truth ——

God has his best prepared for you, and the world can give you nothing to compare. Don't sell out!

I Will Not Leave

Read II Kings 1–3

JOHN KENNETH GALBRAITH was a noted economist in the early 1900s who was called upon by many dignitaries to help sort the economic markets. He wrote the following story in his autobiography about his housekeeper: "It had been a wearying day, and I asked Emily to hold all telephone calls while I had a nap. Shortly thereafter the phone rang. Lyndon Johnson was calling from the White House. 'Get me Ken Galbraith. This is Lyndon Johnson.' 'He is sleeping, Mr. President. He said not to disturb him.' 'Well, wake him up. I want to talk to him.' 'No, Mr. President. I work for him, not you.' When I called the President back, he could scarcely control his pleasure. 'Tell that woman I want her here in the White House.'"

Genuine loyalty cannot be bought, especially in times when that loyalty is tested. Three times in II Kings 2, Elisha pronounces his loyalty to Elijah and tells him, *"As the LORD liveth, and as thy soul liveth, I will not leave thee"* (vv. 2, 4, 6). Little did Elisha know that this would be the last time that he would see Elijah. Imagine for a moment, if Elisha's response had been different. Imagine if he had complained, or questioned his leader, or threatened to leave. Elisha passed the test to remain faithful and loyal to the person and the place God had for his life.

Marriages have a problem with loyalty and faithfulness. Studies show that as many as twenty-five percent of marriages will involve a spouse that is unfaithful. Surely, all those couples made the same or very similar vows at the wedding altar. We don't have a problem expressing our loyalty, but keeping it. Wherever God has you, and whoever God has put you with, just stay. Echo the words of Elisha to the place and to the people God has put in front of you.

—— Today's Truth ——

Loyalty must be declared, and it will be tested. Don't let your loyalty stop with your words.

It Is Well

Read II Kings 4–5

B AD THINGS HAPPEN in life. "That's just life," people will tell you. But amidst those times of trouble are situations that started out good but turned bad quickly. We expect opposition, and everyone knows that hardship will come. The good times are sweeter because of the hard times, but added difficulty comes when it is the good times that turn bad too. Holidays, birthdays, vacations, peak months in business—these are all times that we eagerly anticipate. They are moments we relish and depend on. When the times we long for turn sour, it is often a powerful blow.

II Kings 5 gives the story of the Shunammite woman whom God miraculously blessed with a son in answer to her prayer. That child grew up and went out into the field just like any other day. It appears that he was injured and died in his mother's arms. This answer to prayer turned into a nightmare. She ran to meet the man of God, and when Elisha sent his servant to see if anything was wrong, her response was this: *"It is well"* (v. 26).

This heartbroken mother had no idea if God would heal her son. She couldn't read the end of the story like we can. Before God did a miracle, her spirit was already settled on that statement. It is usually after God does the miracle or answers the prayer that we declare with a shout, "It is well," but that is a superficial form of spirituality. Before you pour out your heart to God, before He answers your prayer, and regardless of how He works in your greatest times of need, trust God that "It is well."

—— Today's Truth ——

Don't wait to see how God works to determine how your heart is toward Him. Have the heart to say, "It is well" no matter what comes, no matter how He answers, and all because of who He is.

People Problems

Read II Kings 6–8

MOST OF OUR life is filled with fixing problems. Chapter six begins with an ax head that fell into the water. This was a problem. It may not seem like much to Americans who can go to Home Depot for most tools, but iron was scarce in these times. Additionally, this ax head was borrowed. While the problem may not be relevant to your life personally, the problem they faced reminds us of some basic truths when dealing with problems.

Problems are *constant*. Cancer doesn't care how old you are. Death doesn't consult with your calendar. Financial stress doesn't wait until your portfolio is prepared. Problems come, and often at the worst of times. Recently, I performed a funeral for three people. Due to the stay-at-home order during the coronavirus pandemic, few were allowed to attend. The youngest daughter, who was out of state, was not even able to attend her own father's funeral.

Problems must be *communicated*. You do not have to tell everyone, but God made prayer possible for a reason. We long to communicate our problems. There may be some person or a few that God has placed in your life to help you, but often we fail to ask for help. Communicating your problem is not complaining about your problem; it is simply asking for help. You need wisdom in how to do this, but you can do this. Unoffered prayers always lead to unanswered prayers.

Problems allows *confirmation*. God made the iron float. For the record, iron doesn't float. Remember that it is in the midst of our problems that we get to see the hand of God at work, not during the times of calm and quiet. God will confirm His presence and His power right in front of you, but it will always be in the midst of a problem.

—— Today's Truth ——

All throughout your life, you will face problems. Instead of complaining, see the opportunity to watch the hand of God move for you personally.

Cut Short

Read II Kings 9–10

A SHORT LIST OF the most wicked rulers in the Bible would include Ahab and Jezebel. I Kings 16:30 shows that Ahab's wickedness even outdid all that were before him. God's judgment came upon this couple, and God used Jehu, a commander in Ahab's army, to replace him and clean house. II Kings 10:28 tells us, *"Thus Jehu destroyed Baal out of Israel."* Jehu was going to work, and God was pleased with him. II Kings 10:30 shows the pleasure from God and His promise to Jehu and to his fourth generation that would succeed him. It appears as if everything is changed and Jehu is the silver lining in this passage, but he failed to live up to his potential.

II Kings 10:31 states, *"But Jehu took no heed to walk in the law of the LORD God...."* After all that he did for the Lord, Jehu sold himself short. He failed to continue to grow in the Lord and to follow God's plan for his life. Verse 32 continues, *"In those days the LORD began to cut Israel short...."* Like a pruner to a plant, God had to continue to cut short His blessings on Jehu and his family.

When you wonder where God is and what He's doing, it would be good to look at what you have given to Him or failed to give up for Him. God will not pour out showers of blessing on a person who will not walk in the way of the Lord. If you feel you are being cut short by God, you can be sure the problem is not with Him; and you may need to do some searching in your life. God doesn't want to cut you short, just like parents don't enjoy taking away privileges and gifts from their children; but He will do no less than just that if you choose to neglect Him.

—— Today's Truth ——

Don't sell yourself short. Follow God with your whole heart and watch as He blesses you fully. If you cut God short in your service to Him, He will cut you short in what He longs to do for you.

The Chariots of Israel and their Horsemen

Read II Kings 11–13

T HE OLD SAYING goes, "You never appreciate what you have until you've lost it." King Joash sees the man of God, Elisha, sick and about to die. To this point, he has not been a king to serve false gods, but he has falsely served the true God. The Syrians made him fearful, and this king feared that when Elisha died, the power of God would die with him.

King Joash repeats the same statement in II Kings 13 that Elisha spoke when Elijah was translated in chapter 2: *"O my father, my father, the chariot of Israel, and the horsemen thereof"* (II Kings 13:14). Joash knew he wasn't right with God, and he knew that a godly man leaving his country was a sign of the judgment that would soon come. The strength of his nation was slipping, and he understood their future was in God's hands. In the end, the Syrians did oppress Israel, but God was gracious (II Kings 13:22–23).

Too often, we wait for trouble to come before we fall on our knees before the Lord. God is good to us in often holding back on what we truly deserve, but His mercy and grace should not be taken for granted. To have God's hand of protection and power on your life, you must fall on your face every day and seek the Lord's presence in everything you do. As a parent, leader, teacher, and with any role that you've been given, be sure to seek the Lord not as a final act of desperation, but as a daily habit.

—— Today's Truth ——

When the presence of God has drifted, we fear because God is the only one to bring the help we need. Don't wait until the final hour to seek Him. Seek Him in the final hour, and seek Him every hour!

Setting the Standard

Read II Kings 14–15

THE MARK OF a good leader is proven by those who follow in his footsteps. Leaders put pressure on their followers to do more, live better, and rise to the standard that has been set by their leader. When a child has a drunkard for a father or a selfish and careless mother, the low standard makes it easy for that child to follow in the parent's footsteps. When an employee has a boss who is driven, exhibits integrity, deals honesty, and strives for growth, the pressure is on the employee to live up to the standard set by the boss.

In the summary given of the reign of Amaziah, God highlights the standard set before this king. II Kings 14:3 says, *"And he did that which was right in the sight of the LORD, yet not like David his father: he did according to all things as Joash his father did."* Amaziah did right, but he did not quite live up to a standard set by his forefather, David. God used the second king of Israel over and over as the standard for the kings that would come after him. Maybe a good standard wasn't set before you in your family, but maybe God can use you to be a David for future generations.

Pressure is healthy. Rules, goals, and other benchmarks create that pressure. God's instruction throughout His Word puts pressure on us all to heed the direction He has given, and we are to do the same for those who follow behind us. Set the standard high in your family, in your work, and for everyone around you. Don't open the door for failure behind you. Put the pressure on for others to live up to the standard you can set.

——Today's Truth ——

People give excuses for why they fail. Don't give those behind you an excuse. Set a godly standard for the people around you to live for God.

The Lord Testifies

Read II Kings 16–17

THE SIEGE OF Syria that overtook Israel takes place in II Kings 17. The sand in the hourglass has finally run through, and the people that God longed to bless required His wrath. We must remind ourselves that God, who is also our Father, does not enjoy giving punishment; but He will punish when there is reason for it. Here, God testifies of the reasoning behind Israel's capture and future captivity.

They *disobeyed* God (v. 13). God gives clear commandments. It is our duty to obey them, not to question them. At the opening of this chapter, God tells us of the present king, Hoshea. Verse 2 describes him as evil, "but not as the kings of Israel that were before him." It wasn't the most wicked king in history that caused God's hand of judgment. Sin is sin, and we must never use a scale on the severity of our sin compared to others. Partial disobedience and petty sin still defies the Lord.

They *doubted* God (v. 14). It must be frustrating to be God. After all that He's done for us, proven before our eyes, and sovereignly orchestrated for our good, we still doubt Him. He's given zero reason for us to doubt Him, yet it's still a battle. It's a battle you must win, and if you trust Him, He remind you there is never a good reason to doubt Him.

They *defied* God (v. 15). Not only did they turn from His instruction, but they also rejected His warnings. Their idols were erected, their children were made to pass through the fire, and they gave undeserved worship to the gods of the world. They sold out, but in all the wrong ways.

—— Today's Truth ——

What reason does God have to bring judgment on your life? Nobody is perfect, but you don't have to experience the pain that comes with the punishment. God longs to bless you and fulfill His promises if you'll listen and follow Him.

Home Invasion

Read II Kings 18–20

Of all the attacks from the world, the home is ground zero. Your spiritual life will never exceed who you are in your home. You can put on a good face out in public, but how you treat your children, what you allow on your television, and how you conduct yourself in the privacy of your home will dictate your future. II Kings 20 tells of Hezekiah's home invasion. However, it wasn't much of an invasion since he invited the enemy into his home. In verse 15, Hezekiah tells the king of Babylon, *"…there is nothing among my treasures that I have not shewed them."* The enemy didn't have to break in. They were invited!

Your home is being invaded, but what creeps in are the things you allow. Parents spend less than thirty-six minutes per day with their children, including time spent in front of the television. Yet, we wonder why children are not being influenced to live for God. Marriages are filled with online secrets, affairs, dishonesty in finances, and growing resentment. Still, we ask ourselves where it went wrong. The invasion that takes place in your home may be forced, but you're still the one to open or close the door to the enemy.

A Christian home is not a Christian home because Christians are living in it. A Christian home is a home that is guided by God's Word and allows God to flow into every aspect of it while closing the door on the invasion of the devil. Colossians 3:16 instructs, *"Let the word of Christ dwell in you richly in all wisdom…."* This is God's Word being integrated into every part of your day and life. Family devotions, teaching children God's Word, praying together, serving and attending church together, and saturating your home with godly music are ways to dwell in God's instruction and fight against a home invasion.

——Today's Truth ——

Your home is your responsibility. What God has entrusted to you, you must guide by His Word. Guard against the invasion of sin into your home.

The Steps to Revival

Read II Kings 21–23:20

LEONARD RAVENHILL SAID, "The only reason we don't have revival is because we are willing to live without it." A revival took place in Judah because of the godly king who began to lead as a young boy, Josiah. Revival didn't come because of a seasoned king or a polished nobleman, but through a boy who didn't know any better than to turn from sin and get in touch with God. I believe revival can take place, but revival doesn't begin with the nation. Revival begins with each one of us. Notice the steps that were taken for this revival:

1. Repair of the temple (22:3–6)
2. Return to the Word of God (22:8–10)
3. Remorse over sin (22:11–13)
4. Removal of idolatry and immorality (23:4–7)
5. Reinstitution of the Passover (23:21–23)
6. Reform (23:8–20)

This revival may have been short-lived, but its impact is traced by the Spirit of God in His Word recorded for us to see. Do you need revival? Revival simply means to bring back the life. What part of your spiritual walk needs some life again? Has sin infiltrated an area of your life that you gave to God and brought spiritual death where there used to be a vibrant and burning life for God? One page won't permit the explanation needed for all of these steps, but as you study God's Word, you can see the need that existed. That same need for revival exists today. It's not the church across town that needs revival, it's us.

—— Today's Truth ——

Revival comes to those who want revival and nothing else. A total transformation was needed for Josiah to connect with God again, and nothing less will result in truly getting ahold of God.

Great Wrath

Read II Kings 23:21–25

"Be not deceived; *God is not mocked: for whatsoever a man soweth, that shall he also reap*" (Galatians 6:7). What Zedekiah, the last king of Judah, learned to be true when Babylon burned the temple, destroyed Jerusalem, and took the valuables and captives is a warning for us to heed today. God will not be mocked. II Kings 23:26–27 states, "*Notwithstanding the Lord turned not from the fierceness of his great wrath, wherewith his anger was kindled against Judah... And the Lord said, I will remove Judah also out of my sight, as I have removed Israel, and will cast off this city Jerusalem which I have chosen, and the house of which I said, My name shall be there.*" This was the end; this was fruit of the wickedness of the leaders and the people of God that they had sown to this point.

It is difficult to read passages like this. Watching God bring a fierce wrath against His chosen people because of their wickedness is an account no one enjoys. If there is a lesson here, let it be determined that your end will not play out like this. There are no shortcuts with the Lord. Proverbs 28:13 says, "*He that covereth his sins shall not prosper....*" The answer is not to cover your sins, but to confess your sins as I John 1:9 prescribes so that you can receive the forgiveness and mercy of Almighty God.

We should shudder in fear at the thought of God's wrath. The end of our Bible gives a future picture of what God's great wrath looks like. I know that it has come to some, and it will come to others in the future, but it doesn't have to come to you. The important lesson to learn in this is that it doesn't have to. You must obey God's Word and live according to His commands. God's way is still the best way. There's no need to test or try where the other roads will lead.

—— Today's Truth ——

You don't have to experience God's wrath; you can experience God's favor, forgiveness, and fellowship instead.

The Chronicles

Read I Chronicles 1–2

J. VERNON MCGEE SAID of the books of Chronicles, "When the Holy Spirit gave us the Word of God, He gave us a telescope. He surveys the landscape with us, then zeroes in on a particular portion and puts it under the microscope and lets us look at it in detail. This is what is happening in Chronicles." I and II Kings give a political view of the nation. The Chronicles give a religious view of the nation. I and II Kings show man's point of view while the Chronicles show God's. I and II Kings are told from the standpoint of the throne and the Chronicles from the standpoint of the altar. In I and II Kings, the palace is the center. In the Chronicles, the temple is the center.

The Chronicles are said to be the interpretation of I and II Kings. In some ways, they are similar to Deuteronomy, the second Law, that interprets and retells the experiences of the wilderness. All throughout the books of Kings you see the statement, "Is it not written in the book of the chronicles of the kings of Israel?" This sets up Chronicles to interpret what has taken place, and to do it in a different light.

Greek translators have referred to *Chronicles* as "things omitted." This is probably an improper title, since God has determined what is in His Word and what is left out. However, God saw it fitting to give us a book to retell old stories of the past with a new meaning. God's Word comes alive when you see the countless lessons and truths from a single passage or story.

But why all the genealogies? Many lessons can be learned in genealogies. The main truth here is the detail of God's plan and the people He used. God sees all people. God knows His children. God has everything figured out to fulfill His work, and He does it through His own.

—— Today's Truth ——

Reading a list of names may not stir you to do a great work for God, but God's sovereign plan sure can. Seeing life from God's point of view, in all its stages, can change a person.

How to Get a Hold of God

Read I Chronicles 3–5

WHEN I BECAME a pastor, I had a friend who wanted to move to our city to come help us, but his spiritual leader advised him not to come. I'll never forget the advice he told me he was given: "He doesn't need a friend right now. He needs to learn to get ahold of God and no one else." In a roundabout way, that man's counsel had a great effect on me. When you have no one else to turn to, do you know how to get ahold of God? I Chronicles 4 speaks of Jabez and how he got ahold of God.

First, we see the *person* of Jabez. Verse 9 calls him *honourable*. God isn't interested in what you do as much as He is who you are with. The draft is a big deal for sports. However, teams get in trouble many times by focusing on what players can do and overlooking who they are as people. Some of the most talented athletes have ruined their careers for being involved in nonsense.

Then, we see the *production* of Jabez. We don't have much insight into his life, but based on his prayer, Jabez already worked toward some goals and produced. God's not interested in laziness or slothfulness. He has given you the ability to do some things, and you can have the strength to produce in this life.

We hear the *petition* of Jabez. This wasn't only a prayer of adoration, but a prayer of asking. Prayer is not just thanking, worshipping, and uplifting God, although those things must be included in prayer. Prayer also includes asking. Jabez was bold in his petitions to the Lord, and the answer came because of the petitions he made.

Finally, we see the *provision* of Jabez. He lived in a way that pleased God, worked with what he could control, and then came to God to do what only God could do. Verse 10 ends, "And God granted him that which he requested."

—— Today's Truth ——

Get ahold of God, and you'll be amazed at what He'll do. God is ready to do a work in your life if you'll seek to get ahold of Him.

The Music Ministry

Read I Chronicles 6–7

THE COMMUNISTS OF the Soviet Union wanted to wipe out Lithuania. They made it illegal to publish a paper in the Lithuanian language. They tried to force intermarriage between Russians and Lithuanians to weaken the culture. They did everything in their power to destabilize the tiny nation. Their nation had only 25,174 square miles compared to the Soviet Union's 8.1 million. They had about 3.5 million people while the Soviets had 190 million. The Soviets had enough nuclear power to annihilate Lithuania many times over. Still, the Lithuanians kept their folk songs and folk tales alive. The mothers were known to always be singing to their children. They kept singing the songs of their heritage to keep their national spirit alive. Lithuania eventually achieved their independence, and the Soviets began to fall.

Music is important to God, and it is an important ministry in the work of God in how it speaks to the hearts of people. Music is prominent throughout the Bible, and in this passage, God references those who were involved in Israel's music ministry (I Chronicles 6:31–48). You may not have musical talent, and that's okay. You don't need an angelic voice to understand the importance of music. We all enjoy music, and I believe we can easily agree that something this universally appreciated is a powerful tool in the ministry.

The music ministry may be people who sing in a choir and who in church, but music should be a ministry to the heart of every person. God commands us to sing, to glorify Him through music, to use music to be a witness, and to encourage ourselves and others through music. Music is an expression of and a ministry to the heart. Live with godly music in your home and in life continuously.

—— Today's Truth ——

The music ministry is a ministry for all Christians. We must use this tool to make an impact on ourselves and others for the glory of God.

Just a Name

Read I Chronicles 8–10

NAMES LIKE MICHAEL Jordan, Tom Brady, and Tiger Woods likely turn your mind to sports. Names like Steve Jobs and Bill Gates make you think of technology. Names carry a reputation. This list of names in I Chronicles may seem irrelevant to you as you read it, but stop and think about how you would feel if your name were inserted in the middle of this list. Having your name etched in Scripture for future generations to read would mean a great deal to you.

Proverbs 22:1 says, *"A good name is rather to be chosen than great riches, and loving favour rather than silver and gold."* Instead of living your life focusing on building a business, put your efforts on building a good name. We could spend quite a bit of time listing successful companies and entrepreneurs, but the list shrinks when you think of those who have built a good name. The value of a good name reaches farther than any success you can obtain in this life. It should be a top priority for every Christian to build a name that will be used as an example for God's people for generations from now.

Think of a ceremony. During events, such as graduations, award ceremonies, or parties, your name is called and the spotlight is on you. You are nervous, maybe even a little embarrassed, but you feel accomplished for your recognition. It feels good to know that your name is called for something good, but God's recognition should mean more to us than anything else. Your name may not be written in God's Word, but God can use the testimony of your name to be a beacon of light to many. To you, it's just a name, but to others, your name carries a reputation. What kind of name have you built, and what kind of reputation are you building for your name?

—— Today's Truth ——

Your name carries a great weight, and you are the only one who can control what reputation is paired with your name. Set your ambition on building a name that brings glory to God and draws others to Him.

Recruits for King Jesus

Read I Chronicles 11–13

THE BOOKS OF the Chronicles deal primarily with David and give only one chapter to Saul. It is clear that David was the man after God's heart and the man that God used to lead the nation that would lead to the Messiah's first advent. Chapter 12 records the men who joined David.

Verse 15 tells of the men who valiantly crossed the Jordan River to join David in a month when the water was deep and the current swift, but this didn't stop them from showing their heart for their king. After salvation, we should publicly and passionately declare to Jesus and to all that we are on the side of the Lord Jesus!

When the men came to David, he was cautious. He didn't know who was sincere and who came to attack. It is sad to think of how many churches have been split, injured, and attacked from within. People who appeared to be loyal to God and to their local church revealed themselves to be wolves within the flock. They have their own agenda. They don't get on board with the ministries. They are never fully invested. They question the leadership. They may be present in body, but they are not a part of the loyal body. Jesus wants followers, but He wants the right kind.

After they were questioned, the men responded in verse 18, "...*Thine are we, David, and on thy side, thou son of Jesse: peace, peace be unto thee, and peace be to thine helpers; for thy God helpeth thee.*" There was no questioning where they stood, and there should be no room for question with your life. Decide what side you're on, and declare your allegiance to King Jesus and to the church that God has given you.

——Today's Truth——

You can give yourself to only one side. King Jesus has room for you, but you have to be the one to determine that you are going to live for Him.

David Inquired of God

Read I Chronicles 14–16

Y OU'VE PROBABLY HAD a few instances in your life where you look back and think to yourself, "It seemed like a good idea at first," only to find yourself in a mess. If you had just asked for a second opinion, advice from a friend, or outside help of any kind. There's good news! God is there for you with every decision you make, and He will confirm in your spirit whether or not your actions are a good idea.

The Philistines heard of David being anointed as the king and prepared to come see this new king. They were prepared to show him how powerful they were, but before David reacted, he inquired of God. In verse 10, God told him to go to battle, and God gave him the victory. In verse 14, God tells David not to go meet them in the valley, but gave David instructions for how to go up against the Philistines. The victory was one in different ways, but for the same reason. David asked God if his actions were approved by God, and He followed the instructions that were given.

It's usually the big decisions that we bring to God, but it should be a daily habit to inquire of God before we do anything that may be in question. Before you buy a vehicle, purchase a home, change careers, or make any big decision, ask God to give you confirmation before you move. Whatever He instructs, you will win if you follow Him. How about the little stuff? I believe that God wants to be a part of our lives not only in big ways, but in every way. When was the last time you stopped before acting on an impulse and asked the Lord, "Is this okay with You?" Wait for God to give you confirmation in your spirit before you do anything. Victory comes to those who follow His leading, and He will lead if you look to Him for direction.

—— Today's Truth ——

Action without approval can quickly lead to a disaster. Look to God to guide you through every decision you make in life. Inquire of Him the next time you look to act, and wait for His Spirit to lead you.

Shattered Dreams

Read I Chronicles 17–20

W HEN YOU SET your heart on something, it's hard to steer it in another direction. In 1 Chronicles 17, David expresses that he wants to build a house for the Lord. In the night, God told Nathan, *"Go and tell David my servant, Thus saith the Lord, Thou shalt not build me an house to dwell in."* (v. 4). I'm sure when David got this idea, he was excited at the opportunity to do something so special for the Lord. Surely, God wouldn't turn this down. This would be a great work for Him. But God had other plans for David.

You may have your heart set on something. It may be a job or some future vision for your life. Ambition is a good trait to have, and there is nothing wrong with aspiring to reach goals in life, especially when those goals bring glory to God. David's dream was a good one, but it wasn't in God's plan for David life. David didn't do anything wrong by wishing to build the temple for the Lord. It just wasn't what God had for David.

I'm certainly not telling you that you should not dream or aspire to do great things, but if God sets your course on a path that shatters your dreams, you don't have to be sad. God is doing something bigger in His will than you could have imagined in your dreams. God says in verse 10, *"...Furthermore I tell thee that the LORD will build thee an house."* In other words, "Thank you for wanting to build Me a house, David. But, no thanks. Instead, I will build you a house." This was a promise on David's life for many years to come. David's dreams were great, but God's plans were better. Don't be discouraged if your life doesn't pan out the way that you planned when you set your eyes on your goals. God always has something better in store.

—— Today's Truth ——

Do all you can for the Lord, but if your plans don't work out, you can always trust that God is working a better plan for your life.

David's Census

Read I Chronicles 21–23

In I Chronicles 21:1, the name *Satan* is used in the Bible for the first time. David was tempted by Satan to number the people. James 1:13 reminds us who temptation comes from: *"Let no man say when he is tempted, I am tempted of God: for God cannot be tempted with evil, neither tempteth he any man."* What exactly did David do in numbering the people that displeased God?

It was a sin of **anger**. The parallel passage here is II Samuel 24. The Lord was upset with Israel, and David acted in anger. His spirit wasn't right, and his emotions got the better of him. People make foolish decisions in times of anger. An old Chinese saying goes, "He who flies off handle makes bad landing."

It was a sin of **arrogance**. Pride is always at the root of our sins. Scripture isn't clear about this, but David could've also numbered the people to remind himself how big of an army he had or to make comparisons to other armies.

It was a sin of **aggression**. Joab pleads with David, *"Now the Lord thy God add unto the people, how many soever they be, an hundredfold, and that the eyes of my lord the king may see it: but why doth my lord the king delight in this thing?"* (v. 3). But David was the king, and he did what he wanted. People will try to warn you, guide you, and remind you of the truth; you would be wise to listen to those people God has placed in front of you. That friend's words could save you from making a costly mistake.

—— Today's Truth ——

Temptation comes in many forms, but it will always come from Satan, and it will always be aimed at hurting the Lord. David had great regret following his sin, because sin will always leave you wounded. Don't give in to the temptations you will face. Choose to do right, and look to please God in all that you do.

Music in God's House

Read I Chronicles 24–26

WHEN YOU MISUNDERSTAND the purpose of something, you will misuse it. Music is widely used in a wicked fashion. How do we go about fixing the problem? We must start with understanding the reason God created music in the first place. I Chronicles 25 lists the musicians for the temple. Understanding the purpose of the music in God's house will help us to determine the kind of music we ought to listen to and why this subject is so important.

Music is to *exalt the Lord.* Music is from God and for God. Ephesians 5:19 makes it clear that Spirit-filled music is directed *"to the Lord."* The question isn't what it did for you, but what it does for His name.

Music is to *educate us on the Bible.* Deuteronomy 31:19 shows the Lord instructing the people to teach their children the Word of God by putting it to music. There's a reason for all those kids songs that sing about the power of God, using lyrics from Bible verses and stories. You're teaching the Bible through music. Many of our hymns are theological gems. These modern 7-11 songs are so shallow and vague in their doctrine and message, it's hard to see what they're really teaching.

Music is to *edify God's people.* Saul was edified when David played for him. We will be helped by singing and listening to God's kind of music. Music will speak to you if you listen to it and allow it to get into your heart.

Music is to *evangelize the lost.* Psalm 40:3 speaks of the power of music causing people to turn to God. We have a great tool in music when it's properly used to accomplish the purpose for which it was created.

——Today's Truth——

God's house was to be filled with music, with great reason. Understand the importance of music, and honor God with yours.

Keep Searching

Read I Chronicles 27–29

W'RE ALL TOO familiar with the feeling that comes after knowing that we've lost something of importance. We check all the normal spots, but our keys are nowhere to be found. We look everywhere in the house but can't find our kid's other shoe. We retrace our steps only to find ourselves more confused. Looking diligently and coming up empty-handed is undoubtedly frustrating.

After David's charge to Israel to continue to follow the commandments of the Lord, he instructs his son with great wisdom, *"If thou seek him, he will be found of thee"* (I Chronicles 28:9). If you're searching for God in your life, this is good news. You may not find your jewelry in the black hole inside your couch, but you have a promise that you will find the Lord if you seek Him. Here's how to start your search:

Seek the right **person**. David said, *"Know thou the God of thy father."* Don't look anywhere else. It's a waste of time. Others have tried the way of the world. You will continue to search, but always come up empty-handed. Set your eyes on God today and nothing else.

Seek with a **pure** heart. Why do you do what you do? Most of our intentions are selfish if we're honest. I willingly include myself, because I know my flesh is more interested in pleasing my desires than the needs of others. Your intentions will eventually show in your actions. Let God do heart surgery on you today. Your heart is messed up by sin, and you need God to give a diagnosis and provide a transplant.

Seek with the **possibility** for God to do His will when you come to Him. David told his son to have a willing mind. Be careful about having everything too figured out in life. I'm all for planning, but it's more often true that my plans don't pan out because my plans weren't in line with what God wanted.

—— Today's Truth ——

Set your eyes on Him, set your heart in the right place, open your mind to His Spirit, and truly seek His presence today. You're going to like what you find.

Give Me Wisdom

Read II Chronicles 1–3

PEOPLE OFTEN ASK, "What do you want for your birthday?" We often reply, "Oh, I don't need anything," "I'm fine," "I don't know. I can't really think of anything." But if you're truthful, you've had your eye on something. It may be a computer, a piece of furniture, a boat, or even a new car. If God gave you what you really wanted, what would your request be? Would it be a materialistic desire that will soon wear out or would you desire something else?

II Chronicles 1 recounts the time God came to Solomon and told him, *"Ask what I shall give thee"* (v. 7). Without any hint of hesitation on Solomon's part, he asked God for wisdom to lead his people. People think that a position makes you feel big and mighty. This may be the case for some, but that's not the case for real leaders. The truth is that big positions make real leaders feel very small. The position and the responsibility it carries seems to dwarf your abilities. Solomon realized that he was in over his head from a human standpoint. He needed a heavenly wisdom. He needed God's help. The answer wasn't riches, military advancements, or power. What he needed was the wisdom to know what to do, when to do it, and how to go about doing it. Through all of his daily decisions, he understood his greatest need, and God granted it to him for seeking the right kind of help.

Earthly riches will not bring you joy in life. Proverbs 3:13 states, *"Happy is the man that findeth wisdom...."* Parents need wisdom for raising their children. We need wisdom while working with others. Leaders need wisdom in how they lead their followers. We need wisdom for how we should handle the difficult situations we will face. What is the great need for the day? The need is wisdom, and God will give it to those who simply ask for it.

—— Today's Truth ——

God's wisdom is available for those who seek it. Turn your eyes from the glamour of the world, and ask God for wisdom for anything and everything you face.

The Old-Fashioned Altar

Read II Chronicles 4–6

THE FIRST THING that you would see upon entering the temple was the altar. Chapter 4 begins by describing the bronze altar and its size. It was noticeable and demonstrated that the way to approach the Lord is by the altar. The Hebrew word for *altar* essentially means killing place. This was a place where blood was shed, and of course this would lead to our ultimate sacrifice, Jesus Christ. It was by His death that we have access to God. He fulfilled the need and gave us an open door to commune with God.

What we refer to as the altar in church today has a quite different purpose than that of the altar in the temple. However, the purpose does have striking similarities. The altar was the place where sin was taken care of, and that is the exact purpose of the altar at the close of a church service. Some look to the "invitation time" as an old tradition that is out of style, and one that holds no Biblical credence. This way of thinking misses the importance of the altar. It is still a "killing place." It is a place to die to your own agenda and turn your life over to God. Using the altar is a time to reflect on what needs to be removed from your life so that the Lord is pleased with you.

The altar is not just for those who are ready to get saved or for those making life-altering decisions. The altar is a place that symbolizes that every time we are in God's house, there is some killing in our life that needs to be done. Respond every time the Word of God is preached by going to the altar, and give yourself as a sacrifice so that He may use you.

—— Today's Truth ——

The altar doesn't have to be a tradition of the past. The altar is available for you at church, but also every time you approach the Lord in prayer. Always be ready to offer yourself to the Lord in whatever way pleases Him.

The Good Old Days

Read II Chronicles 7–9

A SECURITY JOB I had in college required me to drive to a few dozen office buildings every night to perform a variety of security checks. About half of the sites I was assigned to were vacant, and it was evident they had been that way for a long time. Now, I'm not an expert on building, but I know that buildings aren't designed to sit empty. Something went wrong. Something didn't go according to plan.

At the close of chapter 7, God warns Solomon what will happen if he doesn't walk in the way of the Lord and turns to another way. He tells Solomon in verse 21, *"And this house, which is high, shall be an astonishment to every one that passeth by it; so that he shall say, Why hath the LORD done thus unto this land, and unto this house?"* In other words, this temple will be a reminder to everyone who sees it of what used to be here, but is now gone. What a tragic picture after all the sacrifice that went into this place!

We should never come to the place where all the great work for the Lord can be seen only in the past. When you talk about ministry, you talk about what you did years ago. It should be a part of your life today, and it should be something you're striving to do more of the longer you live. Don't allow your stories to all be about yesterday. What have you done for God lately? Within the last year, month, or even the last week? I pray that my children will grow up to see God work in their church and in their family right before their eyes instead of being some kind of story that their parents talk about at bedtime. We know the end for Solomon, and because he turned away from God, that is exactly what became of the temple. It was a mighty, glamorous reminder of how things use to be.

—— Today's Truth ——

Thank God for what He did in the past. Don't forget about that. But don't let your life be all about how it used to be. The past is passed us, and you must choose today to walk in the way of the Lord.

Listen to Your Elders

Read II Chronicles 10–13

WHEN I WAS four years old: "My daddy can do anything." When I was six years old: "My dad is smarter than your dad." When I was eight years old, "My dad doesn't know exactly everything." When I was fourteen years old: "Don't pay any attention to my dad; he is so old-fashioned." When I was thirty years old: "Maybe we should ask Dad what he thinks; after all, he's had a lot of experience." When I was forty years old: "I wonder how Dad would've handled it? He was so wise." When I was fifty years old, "I'd give anything if Dad were here now so I could talk this over with him. Too bad I didn't appreciate how smart he was. I could've learned a lot from him."

Someone said that gray hair is just wisdom highlights. There is certainly something to be said about the wisdom one accrues after living through the ups and downs of life. The older generation may not know everything, but you are a fool to discount the wisdom they could share with you.

Rehoboam's downfall came when he neglected the counsel of the old men and listened to the young men. While I am thankful for the peers around me and all the help they give me, those are not the people I look to for the vast majority of the counsel I seek. God has given me some great older men in my life that have passed down their wisdom to help me through various life situations. Their style may be out of date…way out of date. But the wisdom they can give is timeless. You need to look to and listen to the elderly men and women in your life. Instead of writing them off because they don't seem to fit in, put down your phone, look them in the eye, ask questions, and listen to what they have to say.

——Today's Truth ——

The older generations have something they can teach you. It will likely come in areas you do not expect, and it is certainly something that cannot be replaced by the young, hipster, man-bun crowd around you. Listen to the counsel of the elders around you!

Your Work Shall Be Rewarded

Read II Chronicles 14–17

A S MUCH AS you may claim to love your job, you wouldn't do the work if the reward of money was not involved. Money is not the overall goal, but you need money to provide for you and your family. Still, it's not necessarily the money that drives you. It's the reward.

I worked for my dad every summer of my childhood. Looking back as an adult, I owe him a lot. As a child, I wasn't too thrilled about waking up early on my summer vacation, but my dad knew how to motivate me. There would always be a reward. When I was little, it was an ice cream at the gas station in the middle of the day or a donut at my favorite bakery before we got to the first job. If I was ever in a bad mood about work, it didn't last very long, because the reward was always there. As I got older, the reward became money. The older I got, the more money I earned. When I was a sixteen-year-old purchasing my own car with cash, it hit me how wonderful it feels to be rewarded, but even how much better it was to know that you earned your reward.

In II Chronicles 15:7, God tells Asa, *"Be ye strong therefore, and let not your hands be weak: for your work shall be rewarded."* Rewards are a motivating factor, and if God used this method, I think we can as well. He has promised that our labor for Him will not be in vain. Years may pass, and you may think that you have nothing to show for the life you gave to God, but a reward is coming your way. We think of money. However, I believe God's rewards are bigger than a printed piece of paper. His rewards will dwarf the world's rewards. God's resources are bigger. God's capabilities are broader. God's special interest in giving you what no one else can is better than anything you can imagine. God will reward your faithfulness to Him!

—— Today's Truth ——

The long hours, the moments you felt like quitting but pressed on, the dark times, the stressful days, and all that you've done to prove yourself faithful to God—it will be rewarded!

MAY 26

Ask Forgiveness, Not Permission?

Read II Chronicles 18–20

I RARELY CHECK our mailbox. For whatever reason, my wife has always gotten the mail. With one exception. If I have something coming that I'm looking forward to, I will check to see whether the item I'm expecting has arrived. I don't want to get the bills or the ads. If it's not what I want to see, I'm not taking it out of the box.

The kings of Judah and Israel want to know if God is going to give them victory over a dispute with Syria in II Chronicles 18. Jehoshaphat knows that if they are going to have victory, they need to find out if it is God's will. They felt if God wanted them to have the victory and they honored Him, He would give the victory. But they knew they must seek His will first. This was a wise move by Judah's king.

Ahab, however, wasn't as enthusiastic about this. He didn't want God's desires to be different than his desires. He felt if he didn't ask, he wouldn't know. If he didn't know, he wouldn't have to battle knowing he was doing something against God's will. Here is Ahab's response: *"And the king of Israel said unto Jehoshaphat, There is yet one man, by whom we may enquire of the LORD: but I hate him; for he never prophesied good unto me, but always evil: the same is Micaiah the son of Imla."* (II Chronicles 18:7)

Many don't want to be in church for the very same reason. They don't want to know that what they're doing at home, on their phone, or on the beach is against God. They'd rather ask for forgiveness than permission (if they even ever seek forgiveness). You may not want to hear that drinking alcohol, dressing half naked at the beach, listening to Taylor Swift, skipping church, and using foul language is sinful; but that doesn't change what God is for and against. "Your truth" doesn't change what the real truth is. You've only deliberately shielded yourself from God's truth, the only truth, and chosen to live in ignorance.

—— Today's Truth ——

Look for God's permission and approval on every move you make.

The Quiet of the Night

Read II Chronicles 21–24

THE SUN IS setting, the kids are all clean and reading quietly, the dishes are done, the house is cleaned, the fire is crackling, and your feet are up in your favorite chair. Sounds nice, right? Your house may not be that way every night, and if you have toddlers, it may never be; but the night brings a quiet that is very peaceful.

Athaliah was a wicked woman who killed all the royal seed of Judah after her son was killed. She ruled the land for over six years until payday finally came. Jehoiada the priest had the king's son that was saved, Joash, and put him on the throne to set the stage for Athaliah to realize that her plan had failed. She was put to death and the city had their first "quiet night" in probably a long, long time (II Chronicles 23:21).

That night reminded Judah of the peace they had when the wicked were not in charge, when God's man was on the throne, and when God's will was being followed. After this woman was killed, the house of Baal was destroyed. No more were sacrifices to be given to the false gods made by men. Life wasn't perfect, but for this night, they remembered how good it is to know that you are where God wants you to be.

Proverbs 15:13 states, "...*but the way of transgressors is hard.*" Author Jim Leohr wrote the following in his book *The Power of Full Engagement*: "Researchers have found almost no correlation between income levels and happiness. Between 1957 and 1990 income levels in the U.S. doubled. Yet at the same period, people's levels of happiness did not increase. In fact, reports of depression actually increased tenfold. Incidence of divorce, suicide, alcoholism and drug abuse also rose dramatically." The only way for peace to come and stress, anxiety, and fear to be conquered is for wickedness to be overthrown.

—— Today's Truth ——

Refuse to allow sin to reign in your life. Cast aside anything that is taking God's place. All of your problems can be solved when God is on the throne.

Half-Hearted Christianity

Read II Chronicles 25–27

IF YOU HAD to choose between a Christian that was cold and hardened toward the Lord and one that was a "middle-of-the-road" Christian, which one would you choose? Our logic would certainly assert that coming to church sometimes instead of never is at least doing some good, right? But I believe half-hearted Christianity is the battle of our era. This lukewarm lifestyle does more harm to the faith than those who have completely turned away from the Lord.

King Amaziah was a half-hearted follower of the Lord. II Chronicles 25:2 reads, *"And he did that which was right in the sight of the Lord, but not with a perfect heart."* He did some good, but he certainly wasn't sold out, on fire, dedicated, and fervent in his service. When the standard is lowered by a leader, it will never be greater among the followers. Half is better than none, but in terms of future influence, it is detrimental.

A man wanted to sell his house for $2,000. Another man wanted very badly to buy it, but couldn't afford it. After much bargaining, the owner agreed to sell the house for half the original price with a catch—he would retain ownership of one small nail protruding from just over the door. After many years, the original owner wanted the house back, but the new owner was unwilling to sell. So, the first owner went out, found the carcass of a dead dog, and hung it from the single nail he still owned. Soon the house became unlivable, and the family was forced to sell the house to the owner of the nail on his terms. The moral of the story: give the devil just one small part of your life, and he will make it impossible for Christ's presence to live there.

—— Today's Truth ——

There is no such thing as a half-hearted Christian. You're either in or you're out. Surrender yourself fully to the Lord, and leave no part behind.

Negligence

Read II Chronicles 28–30

NEGLIGENCE IS FAILING to do the work that you are expected and instructed to do. A softer term for this is procrastination. It is putting off and putting aside something that needs to be taken care of. Hezekiah instructed the people and said, *"My sons, be not now negligent..."* (II Chronicles 29:11). Hezekiah was the king who had the guts to prohibit worship in the *"high places"* and restore worship the way it was set up by God. Chapter 29 shows the steps that Hezekiah took for the temple to be used for God's glory again.

He gave them the solution: clean up yourselves, clean up God's house, get rid of the filthiness, and let's start out right (v. 5). There could be no excuse that they didn't know how to get right or what route to take in order to restore their relationship with God. Likewise, you too have been given the solution. .

However, a solution has little worth if it is not followed. Your doctor can prescribe you medicine, therapy, and aid you in your recovery, but unless you follow his instructions, that solution is no more than an idea. If you know what needs to be fixed in your marriage, why wouldn't you do it? If you had the answer to your problems, what would keep you from fixing them? The answer is negligence. Maybe you don't want to put forth the effort to get right. Let me remind you of what you already know: your problem is not going to fix itself without you doing your part. Your negligence will never lead to healing your relationship with God. It cannot be neglected.

—— Today's Truth ——

Knowing the answer and failing to apply it is foolishness. Your pride will keep you from doing the hard thing, but it is only because of your negligence that you will not take action. Listen to the help God is giving you. Don't put it off any longer.

The Battle Is On

Read II Chronicles 31–33

SENNACHERIB, KING OF Assyria, came to attack the people of Judah. Not only did the king come to invade Judah, but the heart of Judah, the city of Jerusalem. Rarely does testing come in insignificant areas in life. You can count on trouble to test you in the areas that mean the most to you. This may sound bleak, and you may feel intimidated to think of these realities. Notice what the leader and the people did in this situation. Your problems may be different, but the approach we take to fight against the enemy remains the same.

They prepared for the attack. It has been said that preparation is the separation. In II Chronicles 32:2–6, we see the great lengths to which Hezekiah and the people went for the coming invasion. Proverbs 21:31 states, *"The horse is prepared against the day of battle: but safety is of the LORD."* This is why no Christian should be ashamed of our Second Amendment giving us the right to bear arms. Safety is of the Lord, but the horse should still be prepared for battle. More importantly though, we must prepare spiritually. This is keeping our hearts right daily with God, confessing our sins, seeking help, and diligently heeding His Word.

They trusted God to fight the battle. Hezekiah reminds the people, *"With him is an arm of flesh; but with us is the LORD our God to help us, and to fight our battles...."* In the end, you're really not the one fighting. Your preparedness is really just to get God on your side. You want God fighting your battles, because no matter the enemy, the victory is always guaranteed in the end. Max Lucado said, "Don't measure the size of the mountain; talk to the One who can move it."

——Today's Truth ——

The battle was never meant to be put in your hands. It may be on your doorstep, but God is the One who will fight for you when you prepare yourself and trust in Him to do what He has already promised.

Standing with Your Decision

Read II Chronicles 34–36

ONE OF THE biggest frustrations in the Christian life and as a leader over others is going forward during the invitation, making a commitment to give up sins and give God your life, only to find that in a short amount of time, you have gone back on your commitment. In II Chronicles 34, King Josiah and those that were with him made a covenant to the Lord. Verse 33 reads, *"...And all his days they departed not from following the LORD, the God of their fathers."* What was their secret? How did they stay true to their commitment to the Lord so that we can learn to do the same?

Declare it. One of the fifty-six signers of the Declaration of Independence was John Hancock, remembered for having the largest signature. He wanted the King of England to know where his allegiance was, with no mistake about it. His commitment was so clear that when King George offered amnesty to those who would cease fighting, John Hancock was one of the few left out. What commitments did the Israelites make? They decided them based on the Bible that was found.

Dedicate to it. In verse 32, Josiah told them all to "stand to it." They had to dedicate themselves to their decision publicly. They made this commitment in front of their leader and in front of their peers. I do not expect our people to share every decision with me, but if you're struggling with a decision and especially if you're making a life-changing decision, you should share that with a leader. They also did it in front of their peers, so that everyone knew where they stood.

Depart not from it. You might slip, but don't fall. Even if you fall, get back up. You made the decision. Why go backwards? One decision can change your life. What is keeping you from making a commitment to the Lord today?

—— Today's Truth ——

Making the decision is hard, but keeping the decision is more difficult. It has been done, and you can turn your life around if you are willing.

A Call to Build

Read Ezra 1–2

THE BOOK OF Ezra gives the record of the Israelites in captivity that were allowed to return to Jerusalem to rebuild the temple under the order from Cyrus. God's design in this event gives great confidence to His Word, as we read of the prophecy of Cyrus some 150 years before he was even born (Isaiah 44:28; 45:1). Zerubbabel then leads the people in this quest to rebuild their place of worship.

The call to build is a call for every life. I don't know how much God cares about building buildings. One thing I do know and have learned through experience is that God is very interested in building people. Through this building project, God was building His people spiritually, and as we do the same in the church and in our lives, we must understand that all of our labor has a purpose beyond the structure that is being built.

Sadly, not all would return to join this building project. Some stayed in their new homes, ignoring the call to build. They had been in captivity for all or most of their lives. Maybe, they had gotten comfortable and didn't feel the urge to labor for those old ways in Jerusalem. All the same could be said of Christians in our day. We have a few who want to be involved in building something, anything that will be used for the Lord, while some sit on the sidelines as life passes by. Jesus told us that we are to pray for laborers (Matthew 9:37–38). We need more workers involved in the Lord's work. There will always be more work to do than there are people to accomplish the task. As the people responded to the task, God provided the funds and He strengthened their hands to do the work. Because where God leads, He will always provide.

—— Today's Truth ——

What are you building for the Lord? There must be a work that every Christian is a part of, a work that God has given you a burden to join, and a vision for what could come from it.

Overcoming Discouragement

Read Ezra 3–5

FORMER HEAVYWEIGHT BOXER James (Quick) Tillis was a cowboy from Oklahoma who fought out of Chicago in the early 1980s. He recalled his first day in the Windy City after his arrival from Tulsa. "I got off the bus with two cardboard suitcases under my arms in downtown Chicago and stopped in front of the Sears Tower. I put my suitcases down, and I looked up at the Tower and I said to myself, 'I'm going to conquer Chicago.' When I looked down, the suitcases were gone."

In Ezra 3, the work began on a high note. The people were unified, the altar was built, and the work began. In chapter 4, adversity came, and the work was stalled for sixteen years. The people fell from their mountaintop, and they were discouraged. Discouragement often comes when things don't work out as planned…when your vision doesn't match your reality. You feel like a failure. You try to think of what went wrong. The answers may differ, but one thing is certain: you can overcome it! How did the people overcome this discouragement that stalled the work in Jerusalem for over a decade, and how can we overcome discouragement?

You need *preaching*. Haggai and Zechariah were the prophets sent to Israel. They preached God's message to the people and stirred them up to get back in the work.

You need a *purpose*. Ezra 5:2 says they *"began to build."* They remembered their purpose and realized there was work to do. You have a purpose. Serving the wrong purpose will never bring satisfaction. You need to fulfill God's purpose.

You need a *problem*. Their work was questioned, and the people stood their ground in Ezra 5. Faith becomes real when faith is tested. Success is sweet because of the determination to get through the hardships.

—— Today's Truth ——

You can overcome your season of discouragement, and God can still use you. Choose to press on and return to the work God created you to fulfill.

The Hand of the Lord

Read Ezra 6–7

IT IS BELIEVED than more than half a century separates chapters 6 and 7 of Ezra. Chapter 6 closes with the completion and celebration of the rebuilt temple. Chapter 7 begins with another group leaving Babylon to join the people in Jerusalem. It isn't until then that Ezra comes on the scene. Ezra is introduced as a *ready scribe*, but there is another description about this man that we must all seek to have said about our lives. Three times in this chapter, God makes clear that His hand was on this man.

Because of his **blood.** Ezra was a Levite, but more importantly, he was a part of the family of God. The touch of God begins with those who are close to Him. That relationship is made possible only by the sacrifice of Jesus. He is the mediator who connects us to our Heavenly Father.

Because of his **Book.** Ezra was a priest without a temple, so he became a scribe. This means that he was a student of the Law, God's Word. II Timothy 2:15 commands all of God's people, *"Study to shew thyself approved unto God…."*

Because of his **behavior.** Ezra 7:10 tells us that Ezra wasn't just an "amen in the church house" Christian. He lived what he studied and obeyed God's commands. Skipping church, neglecting to witness, and failing to pray are all ways to ensure that the hand of God will be removed from your life.

Because of his **boasting.** The chapter concludes in verses 27–28 with Ezra giving God the glory for the temple. The people labored, they fought, and they endured the testing, but they were smart enough to know that their work was useless without God's intervention.

——Today's Truth ——

You must daily desire to seek God's hand on your life. Ezra's name would never be remembered without the hand of God on him. Only with God's hand can we make a difference!

A Little Space of Grace

Read Ezra 8–9

T HERE WAS MUCH to rejoice about with God's people. For a time, they had probably forgotten that they were in captivity. They were given permission from their king to go home, and then they witnessed how God allowed them to accomplish the task at hand. It didn't play out the way they envisioned it, but the job was done. It wasn't long, however, until more bad decisions were made. They mingled themselves with the people of the land. God has commanded us to separate from the world. When Ezra received word, he was devastated. He cried out to God and the people. A powerful phrase is found in his cry where he speaks in Ezra 9:8 of the *"little space of grace"* that God had given them.

Our life can be summed up by that phrase, *"a little space of grace."* Grace is a gift. It is the gift of an opportunity to have a reason to live. The book of Ezra in its own way is a space of grace for God's people. They were enslaved in bondage, but by the grace of God their lives had new meaning again. In reality, we are living in this space of grace and have a short window to do something for the Lord.

In some ways, the people used this window to see God's hand. On the other hand, they caused themselves some major setbacks as a result of their sinful behavior. See your future from this perspective. The next time you are fearful to witness to a lost person, the next time you're afraid to do the right thing in a hard place, or the next time you doubt whether you want to get involved in the Lord's work, remember that you have just a *"little space of grace"* that has been given to you. It can be taken away as quickly as it was given.

—— Today's Truth ——

Billy Sunday made the statement, "What have you given the world it never possessed before you came?" We must likewise ask ourselves, "What have we given God with the space of grace He's given to us?"

Make Confession

Read Ezra 10

Everyone stands guilty before God. It is for this reason that asking forgiveness is a part of the model prayer as Jesus teaches the disciples how to pray in Matthew 6. Because we are not innocent, we must regularly confess our sins to the Lord. This is what Ezra 10 is about. After Ezra arrived, he found that the people had not separated themselves from the people of the land. He was heartbroken, and he knew a change was needed. Ezra tells the people in verse 11, "*Now therefore make confession unto the* LORD...."

During my freshman year of Bible college, which felt a lot like a prolonged youth group trip, I recall hearing the announcement in chapel: "Bro. Oxendine would like to see…Steven Becker in his office after chapel." That meant only one thing—I must have done something wrong. He explained money had been stolen from the dorm room of a friend. He knew I didn't do it but asked if I had ever pulled the door open with force instead of using a key. I had to confess. I got off easy with half the demerits I deserved, but I'll never forget what happened next. A friend of mine got called into the office with me, and we were both questioned. I answered first, and then he replied…and he lied. I was stunned because he knew that I knew he was lying. Still, he sat there and held to his word.

Confession is scary. Not to mention, it's pretty embarrassing, too. Eating crow, admitting you were wrong, and coming clean is a humbling experience. God gives this promise about confession in Proverbs 28:13: "*He that covereth his sins shall not prosper: but whoso confesseth and forsaketh them shall have mercy.*" Mercy is given to those who confess and forsake their sins.

——Today's Truth——

Hiding your sin is like keeping poison. It will stay with you, and it will ruin you. Get clean of the wrong, confess your sin before God and to anyone else who needs to know. It is better to confess your sin than to be caught in your sin.

Put on a Smile

Read Nehemiah 1–3

I T IS OFTEN difficult to know how to deal with troubling news. The older we get, the more difficult it can be to lose those we love. Nehemiah 1 tells of the word that came to Nehemiah about Jerusalem. The news came of the wall that was destroyed and the gates that were burned. Verse 4 shows how difficult this news was to accept. He cried out to God for four months without posting about it or complaining about it to anyone who would listen.

In chapter 2, the king asks Nehemiah about what's troubling him. For four months, he was able to wear a smile, but the burden continued to grow. He couldn't sit by anymore knowing what he knew. Notice something that Nehemiah mentions in verse 1: *"…Now I had not been beforetime sad in his presence."* In Bible college, Pastor Trieber would tell us men, "Don't bring your problems to the pulpit. Don't use that time to complain about what's going on in your life. You might have just received heartbreaking news, but your people need to see the man of God living on the winning side with a smile on his face."

Your emotions shouldn't be worn on your sleeves. This is not hypocrisy. This is maturity. Mourning isn't wrong, but living in a state of discouragement is not healthy for you, nor is it a help to others. We all face discouragement, but there will always be something that we can allow to bring sadness. Put on a smile. Some days, that will be more difficult than others, but one of the traits listed as the fruit of the Spirit in Galatians 5 is joy. Don't be the one that always has to be asked by others, "Are you okay? What's wrong?" Take your burdens to God, and cry out to Him. Your kids need to see their hero smile. The lost need to see God's children with a smile. It is a good testimony to be known as a Christian with a smile.

—— Today's Truth ——

While we can always be sad about something, there is much more about which we can be joyful. Put on a smile today. No problem is worth letting it steal your joy.

A Mind to Work

Read Nehemiah 4-6

William Ward said, "The pessimist complains about the wind; the optimist expects it to change; the realist adjusts the sails." The notion that we pray for God to do all the work and sit back and relax is not how God works. God created all people with an ability to work. Nehemiah and the people built the wall around Jerusalem in fifty-two days because "...*the people had a mind to work*" (Nehemiah 4:6). The wall wasn't going to build itself. Winston Churchill said, "Some people dream of success while others wake up and work hard at it."

Satisfaction comes from labor. Whatever kind of work it is, it takes work to breed results. My wife was asked while in labor with our fourth child, Hudson, "What do you do for a job?" She replied, "I don't work. I'm a stay-at-home mom." The nurse replied, "So, you do work. You just work for free." Work is not defined by what you do to get a paycheck.

Not all work is good work. Social media influencers (whatever that means), professional athletes, actors, and other lines of work do not produce the same fruit as working for the right things. You can give your life to things that have no value or you can work for something that has a real reward. Your job may not feel very noble, but if it's allowing you to feed and house your spouse and children, then there is value in that job. Serving in a ministry in the church takes work, even if you don't get a check from the hours that you donate. Not all good work is paid back with money, but all good work is rewarded. Proverbs 13:4 states, "*The soul of the sluggard desireth, and hath nothing: but the soul of the diligent shall be made fat.*"

—— Today's Truth ——

Give yourself to the work of which God allows you to be a part. There is work that needs to be done, and God will give you what you need to finish the task.

Stand at Attention

Read Nehemiah 7–8

W HEN OUR NATIONAL anthem is played, it shows respect when Americans stand at attention. It also shows great disrespect when some kneel, sit, or leave on their hat. Pastor Steve Nichols, the Singin' Preacher, wrote the song, "That's Our Flag," which speaks of the way his father taught him the great sacrifice that was made for America and how the flag is a symbol of those who gave their lives to give us the liberties we enjoy today.

Likewise, and with even greater reason, the Bible should be treated the same. Ezra 8 tells how Ezra stood behind a wooden pulpit and read the Word of God to the people. Verse 5 says, *"And Ezra opened the book in the sight of all the people; (for he was above all the people;) and when he opened it, all the people stood up."* Respect was given to God's Word being read.

It bothers me to see the Bible treated with disrespect. People will leave their Bible in the rain, in the hot car for several days, stack books on top of the Bible, and even toss it around. This may seem trite to those who perhaps weren't taught this in their early years, but that's just how special this Book is to us, and giving the Bible the respect it deserves is a reminder to ourselves of its importance.

None of this matters though if respect is not given to God's Word the way God intended. The people replied in verse 6, *"Amen, Amen."* This means they agreed with it. They read it, and more importantly, they taught it.

God's Word is not just some book; it is the only book worth such respect, and it is the only book that causes us to respond to its teachings. Understanding the importance of the Bible should make us hungry for it and satisfied when we make it a part of our lives.

—— Today's Truth ——

The Word of God should be paramount in the heart of every Christian. It deserves to be respected, and it ought to be received.

Sign on the Dotted Line

Read Nehemiah 9–10

"I HAVE READ and agree to the terms of this document" may be the most common little fib that we commit. Nearly every transaction has some kind of legal document attached that requires your signature. You may sign without hesitation, but if a problem arises, that signature is consent to the details laid out in that document. So, say goodbye to that full refund, because you signed away that right somewhere in the fine print.

Nehemiah 10 shows the covenant that the Israelites made with the Lord. They confessed their sins and acknowledged that what led them into captivity was solely due to their negligence. They brought out a document so that eighty-four of their leaders could put their name to this new covenant they made with God.

When you sign your name, that shows your commitment and submission to the contents of that document. The people were not making this decision half-heartedly like we so often do in the Christian life. To vocalize their decision was great, but to put it on a document was just another step they took to show the Lord that they were serious.

If the Lord gave you a document and asked you to sign to all the convictions that you hold to personally that are found in the Word of God, where would you stand? If you were going to be held by law to these decisions, what would you be willing to sign your name to? The truth is that if you're not willing to commit like this to a conviction, then it really isn't a conviction at all. Convictions don't change, and our decisions for the Lord change much too often.

——Today's Truth ——

Commit your heart to anything that God has placed in His Word. If it pleases Him, you should be ready and willing to sign your name and give your life for it.

Put on Your Mask First

Read Nehemiah 11–12

I F YOU'VE EVER flown in an airplane, you're familiar with the routine the stewardess goes through before takeoff. She will show you how to buckle your seatbelt (because apparently we still have adults that need to be shown how to buckle themselves). She will show you the life vest and how to pull the red tabs to inflate. Finally, she will show you how to use the oxygen mask—and it is always emphasized that if you have a child or someone near you that needs help with their mask in case of an emergency, you should put on your mask first, before attempting to help others put on their mask. Why? Because you're not much of a help to others if you pass out from lack of oxygen in the process. It may seem selfish, but you can't be as much of a help to others if you do not help yourself first.

It may feel selfish to admit it, but I pray for myself before I pray for others, and more than I pray for any other person. My prayer time with the Lord always begins with thanking the Lord and is followed by confessing sin, yielding myself to His will, and then seeking His help in various areas of my life. After this, I pray for my wife, my children, my family, and so on. In John 17, we see Jesus' prayer patterned the same way. Jesus prayed for Himself, for the saved, and then for the lost.

Nehemiah 12:30 shows that at the dedication of the wall, the Levites purified themselves first, then the people, and then the wall and the gates. You are not selfless just because you help everyone else while your life is in shambles. This is why you should not apologize for paying your bills while others could use that money. How can you help others if you're needing help as well? Make sure that you have your heart right and your life in order if you want to be a help to others. We must help others, but you can be a greater help if your life is in order first.

—— Today's Truth ——

Helping yourself first is not selfishness. Selfishness is when you never help others. Help yourself, and then find somebody else to help today.

Separate Yourself

Read Nehemiah 13

AT THE END of this book, we read about the response of the people after the work had been accomplished. God doesn't want your life only while you're "on the job"; He wants your life all day, every day.

The Israelites made a wise decision to separate themselves from the Ammonites and the Moabites. When the Word of God was brought out and read, Nehemiah 13:4 says, *"Now it came to pass, when they had heard the law, that they separated from Israel all the mixed multitude."* This is the proper response of every Christian after getting into the Bible and getting closer to the Lord.

For those that will question if we are to draw the line, II Corinthians 6:17 clearly states, *"Wherefore come out from among them, and be ye separate, saith the Lord, and touch not the unclean thing; and I will receive you."* The Israelites were commanded to separate from these people, because that command was given back in Deuteronomy 23:3–4 concerning these two groups. They could have convinced themselves, "This command was given a long time ago and didn't apply in my day," "Things are different now," "We don't need to go overboard," or have tried to spiritualize some reason to not separate themselves. Instead, they obeyed.

The reason we have to talk differently, be careful about the appearance of the places we go, be concerned with our appearance, and not get involved in things that could mix our lifestyle with the world is because of this principle. Refusing to separate from the world is choosing to mix yourself with the world. We are to influence the world, not allow the world to influence our lives.

——Today's Truth——

Removing yourself from others may feel extreme, but there was an extreme change that took place when you got saved. You are different now!

Fake News

Read Esther 1–3

THE BOOK OF Esther focuses on the false description of the Jews that Haman gave the king in order for him to agree to the wicked decree that the Jewish people be executed. Haman (described in Esther 3:10 as the "Jews' enemy") fed this false narrative to the king, and it endangered the lives of every Jewish person under his rule.

It is unfortunate, to say the least, to think that there are people who believe that Christians are the enemy and that somehow we are the ones hurting our society and hindering our nation from prospering. He made this clear to Israel, and this is the case with every nation and people in the world. This can cause you to fear what may come as a result of this kind of propaganda, or you can simply understand that there is no telling what wickedness will take place and remember that God is still on the throne.

Mud is slung from political parties every day. We try to point out who is to blame for problems that arise. The answer to that question is simple: sin is the problem, and Jesus is the answer. I don't blame him, but I also don't believe that we have to worry when people target Christianity as the problem. In the end, God took care of His people, and although we will face some unrest in this life, God will take care of His children in the end. Don't lose hope because some people might look to you as the problem. The goal isn't to change their mind about you, but to change their mind to lead them to Jesus Christ. We can so easily get caught up in politics and social issues that we forget that God is working in the background.

—— Today's Truth ——

You can be confident that God will always protect and reward those who follow Him. The world may differ, and this may even cause situations that cause fear. God is still in control, and He is still on the throne!

Courage

Read Esther 4–7

IT HAS BEEN said, "There is a fine line between courage and foolishness. Too bad it's not a fence." Your stand doesn't have to make sense to anyone else if it pleases God. If your conviction and your courage to stand behind it pleases the Lord, then that's all the sense you need. Esther showed great courage when she went to ask the king for a time to speak to him and Haman about the wicked decree that was made against her people. However, simply approaching the king unannounced could have cost her life, regardless of what she had to say. Although the king had always had a soft spot for Esther, she had no way of knowing how he felt on this day.

President Theodore Roosevelt spoke powerfully on courage in a speech in Paris, France, in 1910: "It is not the critic who counts; not the man who points out how the strong man stumbles, or where the doer of deeds could have done them better. The credit belongs to the man who is actually in the arena, whose face is marred by dust and sweat and blood; who strives valiantly; who errs, who comes short again and again, because there is no effort without error and shortcoming; but who does actually strive to do the deeds; who knows great enthusiasms, the great devotions; who spends himself in a worthy cause; who at the best knows in the end the triumph of high achievement, and who at the worst, if he fails, at least fails while daring greatly, so that his place shall never be with those cold and timid souls who neither know victory nor defeat."

Living for God requires courage. It's not always easy to do the right thing. Sometimes, we are tempted to give in and lay down the sword for the sake of peace and tolerance, but following through on God's will demand that you have courage.

—— Today's Truth ——

When fear tempts you to give in, show courage and follow through with God's leading.

Problem Solved

Read Esther 8–10

W HILE WE MAY look for God to get rid of our problems, the answer is usually not for the problem to vanish, but to be dealt with. This is how God saved the Jewish people in the book of Esther. After Esther confronted Haman before the king, the king heeded Esther's request, had Haman punished in the place of his wicked plans to execute Mordecai, and gave a solution. The solution was not to erase the decree, because that was not possible. The answer was to act on top of the decree. A new decree was made for the salvation of God's people.

NBC News reported the following story: "On a Saturday in September, 2013, one of the most deadly terrorist attacks in history took place in an upscale mall in Nairobi, Kenya. Four gunmen, part of the Al-Qaeda affiliate al Shabab, took the lives of 67 people, with over 200 injured." It was by all accounts a horrible tragedy.

But one story of the shooting ended up receiving media attention. It was the story of a young mother named Sneha Kothair-Mashru. Sneha was at the mall having coffee with a friend when the gunfire began. Having dropped to the floor, she heard a cell phone going off near her. Not wanting the gunmen to come closer, she reached under the person next to her to silence the phone. At this point she realized the man next to her was bleeding heavily. "When I put my hand under him, that's when I realized that this guy had been shot because he was bleeding," she told *NBC News*. "He was bleeding heavily. There was a lot of blood there." At this point, the woman made a difficult, life-changing decision. She decided to smear the blood of the man on her own body, in hopes that the terrorists would assume she was dead, and they would "pass over" her body. Her grisly camouflage probably saved this woman's life. "I'd love to know who he was because I think his blood protected me, saved my life," she said.

—— Today's Truth ——

Your problem may not disappear, but Jesus is ready and willing to help you. Turn to Jesus. He has the solution!

Everything Happens for a Reason

Read Job 1–4

ONE OLD STORY recounts a man reciting a litany of woes to his friend—he has lost his job, his house, his money, his fiancée—and his friend keeps saying, "It could have been worse." Finally, the man screams, "How could it be worse?" and his friend mutters, "It could have happened to me." Bad days and bad seasons are a part of life with which we are all too familiar. Some have asked the question, "Why do bad things happen to good people?" It is true that bad things happen to good people. Job, one of the prime examples of someone having a bad day, faced incredible hardship when he lost nearly everything he had, including his children, in just one day.

We can look at many reasons why God may have allowed this to happen to Job specifically, but the problem is that the reason God allowed Job to be afflicted may be different from the reason He has allowed affliction to plague your life. How Job responded is the example that we must note. Job 1:22 states, *"In all this Job sinned not, nor charged God foolishly."* Job didn't know the reason, but he didn't allow his lack of understanding to cloud his faith and confidence in the Lord.

Fast forward to the end of the book of Job, and you will find that God rewarded Job; but He left something out of the reward that I'm sure Job sought. God never told Job the reason why He allowed what He did. He rewarded Job for not turning away from God, even if his wife tempted him to do just that. Job knew God had a reason, even if he didn't know what that reason was. God allows us to face these uncertain times for many practical reasons: our relationship with the Lord grows in valleys much more than on mountaintops, our faith is tested and proven to see if we are genuine, we are reminded that God is who He says He is. Whatever happens, God has a reason.

—— Today's Truth ——

God does nothing by mistake. If you are flourishing or just treading water, God has a reason for it. You may not understand it, but there is one.

Speaking Out of Turn

Read Job 5–8

IT IS OUR natural inclination to want to help someone we care about when we see that they are hurting. I have sat in many meetings, been on many calls, and participated in many conversations where people that I care about share great heartache that they have experienced. The vast majority of the time, I am speechless. To be completely honest, I often spin my wheels in my mind thinking of Scripture, words or comfort, or anything that could be a help to this person. I do believe the Lord gives us the verses and words to say when needed. The problem is that too often we speak the first thing that comes to mind as opposed to asking the Lord for the right words to speak.

Job's friends come to counsel him. They couldn't understand why God was punishing Job, and they appear to have not held back on their opinion of the matter. In Job 8, Bildad rebukes Job, insinuating that if Job had been right with God, then this would not have happened? After all, bad things never happen to good people, right? While there are some who preach this prosperity gospel, implying that you'll never face a financial burden or health infirmity if you surrender your life to God, that is not proven from God's Word.

When you see others around you who are hurting, it isn't always what you say that gives comfort. I believe most are sincere in wanting to help, even when they say the wrong thing, but don't spit out something in your own wisdom without asking God how to be a help. It's better to say too little than to say too much in these circumstances. Your presence, your listening, and your actions can be a greater help to people than you may realize.

—— Today's Truth ——

Seek God's wisdom in comforting others around you. Do not speak what you do not know. You can hurt instead of help if you're not careful.

Blessings for the Broken

Read Job 9–12

EVEN WHEN EVERYTHING seems to be going wrong, there is still more to be thankful for than to complain about. Your suffering doesn't have to steal your joy. It brings a heaviness to life, and if you're not careful, your suffering will overtake your life. Joy isn't going to jump at you every day. You need to find ways to have joy and to be thankful. Some days may require a more diligent search to find joy, but it is always there. Job found ways to praise God in his darkest hour. Job 10:12 reads, *"Thou hast granted me life and favour, and thy visitation hath preserved my spirit."* When you are in a time where you feel broken, praise God for these ways that He has blessed your life.

The blessing of *life.* I made it a habit in Bible college to thank God first when I go to prayer. I have a list that I have memorized in my prayer journal that are areas I can thank God for every day. Before I thank Him for my wife, my salvation, or my children, the first thing I thank God for is my life. I am created by God, and any good thing I can do is possible because He loved me enough to give me life.

The blessing of *favor.* God doesn't just give life, but He also gives help to us throughout our lives. Favor speaks of the goodness that God has given you. Spurgeon rightly stated, "I cannot run over the list of God's favors to his people, for it is too long." Just because you are hurting now doesn't erase the goodness that God has granted in your life. We take it for granted, but that's our mistake.

The blessing of *visitation.* Life gives us a chance, favor gives us help in life, but visitation is the icing on the cake. God loves you so much that He not only does good for you, but He also does it with you. Many will write a check or pay a bill without giving up their time, but not God. God longs and chooses to dwell with His people.

—— Today's Truth ——

See His goodness and thank the Lord today for the blessings that He has granted to you. The first thing and the majority of what should come from our lips to God is our praise, not our worry.

Though He Slay Me

Read Job 13–16

JOB RIGHTLY DESCRIBES our lives in Job 14:1 when he says, *"Man that is born of a woman is of few days, and full of trouble."* Trouble is a part of life, and sometimes it feels like it's most of our life. Going through the fire will reveal the contents of your faith. It will reveal if you are a Pharisaical Christian who lives for God on the outside but has no real faith on the inside. Job's faith was put to the fire, and the revealing of his faith is found in Job 13:15, which says, *"Though he slay me, yet will I trust in him...."*

We tend to do good to others who do good to us in return. "You scratch my back, and I'll scratch yours" is the secret motto of too many of us if we're honest. Job committed, "God, even if You were to kill me, I'd still trust in You." Even if God allows you to have a life-threatening illness, you can still trust in Him. Even if your mate walks out on you, you can still trust in Him. Don't tell God that you'll trust Him even if you don't have the best, but tell Him you'll continue to trust His mighty hand even if He brings the worst of troubles in your life.

Trust Him when dark doubts assail thee,
Trust Him when thy strength is small,
Trust Him when to simply trust Him
Seems the hardest thing of all.
Trust Him, He is ever faithful,
Trust Him, for His will is best,
Trust Him, for the heart of Jesus
Is the only place of rest.
– Unknown

——Today's Truth——

Think of the worst possible situation that you could be in, and make the decision that if your worst nightmare came to life, you are still going to trust the Lord.

JUNE 19

How Long?

Read Job 17–20

ROAD TRIPS HARDLY feel complete without the occasional and infamous question, "How much longer?" Job laments in Job 19:2, *"How long will ye vex my soul and break me in pieces with words."* Back and forth Job and his friends went with their opinion on the matter. In Job 16:2, he refers to them: *"...miserable comforters are ye all."* He had enough, and could only wish for the moment when his friends would go away.

What do you do when you long for the negative people around you to go away? What do you do when others scoff at your situation? What do you do when you want to quit because you can't handle the discouragement? Persevere! Michael Jordan is widely considered the greatest basketball player to ever play in the NBA. He stated, "I've missed more than 9,000 shots in my career. I've lost almost 300 games. Twenty-six times I've been trusted to take the game-winning shot and missed. I've failed over and over again in my life. And that is why I succeed." Because he persevered through discouragement and failure, he succeeded in the highest ways in his craft. Just imagine what God can do with a man who will persevere for something bigger than a ball game.

Nobody reaches the end without having to push through quitting times. Enduring through the moments where you are tempted to quit prove to God your commitment to Him. Job was discouraged, but Job was not about to quit. He persevered through the misery of his friends. He made it through another day, and another day, and another day until the Lord brought an end to his storm. No one but God knows how much longer your storm will last, but determine today to just make it another day, and tomorrow do the same.

—— Today's Truth ——

Time seems to move slower in times that are hard. Persevere and continue on another day until you have finished your race for His glory.

The Almighty Troubleth Me

Read Job 21–24

FOLLOWING THE JOURNEY of Job in searching to make sense of his condition is a familiar feeling for most Christians. Job states in chapter 23 and verse 3, *"Oh that I knew where I might find him!"* In verse 9, he continues his search, *"On the left hand, where he doth work, but I cannot behold him: he hideth himself on the right hand, that I cannot see him."* Then in verse 10, he makes this great conclusion, *"But he knoweth the way that I take...."* Job might not have understood the purpose, but he knew that God knew the purpose. Finally, in verse 16, Job states, *"...the Almighty troubleth me."* Job recognized that this trial was a part of God's purpose and that it was allowed by the Almighty.

God is either trying to do something in you or He's trying to do something through you. Jesus sent the disciples into the sea so that they would learn to have a faith greater than their fear. He wanted them to see that He was greater than any storm that they would face. Jesus needed the storm to increase their faith so that He could do something through them.

God does what He does for many reason, and Job recognizes what this trouble has done to him. Job says in verse 16, *"For God maketh my heart soft...."* I believe one of the keys to a godly Christian life is to maintain a soft and tender heart toward the Lord. Something is wrong with a person who hasn't shed a tear in prayer lately or been moved by the Spirit of God through His Word or in His church. Hebrews 3:13 tells how sin can harden our heart, but our trouble can draw us to Jesus. Storms both stir and soften the heart. Don't become bitter and hard because of your trouble. A broken, soft, and tender heart is one that God can use and mold exactly the way that is needed.

—— Today's Truth ——

While a hardened heart will push God away, a soft and tender heart will allow God to mold you. Keep your heart soft toward the Lord today.

JUNE 21

The Cry of the Hypocrite

Read Job 25–29

IT WAS A normal day in Bible college, and I was at my security site getting all situated for the rest of the day at work after a day of classes. I received a call from Alisha (my fiancée at the time, just two months before our wedding). I answered the phone, but instead of putting it up to my ear, I swiped to answer and said loudly, "Hey, could you hold on a minute?" I was getting my headphones untangled so I could talk more easily while sitting at my post for the night. Untangling headphones can be a frustrating, time-consuming, and tedious task. Finally, after a minute or so, I put the headphones in my ear and said, "Hey, how are you?" She was crying, her voice was shaking, and she began to explain how she had been involved in a bad car accident. While at a dead stop in traffic, she was hit from behind very hard, followed by several more cars, totaling five collisions with my soon-to-be bride in the center. I felt so bad for her, but I felt worse that I hadn't been there right away when she called.

Job 27:8–9 says, *"For what is the hope of the hypocrite…Will God hear his cry when trouble cometh upon him?"* A hypocrite is not a true follower at heart, but only for show. Job emphasizes that this way of living has a cost. If you're not real in your relationship with God, He won't be your life raft just because you're in trouble. God is ready to forgive and move on, but He is not the "priest" to whom you can confess your sins, only to go out and continue in that sin, repeating this cycle of confessing your sin and continuing in your sin. Living this way should cause you to fear that God will not hear you if you are not close to Him. Following God's Word results in abiding in His presence. He is there when you need Him because you are already close to Him.

—— Today's Truth ——

It is certain that you will need to cry out to God for help. Will you be close to Him when you need Him most or are you living at the distance?

180 | STEVEN BECKER

What Do Others Think of Me?

Read Job 30–33

WHY DO PEOPLE get dressed up for the day, fix their hair, shower, shave, clean up, and put on their best? Some may say that the way they dress helps them feel better about themselves or even helps them work better. These are valid points, but the truth is that the main reason, and maybe the biggest reason of all, is because of the opinion of others. We join in trends because others think it's cool. Far too much of what we do, how we act, and how we feel is a result of our insecurity. You should be concerned with your testimony before others, but that is far different from being affected by others' opinion.

Job 30 reveals what others thought about Job. Everybody will have an opinion about you, especially when you are going through something difficult. People will make conjectures about your circumstances, and if you let it, it can consume you. It can cause you to be insecure about yourself, and instead of working on your relationship with God, you become consumed with every comment of every person, and you will go mad trying to win everybody over.

Should you care what others think of you? Yes. Should you allow the opinion of others to consume you? No. Christians should have a good testimony before the world. Your example speaks louder than anything you say, and although others may not agree with what I do, I want them to respect that I do what I say I believe in. I'm concerned with whether or not I am a good representation of Jesus Christ. I am not concerned with people agreeing on my stand. When we would take field trips in school, we were always told that we represent ourselves, our family, our school/church, and most importantly, Jesus.

—— Today's Truth ——

Are you too concerned with the opinion of others? Do you change what you do so people will like you? Stand for Jesus, keep a godly testimony before others, and consume yourself with God's opinion above all others.

Speaking on God's Behalf

Read Job 34–37

A<small>S A PASTOR</small>, my job when I stand behind the pulpit is very simple when you think about it. My duty is to be a vessel for the Lord's voice to speak to His people. In Job 36, Elihu claims to speak on God's behalf. John the Baptist referred to himself in John 1:23, "*...I am the voice of one crying in the wilderness....*" John wasn't claiming to be God, but to speak God's truths to the people.

The only way that any of us can be used to speak on God's behalf is when we speak in God's Spirit and by God's Word. We have many "Christian" leaders preaching, writing books, and counseling people on their lives today, claiming to be speaking on God's behalf, but their message contradicts God's Word. That's not speaking for God. That's speaking your interpretation or opinion.

Before every message I preach, I pray for God's Spirit to give me the words He wants me to say. Our people don't need a message from Steven Becker. They need a message from God! I can't tell you how many times God has used a thought, a story, or something I said while preaching on a Bible truth that opened somebody's eyes and heart to the Lord. That's not me, that's God!

Be cautious with who you listen to just because they claim they are "speaking on God's behalf." Just because somebody talks about Jesus doesn't mean that God is speaking through them. You have a Bible to study so that you will know the difference between a real or a false witness. Likewise, you have the Spirit of God to help you determine what you should or should not give your ear to. There's only one voice that matters. God can use people to speak to you by His Spirit, but if it's not of Him, then it's not really worth listening to.

—— Today's Truth ——

God is always speaking to us. Many times, He speaks through people, but it will always be by His Spirit and by His Word.

God Ends the Debate

Read Job 38–40

JOB HAD SAID his peace. Job's friends had expressed their opinions. Now, Job 38:1 says, *"Then the LORD answered Job...."* God didn't answer Job's friends. God answered Job. God doesn't waste time with every critic. I don't know if these men were saved or not, but I believe there is a great wisdom to be learned in how God doesn't even acknowledge the previous several chapters of speculation among Job's friends.

Job questioned the Lord. He asked Him questions for several chapters, trying to understand. God is here to answer, but demands that Job must answer His questions first. God begins in Job 38:4, *"Where wast thou when I laid the foundations of the earth? declare, if thou hast understanding."* You can see very quickly where this is going. God reminds Job that He is the Creator of the universe that He spoke into existence, that He is the One who makes the sun rise every day, that He is the One who knows the mysteries of the sea, that He is the One who causes the wind to blow, the rain to fall, and the grass to grow. He asks Job to explain where he was when God created all of this. He asks Job if he understands the details of the world in which he lives. Clearly, this reminder is a blunt message. Job and God are not on the same level, because mankind and God are not on the same level. This wasn't just a reminder of God's majesty and power, but also of His love and care toward all of His people and His creation.

In Job 40, Job's tone seems to change after God spoke to him. His circumstances didn't change, but his view of God changed. He remembered how wonderful and powerful his God is, and it settled Job. He thought that God had forsaken Him, but then he felt God's presence and knew that God was with Him and nothing was done without His knowledge. No matter what debate or accusation was made, God settled it in Job's heart, and that's all that really mattered.

—— Today's Truth ——

Let God's Word settle your heart and your questions. Don't let yourself be unsettled because of others or even yourself. God will answer!

The Best Is Yet to Come

Read Job 41–42

THE BEGINNING OF Job's story was rough. Sometimes, the beginning of the Christian life is hard. You have to make hard choices, cut ties with people you had relationships with, and turn the trajectory of your life because you're God's child now.

After this, it seemed to only get harder. Life is sometimes cruel, unfair, unjust, and difficult to understand. I'm sure Job had some doubts along the way. Was God going to do what Job believed He would do? I don't believe there is a single Christian who hasn't asked questions like this in times of trouble.

Job's faith was tested, and although Job was not sinless, Job remained faithful and got his heart right with the Lord and even with his friends. Job 42:12 concludes this story, *"So the LORD blessed the latter end of Job more than his beginning...."* God did it! Job saw firsthand that the Lord takes care of His children who remain committed to Him and return to Him even when they stray. The start was tough, but Job learned how God works. Job learned that with God, the best is yet to come!

No person has the faintest idea what God has prepared for those that stay faithful to the end. We talk about Heaven, but we really have no idea how wonderful that place is. We sing about God's goodness, but our imagination can't do it the justice that He deserves. If you're in a time like Job, possibly weighing your decisions on whether or not you're going to continue on for the Lord, remember this—the best is yet to come! You may not see the fireworks in the beginning, because that's not how God works. God blesses in that "latter end." He wants you to prove your love and devotion for him, and every time, He will come through! Hold on another day, because the best is yet to come!

—— Today's Truth ——

He always keeps His Word. He always rewards those who remain faithful to Him. He always gives more and more the longer you serve Him!

The Daily Practice of Dealing with Sin

Read Psalms 1–9

EVERY GOOD THING begins with God. The Psalms can be divided up into several sections. The first group of Psalms are considered to be the "Genesis Psalms." This book is a collection of prayers and songs dedicated to the Lord by the Jews. Psalms is a very emotional book, and it teaches us to bring every emotion before the Lord. Psalm 6 is considered the first of the "Penitential Psalms." Scattered throughout Psalms, they reveal the heart-cry of man. The Psalmist is beaten down by sin and turns to God for repentance. All men deal with sin, and all men can overcome sin by turning to the Lord.

We know that the longer we live, the more we sin, the more baggage we carry, and the more regret we have. Picture David at the end, looking back on his life, expressing his heart to be right with God and clean from sin. We never should get to the place, in the beginning of life or the end, where we think we don't need to cry out to God and get right with Him. God doesn't deal lightly with sin. God convicts us of our sins, but He also can deliver and cleanse us of our sins.

David's sin caused an uneasiness in his heart and in his body. In verse 6, he says, *"I am weary with my groaning; all the night make I my bed to swim; I water my couch with my tears."* Sin makes life uncomfortable, and the only way to get peace and comfort is to bring your sin before the Lord every day, morning or night, asking Him to search you so that you can get right with Him. This is not just to be done at the end of a life, but every day of your life. Confessing your sin should be a daily discipline in your walk with the Lord. Verse 9 gives assurance, *"…the LORD will receive my prayer."* God will hear you. God will answer you, and God will forgive you and bring you close in your fellowship with Him.

—— Today's Truth ——

Make confession a daily practice between you and the Lord.

Atheism 101

Read Psalms 10–17

ROMANS 1:20 MAKES IT clear that God's creation alone causes us to be "without excuse" regarding His existence. The world screams at us of a grand Designer who so perfectly and beautifully put life together in this universe of His. Psalm 14 fittingly refers to the one who reject God's existence as a foolish man. Verse 1 says, *"The fool hath said in his heart, There is no God."* We were made to believe in something.

Atheism is the denial of the God of the Bible, whether that lifts up man as a form of a god or another false man-made god. The atheist denies the thing inside of himself that tells him there is a God. This person is a fool. It is a very stubborn form of pride that causes someone to adhere to this belief. They are gods in their own minds.

Moreover, we must note that there are two types of atheists—professing and practicing. Professing atheists openly declare their denial of God, while practicing atheists prove by their lifestyle that they do not believe in God. This fool was not professing atheism with his mouth, but in his heart. The Psalm concludes in verse 7, *"Oh that the salvation of Israel were come out of Zion! when the LORD bringeth back the captivity of his people, Jacob shall rejoice, and Israel shall be glad."* It may be frustrating and discouraging to hear the mocking and denial of God all around you, but salvation is near. It is believed that this Psalm was written during the Babylonian captivity. God's people were living in a God-denying world. They needed to remind themselves of the hope that they would one day be saved. Jesus will come again and remove all His children from the captivity of a sin-cursed world.

—— Today's Truth ——

God is real, regardless of the opinion of man. We must seek to draw all men to Him without becoming discouraged by those who deny Him.

The Heavens Speak

Read Psalms 18–22

GOD IS THE grand Designer of this magnificent universe in which we live and everything beyond our reach that is completely unknown to us. Psalm 19:1 declares, *"The heavens declare the glory of God...."* Quite powerfully, God's creation sends a message to the people living in it.

The message that nature and all matter around us speaks is a language that all people can see and understand. Creation is so grand and beautiful that it not only is not constrained to a particular language, but it is beyond what mere words can describe. Has anyone ever tried to explain some place to you and in frustration said, "You just had to be there"? God's creation speaks to all people because the gospel is for all to understand God's goodness. II Timothy 2:3–4 says, *"For this is good and acceptable in the sight of God our Saviour; Who will have all men to be saved, and to come unto the knowledge of the truth."* All means all. Calvinists may claim some are just destined to hell and nothing can change that, but Jesus said otherwise. Psalm 19:3 continues, *"There is no speech nor language, where their voice is not heard."*

This message that the heavens declare is God's glory. The bigger the construction, the bigger the praise. My wife had her appendix removed and, while she was in surgery, I googled the purpose of the appendix. Google, man's direct line to answer all of life's questions, claimed that this organ's purpose is still unknown—and that's just the human body. Our God is so great and powerful, and we are reminded all around us every day of His majesty.

—— Today's Truth ——

God's handiwork is all around you every day, declaring a message for all the world to see and to learn of Him. We must take notice and not pass by the glory of God surrounding our world and universe.

A Godly Home

Read Psalms 23–30

DAVID DESIRED TO build a house for the Lord, but God did not allow David to be the one to build the temple. Instead, God told David that He would build him a house. When his home was finished, David dedicated his home to the Lord and this is the context of Psalm 30.

Every Christian should have a home that is dedicated to the Lord. Our nation and our churches will never exceed the spirituality of our homes. To see God more in our world and our church, we must begin with the home.

One of the ways David dedicated his home to God was by remembering his past and what God had done in his life. Get alone regularly and ponder God's goodness on your life. Think of the big picture. Remember how fearful you once were and look now at how God has taken care of so many of those fears. David wasn't in a perfect place, but he was in a good place; and God deserves the credit.   In verses 8–10, David prays as a part of his dedication. When was the last time you prayed with your spouse or children? I love hearing our children learn to pray, but I know that I must pray for my family and with my family. Make it a daily habit, aside from praying over a meal, to pray together and for one another.

Lastly, David ends by praising the Lord. Verses 11 and 12 say, "Thou hast turned for me my mourning into dancing: thou hast put off my sackcloth, and girded me with gladness; To the end that my glory may sing praise to thee, and not be silent. O Lord my God, I will give thanks unto thee for ever." Praise Him in your home!

—— Today's Truth ——

Any home can be a godly home if there are godly people in it. Determine to have a godly home and dedicate it for God's glory.

The Rest of the Story

Read Psalm 31–35

PSALM 51 IS THE famous "get right with God" Psalm. It is David's repentance after committing adultery and having that woman's husband killed. Psalm 32 fits in chronologically after Psalm 51. It is the rest of the story. So many may think that, because they have failed, life is over and they cannot continue. You may be so discouraged because you fell so hard that you think there is no way to recover. Remember, you will fail, but you are not a failure. Failure is not a person; it is an event. You are not a failure because you failed. David's life wasn't over because he sinned.

The very first word of this Psalm is "blessed." The beauty of obtaining God's forgiveness is having His hand on your life. You are blessed because God has blessed you. David didn't say he was blessed because he was perfect, but because he was forgiven. Stop measuring yourself against celebrities and others you may envy.

Why is it so hard for people to get right? Verses 3 and 4 show the battle in David's heart when he kept his sin to himself. His sin weighed on him, just like sin weighs on you when you carry it without getting right. How did David rid himself of this pain? He acknowledged his sin. He owned up to his failure. This is hard for us to do. We don't like to admit that we were wrong. We'd rather give excuses or maybe try to downplay the severity of the situation. Don't play games with God. Tell it to God the way it is and come clean.

David confessed, and God forgave. In verse 7, David calls God his *"hiding place."* He realized that his sin was not more important than being close to God. When you are far from Him, He won't protect you or bless you the way He wants. Don't miss out on your hiding place in Him. There can be more to your story too.

—— Today's Truth ——

David's story continued because he confessed his sin and was forgiven. Your life may continue, but it won't be much if you don't get right. Come clean with God!

JULY 1

Good News in a Bad Day

Read Psalms 36–39

WOULD ANYONE AGREE that 24/7 news is really a good thing? The sad part about the news is that it is overwhelmingly negative. Murders, scandals, and crises drive ratings, so bad news, bad news, and more bad news they give. Setting your focus on the good news does not mean that the bad news goes away. In Psalm 36:1–4, David describes the wickedness of his day. The reality of sin and its destruction was all around him, but that isn't the subject of this Psalm; and that doesn't have to be the center of your life either. So many are inundated with bad news, and it begins to show in their attitude and outlook on life.

In verse 5, David directs his focus on the mercy of God and other attributes of the Lord. What a man thinks in his quiet moments says a lot about who he is. David's flesh probably was discouraged by seeing the wickedness of the world, but his spirit set his heart and his eyes on the things of God. God's goodness is always worthy of praise, so you will never fail to list the wonderful attributes of God. That's what David does in verses 5–9.

Finally, the Psalm ends with a prayer. David prays for the blessing of God to continue on those who are righteous. He prays for his own heart to be right and for God's protection on his life. Then, he prays for the defeat of the wicked. Prayer has a way of removing the dross and giving you joy in every day. Talk to your phone and watch your TV, and you'll be filled with negativity and darkness. Talk to the Father and you will be reminded of the good news of who He is and what He is for His children who follow Him.

—— Today's Truth ——

Learn to look at the good news even though bad news may be all around you. Joy is a choice, and it is often a result of what we set our focus on. Look to God today and bring yourself into the goodness of His presence.

Characteristics of Godly Music

Read Psalms 40–45

W HETHER YOU SING like an angel or like a hyena, God made you to love music. God created music for a purpose. The primary purpose is to worship Him, but another benefit is what music does in your heart. Look at Psalm 40:3 and see the characteristics given about their song.

Godly music is derived from God. Psalm 40:3 begins, *"And **he** hath put...."* Good music comes from God, and it is for God as well. But not all music comes from God and not all music is pleasing to God.

Godly music is distinct from the world's music. Verse 3 continues, *"a new song."* The lyrics should be different, the purpose should be different, and the sound should be different. Putting lyrics about Jesus in a song that sounds like a pop or country song is not distinct from the world.

Godly music is directed toward God. The text goes on, *"even praise unto our God."* Most people who have difficulty accepting that CCM is wrong use the excuse, "It speaks to me, so God must be okay with it." Remember, we are benefited by music, but the primary purpose is not to make us feel good, but to give God the glory. If music is for Him, we should first be concerned with what pleases Him.

Godly music is displayed in public view. Verse 3 says, *"many shall see it."* Our song is a testimony of the joy in our heart and praise to the Lord. While you should not be consumed with the opinion of others, you should be aware of what they see in your life.

Godly music is designed to bring others to Christ. The verse ends, *"many shall see it, and fear, and shall trust in the LORD."* This could apply both to the saved and the lost. Music has great power. It can be used either to help or hurt others in their walk, but music is not only about you. Godly music edifies others in their spiritual walk.

—— Today's Truth ——

Music is a tool, and God's Word helps us to determine the traits of the music that brings glory to God so that we can ensure that He is pleased.

Do You Know God?

Read Psalms 46–51

KNOWING ABOUT GOD is not the same as knowing God. To know my wife, I need to know her likes and dislikes, her habits, and things about her. However, I can know a lot about her without knowing her personally.

Psalm 43:10 says, *"Be still, and know that I am God...."* Have you ever pondered the fact that God wants to have a relationship with you? How wonderful it is to think that the magnificent God of the universe wants you to know Him.

Life can be hectic. The only way to truly know God personally is found in this verse. God tells us that we must "be still." That means turning off the TV, putting down your phone, and quieting the noise around you. This is why I can't have my daily devotions on a device. It's too distracting. It's hard enough getting work done on a computer with notifications, messages, and emails popping up every minute. How do you expect to build a strong and lasting relationship with God if you never give Him time that is 100% focused on Him? It's like talking to someone while they're texting. I've been guilty of this and have been convicted at how rude it is to the person trying to talk to me, because I know how I feel when someone does that to me.

James 4:8 gives us this promise: *"Draw nigh to God, and he will draw nigh to you."* If you give yourself to truly knowing God, you can be sure that the Lord will draw Himself close to you. He wants to know you, but you have to put forth the effort.

—— Today's Truth ——

Getting to know God is not difficult, but it does take effort. It is giving yourself to Him fully and quieting what distracts your attention from Him.

Prepared for the Emergency

Read Psalms 52–59

EMERGENCIES HAPPEN, and they are completely unpredictable. I'm sure you could trade stories with others about car accidents, broken bones, identity theft, and other unpleasant experiences you've endured. It's impossible to truly plan for every emergency. You can be paranoid to the place where you never leave your home, never see other people, stay "off the grid," and take every extreme precaution. However, this will not be enough. Emergencies will happen, but you can prepare yourself in other ways.

Psalm 56 was written in the time that David was taken by the Philistines. In this passage, we learn how the man of God dealt with an unexpected emergency. In verse 3, he states, *"What time I am afraid, I will trust in thee."* He may have not known what the future held for him, but he resolved to continue to trust the Lord, no matter the circumstances. When you find yourself wondering, "How did this happen?" or "What do I do," determine that no matter what, you're going to trust the Lord to see you through. Your emergency doesn't have to be the end. It may be a bump in the road, and some may take you on a long detour, but God is still with you.

Eighteen times in thirteen verses, David mentions the Lord. He didn't forget God in his emergency; he turned to God in his emergency. Not only did he remember the Lord, but he also praised Him. Verse 4 reads, *"In God I will praise his word, in God I have put my trust; I will not fear what flesh can do unto me."* He didn't complain or worry, but praised the Lord, and as a result, his fear was conquered.

—— Today's Truth ——

When emergencies come and you don't know what to do, determine that you will turn to the Lord. He will see you through.

My Rock

Read Psalms 60–66

I**N 1799, C**ONRAD **R**EED was fishing in Little Meadow Creek and found a seventeen-pound rock that caught his attention. Unaware of its value or even what it was made of, that "rock" served as a doorstop at his home in North Carolina for three years. Eventually, his father took it to a jeweler to find that this "rock" was in fact a golden nugget worth $3,600 and one of the biggest nuggets found east of the Rockies. Much like Conrad Reed, many Christians miss the value of the true Rock in their lives, Jesus Christ.

A rock is **secure**. Psalm 62:2 says, *"He only is my rock and my salvation; he is my defence…."* Rocks can give security. The defense and protection they can give can be a great help to someone. God is your defense against every adversity you will face in life. He doesn't guarantee that you will not get attacked, but He does guarantee that you will be delivered.

A rock is **steady**. Psalm 62:2 and 6 says, *"He only is my rock…I shall not be greatly moved."* The bigger the rock, the less likely it is to move. Bigger rocks such as boulders, cliffs, and even mountains, have stayed fixed on certain locations for centuries. God doesn't change. He doesn't change direction. You can always find Him in the same place. Secure yourself to the Lord as closely and as much as you can, and you will find a steadiness in your life.

Finally, a rock is **strong**. Psalm 62:7 refers to *"the rock of my strength."* The Lord's strength is unmatched. We see weightlifting competitions, boxing matches, and MMA fights to determine who is the strongest or most skilled in their physical capabilities. Satan and his minions have tested God over and over but, in the end, God will display His strength for all the world to see.

—— Today's Truth ——

Get yourself close and fixed to the Rock, the Lord Jesus. He is your security in times of trouble, your steadiness in the storm, and your strength against all opposition.

A Word to the Youth

Read Psalms 67–71

Y OUNG SEEMS TO be a relative term the older you get. In Psalm 71, David talks about how God worked in his life in his youth. Every young person needs to know that God desires to work in their lives. Notice some truths we can glean for the youth:

God created you. Verse 6 says, *"By thee have I been holden up from the womb...."* God has a purpose for why He created you and gave you life.

God is your hope. In verse 5, David says, *"For thou art my hope, O Lord GOD...."* The dreams you aspire toward are in vain if they are outside of God's will. The things you hope for, the things that really matter, come with God's help.

God was his trust. The greatest decision anyone makes is the acceptance of God's free gift of salvation. Verse 5 ends, *"thou art my trust from my youth."* The sooner you become a child of God, the better.

God wants to teach early. Children are moldable when they are young. Every child needs a teacher. Either that teacher will be Disney, a friend, a voice on social media, or it can be a godly parent or leader that God uses to teach His Word. Verse 17 says, *"O God, thou hast taught me from my youth...."*

Lastly, what you do in your youth will largely determine what you do the rest of your life. If you instill God's truths into your life early, you will continue to increase all your life. Few will change the course that they set from their youth. Verse 17 ends, *"and hitherto have I declared thy wondrous works."*

—— Today's Truth ——

Wasted years can never be reclaimed. Whatever stage of life you're in, determine to live for God from this day forward.

One Final Request

Read Psalms 72–77

PSALM 72 IS THE end of the second section of Psalms known as the *Exodus Psalms* (chapters 42–72). The purpose of this section causes us to remember our Redeemer. Psalm 72 is entitled "A Psalm for Solomon." This is King David's charge to his son as his life comes to an end. David's focus at the end of his life was not on his own life, but on his son, Solomon.

David had a heart for the generation after him. This was David's impact on what would be left when he was off the scene. Live for today, and you are selfish. Live for your life, and you are short-sighted. Live for eternity, and you are focused on God's plan and the difference you can make in the lives of others.

It is clear through this final prayer of David that he wanted to see his son succeed. His success wasn't determined by a majestic reign. His prayer is centered around how he would judge and lead his people, how righteousness would flourish, how he would help the needy, and how God would get the glory. Your desire should be for the generation behind you to do more than you have done, and to take your legacy as an opportunity to lead well.

I've conducted enough funerals by now to see those who have left behind a godly legacy that sets up the next generation to do more for God, and I've seen those who have lived for the temporary, and in their selfishness failed to do anything that would last beyond their lives. Who would stand up at your funeral and say, "I would never be where I am today if it wasn't for the godly example and leading of this person"? While we must look to live for God today, our focus must be greater than just the present or even the span of our lives.

—— Today's Truth ——

Invest in the next generation so they will succeed beyond your life.

Refusing Help

Read Psalms 78–80

IT HAS BEEN said that unsought counsel is usually rejected. We often get bad advice, but sometimes people are sincerely trying to help; and we should listen to the wisdom that they have to offer. In the end, God is always available to be a help to you in your time of need. However, the sad truth is that not only will some reject the help of others, but they will also reject help from God.

Going back to Psalm 77, he states in verse 2, *"my soul refused to be comforted."* Imagine a doctor handing you the cure to your sickness and pain, and it is guaranteed to be successful. There are no risky side effects. It is a sure thing. But you refuse it. You decide to continue in your agony and sorrow, complaining to others, feeling pity for your own misery… all because you refused to be helped. This sounds foolish, doesn't it? Sadly, this is how many of us treat God. Through our pain and suffering, He gives us promises like he gave Paul in II Corinthians 12:9, where He said, *"My grace is sufficient for thee."* Yet, we try to get through the storms in our own strength. God is trying to help you carry your burdens. He may not always remove the burdens from your life, but He is always there to help you. Call it whatever you want, but it takes a truly prideful and foolish person to deny the help that God offers.

Think of the problem you're facing. Are you *"refusing to be comforted"*? Is God trying to help you, but you'd rather throw your pity party than allow the Holy Spirit to comfort, uplift, and strengthen you? Imagine sitting at the table refusing to eat while complaining about your hunger or refusing help from others while complaining that you're overworked. Don't refuse the helping hand the Lord extends to you every day.

—— Today's Truth ——

God is there to help you, but you have to be willing to accept His help.

Keys to Answered Prayer

Read Psalms 81–87

GOD LOVES WHEN we pray, and God also loves to answer our prayers. David confidently stated in Psalm 86:7 in his prayer, *"thou wilt answer me."* Notice the reasons that David was so confident that his prayers would be answered:

He humbled himself (v. 1). I Peter 5:5 declares, *"God resisteth the proud, and giveth grace to the humble."* God hears the prayer of the humble. One way to ensure your prayers will hit a brick wall is to allow pride to fester in your heart.

He sought mercy (vv. 2–5). David rightly recognized that he had nothing to offer, but rather that he had sin that deserved to be punished. Don't ignore your sin. Bring it to Jesus and receive forgiveness. Sin only hinders your prayer life.

He asked for help (vv. 6–7; 16–17). Remember, you are not enough in your own strength. You need help in every area of life. Bring your needs to the Lord and ask specifically for His assistance. Prayer is not prayer without asking.

He recognized and praised God's power (vv. 8–10; 12–15). I think because we become so familiar with the stories of the Bible and the truths about God's power, we forget how absolutely magnificent and powerful He is. David reminded himself that He served the God of the impossible. He praised God to give Him glory, and, as a result, his faith in the Lord increased.

He submitted to God's way (v. 11). Another aspect of his prayer that we must notice is that he decided before his prayer was answered that his heart and desire was whatever God deemed best. David wanted the best in life, but he wanted God's best most of all.

—— Today's Truth ——

Answered prayers are promised to all of God's children. However, it matters how we come to Him, what we ask for, and how we respond to the answer.

Why We Sing

Read Psalms 88–91

THE OPENING LINE to Psalm 89 says, *"I will sing...."* Music fills the pages of Scripture. The book of Psalms is the biggest book in the Bible, and it is a book of music. God cares a great deal about music. It's a blessing to hear beautiful songs, harmony, and instruments, and it gives God pleasure when you sing.

Singing practices obedience. Singing is not a suggestion. It is a command. How we sing is just as important as the fact that we sing; and when we sing, we are singing for the glory of God. Hymns are beautifully written in a way that makes them easy to follow. This isn't the time for only a select few to sing, but for all to take part in this needful time in church to lift our voices in unison to the Lord.

Singing teaches the Bible. Colossians 3:16 says, *"teaching and admonishing one another in psalms and hymns and spiritual songs."* Great doctrines fill our music. Children learn their ABC's by putting them to a tune, and they can learn the Bible by this method as well.

Singing encourages. Ephesians 5:19 says, *"Speaking to yourselves...."* Singing encourages you and others. It's hard to sing and be a grump at the same time.

Singing strengthens. When Paul and Silas were bound in prison, they sang. This gave them spiritual strength for the valley they were enduring. You may be going through a valley, and you can use this great weapon to fight against spiritual enemies and strengthen your spirit. Have music saturate your home and your life. Play music, sing music alone and collectively, and let your mind and heart dwell on the strength that comes when you sing.

—— Today's Truth ——

Many know how to listen to music, but few understand the importance of personally singing. Great help comes with singing to the Lord, both for yourself and for others.

The Good Kind of Hate

Read Psalms 92–100

Finish the statement, "I hate _____." What comes to your mind when you think about what you hate in life? Many people might say *traffic, long lines, taxes, visits to the doctor/dentist or bills.* Did you know that it is good to hate some things? Loving God means that you love what He loves, but it also means that you hate what He hates. Psalm 97:10 says, *"Ye that love the LORD, hate evil...."*

I will never forget watching the New York Senate in 2019 as they cheered after passing a bill to allow late-term abortions. The kind of wickedness that fills a person to not only allow such atrocities, but to celebrate them is beyond my comprehension.

I will never forget when sodomite marriage was legalized in America by the Supreme Court in 2015. This kind of filthy living and this attack on the nuclear home created by God set America on a scary trajectory. President Barack Obama became the first President in our nation's history to support this kind of evil.

I will never forget where I was on September 11, 2001. I didn't quite understand it fully as a ten-year-old boy, but I began to realize that there are people that hate this nation so much, they would go to these kinds of extreme efforts to kill as many people as they could.

We are not supposed to tolerate evil. We are not supposed to brush it off and say, "Well, I'm just going to agree to disagree" like it's no big deal. If God hates evil, then Christians should hate evil. This hatred should not fill your life so much that it steals your joy and your love for right. It should, however, cause you to lead your family and others against the wickedness in this world.

—— Today's Truth ——

Sin is not something that is just a small mark on our society. It is an evil that you should hate so much that you can't help but do something about it.

200 | STEVEN BECKER

Out of Sight, Out of Mind

Read Psalms 101–105

I ONCE HEARD a preacher asked what to do about the ungodly and sinful things all around us. He made the statement that we might not always be able to control the first look, but a second look should never take place. You can remove yourselves as much as possible, but every so often, your eyes will see something you shouldn't see. You might see an old sin that is tempting for you; you might see something that causes you to covet the wrong things; or you might see something inappropriate that causes you to lust. Psalm 101:3 says, *"I will set no wicked thing before mine eyes...."* That means it is our duty not only to refrain from indulging in sin, but also to be vigilant about not allowing our eyes to bring our focus to that sin.

I have known many people who have talked about past sins that they had to conquer either before they got saved or while they were backslidden. Just viewing that past sin in the world is a temptation for them. In the case of alcohol, some will avoid that aisle at the grocery store at all costs.

Sin traps its victims, and it begins with the eyes. Lot set his eyes toward Sodom before he became a resident of the city. Achan set his eyes on the garments and silver that he coveted before he stole them. Samson set his eyes on the wrong kind of women before he decided to marry a Philistine. It has been said that the eyes are the portals to the soul. The Psalmist here talks about removing people and wickedness in his life, just so it won't even be something that he has to look at, lest he be tempted and succumb to sin. Sin has to begin somewhere; it begins with the eyes, then it moves to the heart, and then it becomes an action. Cut off the temptation at the start.

—— Today's Truth ——

It is not extreme to keep sin out of your sight, because if you keep it out of sight, you will keep it out of your life.

A Reminder to Remember

Read Psalms 106–107

THE STORY IS told of an old Navajo Indian who became rich when oil was found on his property. He took all the money and put it in a bank. His banker became familiar with the habits of this old gentleman. Every so often, the Indian would show up at the bank and say to the banker, "Grass all gone, sheep all sick, water holes all dry." Without a word, the banker would take the old Indian into the vault, show him several bags of silver dollars, and say, "All this is yours." The old man would spend about an hour stacking up the dollars and counting them. Then he'd return the bags to their places, come out of the vault, and say, "Grass all green, sheep all well, water holes all full."

The Israelites' fall came because they forgot to remember. Just like them, your downfall can come easily if you fail to remember several truths about the Lord.

They forgot His mercy (v. 7). God's mercy is the root of the goodness we do not deserve which He gives on a daily basis. The only thing keeping you out of hell and from all the bad in life is the mercy of God. They forgot how good He was to them. We should be in awe of His mercy toward us.

They forgot His works (v. 13). God proved His love and power over and over for His people. Our faith is increased in the midst of the storm when we remember His works in the past.

They forgot their Saviour (v. 21). The most important truth you should and must remember is your salvation. Their salvation out of Egypt is a picture of the believer's salvation from the world into the presence of the Lord. Stop and think about the day you got saved. Think about how little you knew how that decision would change your life forever.

——Today's Truth ——

You cannot afford to forget some things. Remind yourself often of important truths about the Lord and how those truths can impact your future.

Be Glad

Read Psalms 108–118

Dᴵᴰ ʏᴏᴜ ᴋɴᴏᴡ that you don't have to have a bad day? Every day can be a good day. Psalm 118:24 rightly states, *"This is the day which the* Lᴏʀᴅ *hath made; we will rejoice and be glad in it."* Christians aren't supposed to have a spirit of doom and gloom. We have many reasons to be glad each and every day.

Today is a gift from God. It's been said that every day is a gift and that is why today is called the present. Tomorrow is never promised. We shouldn't live in fear of these possibilities, but they are real possibilities. If you're alive today, it's because God chose to give you another day of life. That means you have great reason to be glad.

Today is on purpose from God. God created everything, and everything He created has a purpose. If God gave you another day of life today, then you know God has something for you to do in your life today.

Today is an opportunity to be glad. Nobody enjoys being miserable, but miserable people live that way by choice. Joy is not a result of good things happening to you. Happiness may be determined by happenstance, but joy is a daily decision regardless of your circumstances.

Oliver Wendell Holmes, Jr., was a member of the U.S. Supreme Court for 30 years. His mind, wit and work earned him the unofficial title of "the greatest justice since John Marshall." At one point in his life, Justice Holmes explained his choice of a career by saying: "I might have entered the ministry if certain clergymen I knew had not looked and acted so much like undertakers." Charles Spurgeon said, "There is a marvelous medicinal power in joy. Most medicines are distasteful; but this, which is the best of all medicines, is sweet to the taste, and comforting to the heart."

—— Today's Truth ——

Many things can steal your joy, but we have far more reasons to have joy. Choose to be glad today!

Not Offended

Read Psalm 119

I'LL NEVER FORGET a video shown in a college class showing people in a remote village, removed from civilization, receiving boxes of Bibles for the first time. As they opened the boxes and grabbed a Bible for themselves, they cheered and rejoiced with tears. These were not expensive, leather-bound Bibles, hand cut to perfection. They looked like inexpensive, paper-backed gift Bibles. But the people didn't care about the cover, the size of font, or whether or not they had maps in the back. They had the Word of God in their hands, and their lives were forever changed because of it.

Psalm 119:165 says, *"Great peace have they which love thy law: and nothing shall offend them."* This verse is often quoted to teach that it should not hurt our feelings when the Bible is preached, even if our sin is called out. However, that's not the meaning of this verse. The word *offend* here means "to cause to fall or stumble."

Failure is a real possibility for every Christian. No matter how long you've been saved or how much Bible you can quote, you can fall too. I Corinthians 10:12 says, *"Wherefore let him that thinketh he standeth take heed lest he fall."* At any time, you can be "offended" and knocked off course.

The way to keep yourself on the right path that God has paved for you is found in your spirit toward the Word of God. The verse states that peace comes from developing a love for the Bible. The closer your heart gets to your Bible, the more stable your heart becomes in your Christian walk. Don't treat your Bible reading like a chore or a school textbook. Learn to love the Bible! If your love has faded, pray to God to help you rekindle that desire for His Word. Dive into its pages. You may not feel the emotions on the first verse you read, but if you put your heart in it, you will learn to love the wonderful gift that God has given, and that love will anchor you on the path that He has set for you.

—— Today's Truth ——

Your heart toward God's Word will directly relate to your longevity in the Christian life.

Let's Go to Church

Read Psalms 120–131

FOR 11 WEEKS AND 44 services, we did not assemble for church during the coronavirus lockdown. I will never forget the first service we had together after being apart for nearly three months. I was more glad to be in church that day than I had been at perhaps any other point in my life.

Psalm 122:1 says, *"I was glad when they said unto me, Let us go into the house of the LORD."* Church is not to be something that we dread; it is not just another activity on the calendar, and it is not something that can be replaced.

Do you find your heart spiritually asleep even when you're in God's house? We need a renewed passion for assembling with the body of Christ as the church for which Jesus died!

It is said that every year in America the number of churches that close is three times higher than the number of churches that open. No county in the nation has a higher percentage of church attendance than it did ten years ago. Additionally, more than half of churches in America did not add one person to their congregation. We can attribute these startling statistics to the spiritual decline of our nation, but I believe that the death of the church in our country is due to the way Christians have treated God's house. If we want our churches be a place that people enjoy attending, it must start with us having the spirit of the Psalmist who said, *"I was glad when they said unto me, Let us go into the house of the LORD."* People shouldn't have to fight with you to get you into church.

—— Today's Truth ——

Renew your affection for your church and make God's house the exciting, helpful, and spiritual place that Jesus created it to be.

Biblical Unity

Read Psalms 132–138

UNITY IS NOT the same as harmony. I can live in harmony with the people in my neighborhood, but we do not live in unity. We live peaceably around one another. My kids ride their bikes in front of their homes. They walk their dogs on the sidewalks. We share a neighborhood park. For the most part, there is peace because we live in harmony. Romans 12:18 tells us, *"If it be possible, as much as lieth in you, live peaceably with all men."* Be kind to your neighbors, your co-workers, and the clerk at the bank. You don't have to be unkind just because you can't have a close unity with a person.

It is possible to have true unity only with the brethren. Psalm 133:1 says, *"Behold, how good and how pleasant it is for brethren to dwell together in unity!"* While we can have a limit to how unified we can be with the people of the world, we have the good pleasure to have unity with God's children. This begins with the people in your home. This includes the believers in your church (all of them, not just your friends). This unity creates a pleasant way of living.

People love drama. Say what you want, but look at how successful Hollywood is for portraying their dramatic stories of people's lives. Look at the popularity of social media that is filled with "look at this person." Do you find yourself constantly in the middle of drama or in need of always having the "scoop" on every situation? I promise you that you will not have that "good and pleasant" feeling in life by living with everyone's drama. Unifying yourself with your family, your church family, and other Christians is possible; it is also commanded. Progress isn't possible when there's fighting. More damage is done in drama than good.

——Today's Truth ——

People have their differences, but under Jesus as our Saviour and Shepherd, we can have unity through Him. Unity brings pleasure with it.

Precious Thoughts

Read Psalms 139–143

WHAT YOU THINK about shows what you care about. We all have random thoughts that come to mind, like "Do things catch on fire or is fire just on things?" or "Why do moms get only one special day out of the year, but sharks get a whole week?" What do you think about? It may be a hobby, food you enjoy, a travel destination, memories of the past, people you love, etc. The more you care for something, the more you will be prone to think about it.

The Bible tells us that God thinks about us. Psalm 139:17–18 says, *"How precious also are thy thoughts unto me, O God! how great is the sum of them! If I should count them, they are more in number than the sand: when I awake, I am still with thee."* Notice that these are not just random thoughts. God is constantly and continually thinking about you. It makes you feel special when someone tells you that you've been on their mind. How much more incredible of a thought is it that the Lord of all creation thinks about you and the sum of His thoughts are more than the sand on the seashore!

God's thoughts of you show that He cares for you and notices you. Why is this important? Proverbs 5:21 says, *"For the ways of man are before the eyes of the LORD, and he pondereth all his goings."* When we realize that God notices us and thinks about our lives, this should cause us to ask ourselves, "What does God think about when He sees my life?" So much of our lives is dictated by what others think, but what have you changed because of what God thinks of you? Would your life bring Him thoughts of joy and pleasure or thoughts of sorrow and sadness? The Psalmist was honored to think that the great God of Heaven would take thought of His life.

—— Today's Truth ——

God's mind is filled with thoughts of His children. This is an honor to consider and a challenge to think about what kind of thoughts we bring to His mind.

How to Get Close to God

Read Psalms 144–150

Nothing is still in this world. Our universe is constantly moving. The earth spins on its axis at 1,000 mph and orbits the sun at 67,0000 mph. You may think that you are still when you are asleep or relaxing on your couch, but you are constantly moving. The same could be said about your life, not just physically, but spiritually. Your spiritual life is also in constant motion. Either you are getting closer to God or you are drifting away from God.

God wants to be close to you. He wants you to talk to Him, and He wants to speak to you. As a father, I want so badly to have a close relationship with my children. I have a relationship with a lot of people, but my wife and kids are different. I don't want to have just a relationship with them; I want to have a close relationship with my family. And here's the truth: you are able to have a genuinely close relationship with only a few people in life. If you can have a close relationship with anyone, have it with God.

Psalm 145:18 says, *"The LORD is nigh unto all them that **call upon** him...."* God wants to see that you want it. I can ask my wife to talk with me or ask her out on a fun date, and that draws us closer to each other; but our relationship has grown to its current point because of the efforts both of us have put into it. Calling unto God in prayer is proof of your desire to be close to Him. But relationship is a two-way street!

The second part of that verse says, *"to all that call upon him **in truth**."* Your actions can help or hurt your relationship with people. What I do or don't do can hurt or help my relationship with my wife and children. Your obedience to His Word is directly related to how close your relationship with Him will be.

—— Today's Truth ——

Getting close to God is possible for every person. It isn't difficult, but it does take effort, and it's always worth it!

Wisdom Series: Part 1—Get Wisdom

Read Proverbs 1–3

THE BOOK OF Proverbs is a book written from a father to a son. Just imagine your Heavenly Father writing this book to you as His child. After all, this is actually the case with every book of the Bible. The theme of Proverbs is centered around wisdom. Wisdom is different than knowledge. Knowledge is retaining information, while wisdom is knowing how, why, and when to use that knowledge in your everyday life.

Our world has a dire need for people with wisdom. Leaders need wisdom as they lead others in following them. No matter what roles you have in life, one thing is certain, you need wisdom to be successful. Proverbs 4:7 says, *"therefore get wisdom: and with all thy getting get understanding."* Wisdom isn't just something that's good to have; it is a trait that you must have. The good news is that Proverbs is filled with truths that offer wisdom for our daily lives.

Proverbs 2:6 tells us, *"For the LORD giveth wisdom: out of his mouth cometh knowledge and understanding."* Wisdom comes from the Lord. You might learn worldly wisdom at work or amongst your friends, but what we must seek is heavenly wisdom. I've had people tell me at times, "You're so wise for your age." The truth is that I'm not wise, but God has given me wisdom in areas. I don't have wisdom. I lack wisdom, and I look to God to get more.

God gives wisdom, but He gives it to those who seek it. James 1:5 says, *"If any of you lack wisdom, let him ask of God, that giveth to all men liberally, and upbraideth not; and it shall be given him."* Don't be afraid or ashamed that you lack wisdom. Rather, go to God and ask Him to give you wisdom every day!

—— Today's Truth ——

Wisdom is the great need for our day, and it is available to all who seek it. We must look to God to give us heavenly wisdom for our lives.

Wisdom Series: Part 2—Hold on Tight

Read Proverbs 4–7

THE STORY IS told about the father of a vacationing family who came across a large sign that read, "Road Closed. Do Not Enter." The man proceeded around the sign because he was confident it would save them time. His wife was resistant to the adventure, but there was no turning back for this persistent road warrior. After a few miles of successful navigation, he began to boast about his gift of discernment. His proud smile was quickly replaced with humble sweat when the road led to a washed-out bridge. He turned the car around and retraced his tracks to the main road. When they arrived at the original warning sign he was greeted by large letters on the back of the sign that said, "Welcome back, stupid!"

Proverbs 4:1–2 says, *"Hear, ye children, the instruction of a father, and attend to know understanding. For I give you good doctrine, forsake ye not my law."* The instruction given in Proverbs and throughout the Bible is wisdom for your life for your benefit. It is "good doctrine." This isn't just a different philosophy that you should consider. This is godly wisdom that the Lord is passing along to you.

Proverbs 4:13 commands, *"Take fast hold of instruction; let her not go: keep her; for she is thy life."* The instruction given in God's Word is not something to take lightly. Imagine holding on to the edge of a cliff where if you fall, you will die. That kind of grip and intensity is the mentality that all Christians need as they handle the Word of God. We have a lack of godly wisdom in our society because we have too many Christians who are casual about the Bible. Hold on tightly to the wisdom in God's Word that He has given you!

——Today's Truth ——

The wisdom that God has given us in His Word must be held on to with a strong grip. Heeding God's instruction is a life-or-death matter.

Wisdom Series: Part 3—Where Wisdom Begins

Read Proverbs 8–11

A FRESHLY MINTED lieutenant wanted to impress the first private to enter his new office, and he pretended to be on the phone with a general so that the private would know he was somebody. "Yes, sir, General, you can count on me," he said before he banged down the receiver. Then he asked the private what he wanted. "I'm just here to connect your phone, sir." Proverbs speaks much about pride, because pride is an enemy of wisdom. Proverbs 8:13 says, *"The fear of the LORD is to hate evil: pride, and arrogancy, and the evil way, and the froward mouth, do I hate."* God doesn't want you to just conquer your pride, but to hate it.

All things have a beginning. Proverbs 9:10 tells us where wisdom begins in your life: *"The fear of the LORD is the beginning of wisdom...."* Fearing God is a vital part to the Christian life. Fearing the Lord speaks of a respect and recognition of His power and wisdom. God doesn't want you to fear Him so that it causes you to not speak to Him or get close to Him. That is an unhealthy fear.

Many homes are run by children because they don't fear their parents. They can get away with screaming at their mother, throwing tantrums, and getting their way because their parents don't have the care to discipline their children. Without fear, pride takes over; and the flesh does what it wants. Think of employees who fear their boss. They fear what will happen if they are late, miss work, and don't finish their tasks. They also fear missing promotions, bonuses, and other incentives. Because of this, the employees are diligent in their work, work harder, and do the best job they can do. Similarly, a healthy fear of the Lord is needed to obtain wisdom.

—— Today's Truth ——

Wisdom begins by developing a fear of the Lord that pushes you to be the best Christian you can be for His glory.

Wisdom Series:
Part 4—Wisdom Draws a Crowd

Read Proverbs 12–15

ACCORDING TO THE Terman Study, which followed one thousand study participants from childhood until their death, the people we surround ourselves with are who we become. We see those around us slacking off, we become less motivated. When we see people performing selfless acts, we become selfless. Who you surround yourself with, especially at an early age is likely to make a significant impact on the person you ultimately become. Pastor Jack Trieber has said it this way, "Show me your friends, and I'll show you your future."

Proverbs 13:20 states, *"He that walketh with wise men shall be wise: but a companion of fools shall be destroyed."* Walk with people who curse, and you will find yourself eventually saying those words. Walk with people who listen to ungodly music, and you will develop an ear for that music. There is no way around it. You will adapt to the people in your circle. Although you cannot always control where you work, there are some jobs that I would not work for this reason when I was getting into the workforce as a young person.

If you want to have wisdom, surround yourself with wise people. You're hindering yourself if the closest people in your life do not have godly wisdom. Wise people will rub off on you, but it will also make you want to keep from being foolish. Nobody likes feeling like a fool. That's why many people surround themselves with others that make themselves feel better, because they feel superior. However, you need the opposite. Befriend people who are better Christians than you. Put yourself in the company of wise people, and you will find yourself obtaining their godly wisdom.

——Today's Truth ——

People around us influence us. When we put ourselves in the company of others, we will copy their behavior.

Wisdom Series:
Part 5—What Wisdom Sounds Like

Read Proverbs 16–19

PROVERBS 18:21 MAKES A powerful statement: *"Death and life are in the power of the tongue...."* You've probably heard the phrase before, "Sticks and stones may break my bones, but words will never hurt me." This sounds nice, but I'm sure you can remember some hurtful words that have been said to you in the past. The words, although they did not hurt you physically, might have hurt you deeply.

Our words are mentioned 178 times in Proverbs in a variety of forms (words, mouth, tongue, lips, etc.). Proverbs 16:23 says, *"The heart of the wise teacheth his mouth, and addeth learning to his lips."* Too often, people apologize for what they say in a way that sounds like they couldn't control their tongue. You have control over your words, and a wise person will teach themselves to use their words to speak wisdom.

Your parents probably told you to "think before you speak." Why did they say this? Because we get into trouble with our words when are thoughts in our heart and mind comes out of our mouth without any thought. It's often wise to keep inside some thoughts that come to mind. Some thoughts can be foolish, but some can be very sinful and even hurtful to others. Proverbs 29:11 says, *"A fool uttereth all his mind: but a wise man keepeth it in till afterwards."*

You shouldn't just be cautious to not say the wrong thing, but you should be mindful to speak words of wisdom. Proverbs 16:24 continues, "Pleasant words are as an honeycomb, sweet to the soul, and health to the bones." You can speak words of encouragement, words of comfort, words that are helpful, and use your lips to do good to others. Many don't realize the impact of their words because they don't even stop to consider what they're saying. Wisdom is learning to control and teach yourself to say the right thing.

—— Today's Truth ——

Teach your tongue to speak words of wisdom.

Wisdom Series: Part 6—For Your Own Good

Read Proverbs 20–22

EVEN THOSE WITH the best intentions have a part of them that want good to come to their life. We are commanded to live for God and others, but the Christian life has great benefits. When you get a job, you look at the benefits—What is the pay? Are there opportunities to be promoted? Are there incentives? Is it worth my time and effort? If the benefits don't feel worth the work, then you will not likely accept the job. In the Christian life, not only are there benefits, but they are so spectacular, it would take a fool to deny it. Wisdom is good for the soul. Proverbs 19:8 says, *"He that getteth wisdom loveth his own soul...."* In other words, it's in your self-interest to get wisdom.

You get happiness. Proverbs 3:13 says, *"Happy is the man that findeth wisdom...."* Maybe you're fine with living life as a grump. If you're not happy, it's not because of your circumstances, but by your own choice. Wisdom brings happiness.

You get to know God (Proverbs 2:5–6). Godly wisdom draws you closer to your relationship with God. The greatest benefit of all is that you have fellowship with God Almighty. There is a great difference between knowing about God and knowing God.

You get protection from God (Proverbs 2:7–19). When you act in the flesh and follow your foolish lusts, you remove yourself from God's umbrella of safety. Only you can do this. Having wisdom guides your life in a way that keeps yourself under the security of His wings.

You get to dwell with God (Proverbs 2:20–22). Proverbs 2:21 says, *"For the upright shall dwell in the land...."* God will receive you when you live by His wisdom. Sin tarnishes our relationship, but godly wisdom brings us into His presence.

—— Today's Truth ——

Living by godly wisdom is not a sacrifice. It is in your best interest to have wisdom. You will always receive more than you can give.

Wisdom Series: Part 7—Counsel

Read Proverbs 23–26

THERE ARE FOUR kinds of people when it comes to counsel. First, there are those who will not seek counsel. They would rather live their way than swallow their pride and look to others for help. Second, there are those who seek the wrong counsel. If you are looking for someone who is going to tell you what you want to hear, that is the wrong kind of counsel. The third type of people are those who seek counsel but don't follow it. This is frustrating for leaders, yet all of us have probably done this at some point. Finally, there are those who seek godly counsel and follow it.

Proverbs 24:6 says, *"For by wise counsel thou shalt make thy war: and in multitude of counsellors there is safety."* Every person needs to have counsellors in their life they can go to about certain decisions or situations. A multitude of counsellors doesn't mean you ask ten people for their opinion about every problem, but that you have a number of people in your life you can go to for counsel. You may only go to one of them for a particular situation, and you might seek counsel from another one for something different. It's better to have a few counsellors than to just have one person for counsel. I have about five counsellors in my life.

Proverbs 1:5 says, *"A wise man will hear, and will increase learning...."* Your pride will keep you from listening to counsel, because it's hard to hear some counsel, especially if it goes against your desires or if it exposes your failures. Remember, God speaks to you through the Holy Spirit, but He often uses other people as a vessel to speak to you. He will use your parent, pastor, a godly friend, or a leader to give you counsel. Godly counsel always goes hand in hand with God's Word. You know it's not of God if it's not of the Bible.

——Today's Truth——

Counsel is a safety net to guide you in your decisions and to give you wisdom for every situation you may face.

Wisdom Series:
Part 8—The Hard Lessons of Wisdom

Read Proverbs 27–31

O NE OF THE hardest parts of parenting is disciplining your child. I love my children so much, and it makes it difficult to do anything that will cause them to cry or be hurt in any way. I believe that's why God says in Proverbs 19:18, *"Chasten thy son while there is hope, and let not thy soul spare for his crying."* Parents feel bad, and in return, they don't punish their children.

God uses chastisement to produce wisdom in His children. Without punishment, we would continue in our sin and foolish ways if we didn't have the periodic wake-up call from God. Proverbs 19:15 says, *"The rod and reproof give wisdom: but a child left to himself bringeth his mother to shame."* God tells us that children who are not disciplined with the rod (spanked) and reproof (teaching that goes along with discipline) will eventually bring shame to their parents. If you discipline your children, they will not figure it out for themselves.

We often need the rod of chastisement and the reproof that goes along with it to learn the errors in our ways. Do we enjoy it? No one likes to be punished, but I've heard so many adults say, "I'm so thankful for the spankings and the rules my parents had when I was growing up." However, they look back in the eyes of their parents and see that they received wisdom because of that chastisement.

Hebrews 12:6 states, *"For whom the Lord loveth he chasteneth, and scourgeth every son whom he receiveth."* God doesn't punish you because He hates you. He does it because He loves you and wants you to be wise. . It is these hard lessons in life that we can often learn the most.

——Today's Truth ——

After the punishment, you are wise to learn from your mistakes and make the changes necessary to live in a way that is pleasing to God.

Under the Sun

Read Ecclesiastes 1–4

RECALL A TIME when you went on a great search for something. Maybe you lost your wallet, misplaced your keys, or couldn't remember where you filed an important document. I'll never forget my shock when I realized I had lost my passport less than two weeks before my wedding. We were set to go to Mexico for our honeymoon, which required a passport. I immediately became sick when I realized that it was lost. I paid top dollar to expedite a new passport that I received two days before our wedding, only to find my old passport as soon as we returned back home.

Ecclesiastes can be described best by this grand search to which Solomon dedicated himself. He addresses five main categories in this book: wealth, wisdom, wine, women, and works. Ecclesiastes 1:13 reveals this search of his, *"And I gave my heart to seek and search out by wisdom concerning all things that are done under heaven...."* Solomon was a king seeking fulfillment, joy, and purpose. He was searching for what all men still search for today—what money cannot buy, what the world cannot manufacture, and what cannot be replicated.

Solomon uses the phrase "under the sun" twenty-nine times in this short book. He realized the hard way that the missing piece to his life was something that could not be found on this earth. No eternal purpose could be filled by temporary measures. The cheap thrill of liquor and the pleasure of women could not fill that hole inside his heart. As he looked back on his search, he understood that he was looking in the wrong place all along. Likewise, people all over are searching for these same things to bring meaning to their lives, while searching in the wrong place all along.

—— Today's Truth ——

True joy, a meaningful purpose, and real satisfaction cannot be found by money, fame, pleasure, or cheap thrills. Nothing "under the sun" can truly satisfy.

A Man of Few Words

Read Ecclesiastes 5–8

Y OU'LL ALWAYS BE better off to speak too few words than to speak too many words. Maybe you've asked someone who wasn't pregnant when the baby was due and wished you had held your tongue. We get in trouble with our words more than we do with our silence. It is not wrong to speak, but trouble comes quickly when we misuse our tongue. Ecclesiastes 5:3 states, *"a fool's voice is known by multitude of words."* That doesn't mean you're a fool if you like to talk, but if you think of foolish people, it's easy to think of the foolish words that they say.

Ecclesiastes 5:1 tells us, *"Keep thy foot when thou goest to the house of God, and be more ready to hear...."* We like our voice to be heard, our input to be submitted, and our burdens to be conveyed. Far more people are good at talking too much rather than listening too much. Did your parents remind you often that you have two ears and one mouth for a reason? I was taught by an older man that when children talk to you, give them your ear. Don't look around at what you're doing, but look them in the eye when they're talking. They are people, too. Your ears aren't just for the elite, they are for people all around you. You can learn a lot by simply listening.

Verse 5 goes on, *"Better is it that thou shouldest not vow, than that thou shouldest vow and not pay."* We say it like this: "Don't make a promise you can't keep." Better to not make a promise if you can't keep it. If you're going to promise God something, you better be fully committed to keeping it. God isn't interested in your lip service.

Finally, verse 6 warns, *"Suffer not thy mouth to cause thy flesh to sin...."* Your tongue carries more weight than you may realize. It could be lashing out in anger, tearing down someone, or speaking in lust. Your mouth can hurt others, but it can also hurt yourself.

—— Today's Truth ——

Give thought to the words that you speak. Problems come more from words that are spoken than from words that are kept in.

Working God's Way

Read Ecclesiastes 9–12

LIVING A LIFE of faith calls you to a greater work, but the Christian life is a life of work. You cannot separate God's will from work. Ecclesiastes 9:10 gives a great formula of godly work in a book that is written about how so many can waste their lives on the wrong thing.

"Whatsoever." God isn't interested in titles. You can do a lot for God by being willing to do the "whatsoever" tasks. Don't wait for the perfect job. When I went to Bible college, I went to get a security job. I completed all the training beforehand, but when I arrived I took the first job I could get because I needed to pay the bills.

"Thy hand." You can think through things, but you have to be willing to put in the work. Work takes time and energy. Whether you're behind a computer or running heavy machinery, put in the effort and get to work.

"Findeth to do." Delegating is required because there aren't enough volunteers. In my time as the pastor of RBC with a bus ministry, I have not had to ask someone to clean the buses, fill the gas tanks, or check the buses one time. Burnie Row, who has driven over twenty-five years without missing a Sunday, has put his heart into those buses.

"Do it." Once you start it, finish the work. Writing my first book was exciting for me, but finishing it was much more fulfilling. Anyone can begin something, but fewer will see it through to completion.

"With thy might." Don't do anything half-heartedly. It's more frustrating to have a job halfway done than for it to be left completely undone. It takes more time for someone to come behind and pick up the pieces than to just do the job right in the first place.

—— Today's Truth ——

God's will requires God's people to work. Get involved in the work, and give it your best.

Marriage Series: Part 1—Oneness

Read Song of Solomon 1–8

S ONG OF SOLOMON is one of the closest insights into the personal relationship between a husband and wife that we have in Scripture. Over the next few days, we will stray from the protocol in the scheduled reading to study some Biblical truths about marriage. I tell the youth in our church all the time that after salvation, who they marry will have more impact on their future than almost any other decision. Not only is choosing the right mate paramount, but it is also just as imperative that we keep this sacred bond right in the eyes of the Lord.

Dwight Eisenhower said, "Only two things are necessary to keep one's wife happy. The first is to let her think she's having her own way. The second is to let her have it." You will not find a void of jokes about marriage, but the world's view of marriage is a relationship of constant conflict. This is not God's design. I emphatically believe that marriage is one of God's greatest gifts in life outside of salvation. You can have more children, you can find another way to make a dollar, but you can have only one mate. The answer in marriage is to become "one flesh." Genesis 2:24 states, *"Therefore shall a man leave his father and his mother, and shall cleave unto his wife: and they shall be one flesh."*

Oneness with Jesus. Since God created marriage, He is the only One who can help you have a successful marriage. Couples will try anything to mend their relationship, but those solutions often include more activities or secular helps than reading the Bible, praying, or serving in church together. Spiritual unity takes place when two Christians make Jesus the center of their marriage and allow His Spirit to bring them together. The Trinity is our perfect example of different people living in unity. It may seem odd, but remember that the picture of marriage is how Jesus, the Bridegroom, has given Himself to the church, His bride.

Oneness by Commitment. Marriage is not for test runs until you get it right. You pray, fast, and yield to the Holy Spirit while you date and court someone, knowing that when you say "I do," you are committed to that person for the rest of your life. The word divorce should be treated worse than any curse word in your home. I truly believe that many of America's problems would be solved if marriages started right and stuck together God's way. Your spouse should never be fearful that you might leave, nor should you ever entertain the idea. Whatever problems you face, determine in the beginning that you will work through them by God's grace.

Oneness by Transparency. Genesis 2:25 continues, *"And they were both naked, the man and his wife, and were not ashamed."* Intimacy in marriage isn't possible without having complete openness with one another. How can you expect your husband/wife to accept you fully if you are not fully open with them? This is often natural in the beginning, but then hearts become closed and hardened after years of hurt, fighting, and division. Openness diminishes little by little, and couples don't have oneness because transparency with each other is lost. Closing off spiritually, emotionally, or physically to your spouse is a hindrance to that perfect unity God created in marriage.

——Today's Truth ——

To be "one flesh" as a couple, you must follow God's pattern and principles to create oneness with your spouse. You begin to think alike and rub off on one another because you become one with each other.

Marriage Series: Part 2—Needs

Read Isaiah 1–4

E VERY GUN IS made to hold a specific caliber round. You cannot put a 9mm round in a gun that is made to shoot a .45 caliber round. Likewise, screws are made to be turned by specific screwdrivers. Now, to illustrate from a woman's perspective, I have learned that women use all kinds of makeup. I won't try to act like I know the purpose, but I understand one goes on first, one is used for your eyes, another is used for your cheeks, another for your lips, and so on. Different parts of your face need a specific kind of makeup, just like a gun needs a specific size round. Now, imagine putting lipstick on your eyes, eye shadow on your lips, or driving a Phillips-head screw with a hex head drill bit. The needs are different and require something specific to meet those specific needs.

There's no debate that men and women are different. Our world is fixed on the quest to make women more like men and men more like women, but we're just not the same. Men and women have different needs. While a woman might feel like her needs are met by vocalizing her emotions to her husband, he will likely not have the same satisfaction from that. That doesn't mean that men are emotionless creatures. It just means that men might not need that like women do. Needs that commonly bring satisfaction to men might not have the same impact on women. While every individual person will have their own specific need due to their past or current state, men and women have general character traits that are created by God, and your spouse was created to meet your needs. Try meeting the needs of your spouse with what fulfills you the most, and you will not succeed. You need to know that your spouse's needs will almost certainly differ from yours, and it is your duty to learn what fuels your spouse the most and commit yourself to meet those needs.

Men need **admiration** (Ephesians 5:22–24). Men are naturally born leaders, and this is a result of God creating man to lead the home. If you treat them as such, they will thrive. If you tear them down, demean them, and neglect to praise their accomplishments, they will struggle. Why are there cheerleaders in nearly every major sport in America? Men love to be cheered, no matter how modest or macho they appear to be. Watch the high fives after a big touchdown or the applause after a big project. Wives must learn to be their husband's biggest cheerleaders. You don't have to treat him like a child as if he won a participation trophy for just trying, but you can find areas to praise in what he does to provide for, protect, and give security to you, and to lead your home by God's grace. Give him respect as God's man in your home instead of battling his leadership. He is not to be a tyrant, but you have to submit to his leadership to give him the ability to lead.

Women most need **adoration** (Ephesians 5:25–29). This is not always shown by materialistic acts of love like putting food on the table, fixing the hole in the wall, or putting a car in the driveway. Women need frequent expressions of love and affection, through both words and actions. We read in Song of Solomon how this couple talked about one another. As you read that, think of the way you talk to your wife and about your wife. How do you describe her beauty to her? How do you describe the parts about her personality that you love? How do you express your affection toward her? In courtship, we write letters, poems, and songs to win the love of a woman, but where does that effort go after marriage? You don't have to be in the honeymoon phase all the time to make her feel loved. Our relationship grows, as does our love for one another, and it should be expressed. Take her out, sit away from the TV that airing the ball game, and remind her that she's the most beautiful woman in the world to you; tell her how much you appreciate what she does for your home, your children, and you. Express to her that your life would not have an ounce of joy without her. How sad that many men can talk for hours about their favorite sports team, but struggle to come up with a paragraph to describe their love for their wife.

—— Today's Truth ——

Put the right fuel in the tank for your spouse. Look for what fulfills that person the most, and commit yourself to fulfill those needs for their sake and for yours.

Marriage Series: Part 3—Communication

Read Isaiah 5–9

WORDS THAT ARE spoken in just a few seconds can have an impact on your spouse for many years to come. You could probably think of a time in your life when someone said very hurtful words to you, even from long in the past. Our words carry great weight. On the other hand, you may also be able to remember meaningful words, like when your spouse first said "I love you," or when you both said "I do" on your wedding day. The greatest part of our walk with God is communication. Your time in your Bible and your time in prayer are how you communicate to God and how God communicates with you. I believe this is absolutely paramount after salvation to sustain any kind of a healthy relationship with God. To have a lasting and happy marriage, you must also have a right and good communication with your spouse.

Words that should not be spoken. Speaking your mind can be dangerous. It is important to be transparent and open with your mate, but there is a limit to what you should say. Words spoken out of frustration and anger can wound the heart. Words like "divorce," "I hate you," or other words that attack and demean should never come out of your mouth. Once they are spoken, they cannot be taken back. You can always seek forgiveness, but that doesn't mean it's right to lash out every time you're upset and then just apologize later. The wounds you leave will put a great strain on your relationship and on your spouse's heart. It's also not just what you say, but how you say it that's important. If you can't have a conversation without raising your voice, especially in front of your children, then take time to calm your emotions before you talk. Don't allow yourself to fall into the trap of attacking your spouse. That is the person God created just for you. Your attitude during your conversation is just as important as the conversation itself.

Words that must be spoken. Ephesians 4:25 says, *"Wherefore putting away lying, speak every man truth with his neighbor…."* Your spouse has the right to know the truth. My wife should never wonder where

I am, whom I am with, and what I am doing. If she doesn't know, I should not hesitate to be open with her. Marriage is not a place for secrets. Social media, email, texts, bank accounts, friendships, business decisions—all of this should be open to your spouse. It has been said that "sin thrives in the shadows." Trust is built from openness, and secrets are a sure way to close off your closeness and trust with one another. Additionally, this means you should be able to share things with one another that you cannot and should not share with others. Your friends shouldn't know more about you than your spouse does, and they shouldn't know as much as your spouse either. Without the ability to be open and share your heart with each other, marriage has no real depth. You also should speak words of kindness and encouragement every day of your lives together. Give compliments regularly. Give praise for the little things. Speak words of affection as a reminder of your heart for that special person.

——Today's Truth ——

Your words have power like little else in your marriage to be a help or a hurt.

Marriage Series: Part 4—Healing

Read Isaiah 10–14

Marriages are crumbling in divorce, affairs, damaged relationships, and bitterness toward one another. There is good news! God is the great Physician, and you can have healing through Him. It's no secret that marriages have their problems, and how people work through those problems will determine whether the problem grows bigger in each partner's heart or whether healing is achieved. Whether your spouse has hurt you or you've hurt your spouse, God has a remedy for your marriage.

One of the reasons that married couples struggle is due to unrealistic expectations of each other. After seeing too many movies and picture-perfect couples (spoiler alert: there are none), disappointment hits hard when your dream husband/wife doesn't meet all the criteria like you imagined. After all, marriage has no training requirements. It takes training to be successful in every line of work, but marriage (the most important work you have) requires no training at all.

People fail us every day, but these failures seem to be more challenging and discouraging when coming from the person we expected to meet our every need. Working through hurt and finding healing through the Lord is not always simply and certainly not easy, but it is possible. Divorce doesn't have to be an option. You may even have Biblical grounds for divorce, but that should never be the first option. God never commanded divorce, even if He does permit it in a specific circumstance. You are foolish, however, to not attempt to find healing with your mate. God can mend relationships.

Humble yourself. I Peter 3:1 commands the wife to live in submission to her husband. Verse 7 commands the husband to dwell with his wife according to knowledge. Wives must put their personal agenda aside to submit to their husbands, and husbands must have the care and compassion to live for their wives. At some point, you have to put aside pride and selfishness and determine that your spouse is not given to meet your needs, but you are there to meet your spouse's needs. Humility is having a spirit for others. Frustration builds because we are focused on what is being done or not being done for us. That's pride, not humility.

Help one another. Most people would say that marriage is a 50/50 relationship, with each partner giving half. Marriage has some compromise after all, right? This kind of mindset is a recipe for disappointment. Unless you are willing to give yourself 100% to your spouse, you are not fulfilling your God-given role.

Think of a neighborhood with houses close together. Many will share a lawn if their yard connects. My parents had a home like this. I would mow our yard and follow the fence line where the yard line was. After I mowed the lawn, our side looked nice, but the neighbors' looked like it needed work. Before too long, I'd look out to see that their lawn had been mown, too. You take care of your job, and your spouse will be more motivated to do their part as well. When you give up, your spouse will be stirred to do the same.

Give honor. It doesn't matter what you think your spouse deserves, but what is commanded by God. I Peter 3:7 says, *"Likewise, ye husbands, dwell with them according to knowledge, giving honour unto the wife, as unto the weaker vessel, and as being heirs together of the grace of life; that your prayers be not hindered."* Honor is not earned, it is given. I must give myself to know my wife, respect her, and seek to understand her needs. Your effort shouldn't be just what you do to impress or win your spouse, but to understand them better and live to meet those needs. Ask God for wisdom as you live for the mate He has given you. James 1:5 promises that God will guide you by wisdom if you ask. Be willing to listen and learn. If something is wrong, you should be the first to see it and ready to listen instead of jumping to "your side of the story." Be careful with how you speak as you work through times of hurting and healing. Let your words be spoken with grace, instead of in the flesh, as you work through problems.

—— Today's Truth ——

God gives a prescription for healing. Hurt doesn't have to continue to grow. Your marriage is too important to let it fail.

Marriage Series: Part 5—Storms

Read Isaiah 15–21

EVERY MARRIAGE HAS its rough patches. When you fly in a plane, you don't expect turbulence to come, but without warning, it often arrives. Sometimes, it's mild. Sometimes, it makes you fear for your life. The great news is that, in marriage, God has given you a partner to go with you through that turbulence. You don't have to go through it alone, although that may be the case for some. Suffering is hard, but it's more difficult when you're alone. As a Christian, you are never alone with the presence of the Lord in your life, and in marriage you have companionship through the fiery trials of life.

My attraction toward my wife began when we were in high school. We were always good friends, but one day, it was like a light switch flipped on and I realized what an incredible young lady she was. From that moment, I knew almost instantaneously that she was the one I wanted to marry. During the ensuing years, I can recall several times when she and her siblings came to school with bloodshot eyes from tears they had shed when their father was severely ill. I wanted to help, but I felt helpless. When we got married, I was able to witness firsthand the hurt that she faced watching her father and sister go through serious health issues. At times, I have been the one going through the fire, and she had a similar experience. Whether it is you, your spouse, or even both of you going through a struggle, we have guidance from God's Word as we endure these times of testing.

Give encouragement. The saying goes, "Hurting people hurt people." Job's wife was likely a godly lady. However, her only words that the Bible records was when she lashed out at her husband in a season of despair and told him, *"Curse God and die"* (Job 2:9). Don't belittle what your spouse is going through, even if you are hurting, too. What everyone needs in the midst of the valley is someone standing beside them speaking words of hope. This isn't the time to point out all of their flaws, nor is it the time to load them up with more work. Find ways to be encouraging by what you say and what you do. Even if you're the one feeling the heat, encourage yourself in the Lord for your sake and for your mate.

Endure together. One of the things I've admired most about my in-laws is how the greatest seasons of hardship they went through as a family brought them closer together. They determined that they weren't going to draw farther apart in the storm, but that they would huddle together. Pray together. Read the Bible together. Spend extra time just sitting down and talking with one another. Listen to music together. Your spouse might need some time to himself/herself with the Lord or to grieve, but you can be there for them. It has been said that the greatest ability is availability.

Lighten the load. Galatians 6:2 tells us, *"Bear ye one another's burdens...."* If my wife sees that I'm overwhelmed and stressed (she can read me like a book), she will do little things to relieve the tension. She may take the kids on a drive if I'm working from home, get me a coffee, or make my favorite dessert (after all, the way to a man's heart is through his stomach, right?). On the other hand, I may book her an appointment at a nail salon, take the kids so she can take a nap, or take care of dinner for her. It doesn't have to be the biggest burden, but helping your spouse in the smallest way can take weight off their shoulders.

Determine to finish. God's grace is sufficient. God's Word is enough. Prayer is powerful. The Holy Spirit will help. There is no reason that your trial has to win. Whatever storms you may face personally or together as a couple, make the commitment to God that you will make it through. I John 4:4 tells us, *"greater is he that is in you, than he that is in the world."* With God's help, you can make it through anything. This is why Christ must be the foundation and center of your home. Without you, we really can do nothing. Defeat is never an option. The devil doesn't have to win. You can have victory!

—— Today's Truth ——

Through every storm that life may bring, God has given you a mate in marriage to be a help to one another through the tough times. Look for God's strength and wisdom to navigate through the storms so you can reach the other side.

Perfect Peace

Read Isaiah 22–26

THE BOOK OF Isaiah is written from the prophet to the people of Judah. This book mirrors the Bible, having 66 books, and picturing the Messiah more than any of the prophets. Isaiah lived about 700 years before Christ, yet God used Him to warn Judah of judgment if they continued in their rebellion, and to set their eyes on the future promise of God's plan for them. A prophet is like a preacher. Isaiah was a messenger of God sent to the people to preach His Word. Change never comes by trying to reason with people. Real change takes place when the Bible is preached!

Our world is chaotic. However, chaos, judgment, and destruction are still all around us in this life. God's people don't have to live in fear or worry during times of distress. What is causing stress in your life doesn't have to be what's going on in the world around you; it may be something going on in your life personally. God has the solution for the Christian who is uneasy, worried, and even afraid. Isaiah 26:3–4 states, *"Thou wilt keep him in perfect peace, whose mind is stayed on thee: because he trusteth in thee. Trust ye in the LORD for every: for in the LORD JEHOVAH is everlasting strength."*

Focusing on your problem, stressing about your situation, or consuming yourself with your burden doesn't fix what you may be going through. Like the great hymn goes:

> *Turn your eyes upon Jesus,*
> *Look full in His wonderful face,*
> *And the things of earth will grow strangely dim,*
> *In the light of His glory and grace.*

——Today's Truth ——

Get your heart and mind focused on the Lord, and He will give you peace in this life. The result of setting your eyes on Him is that you will trust Him. You remember who He is and what He can do, and so you realize you can trust Him.

Spiritual Slumber

Read Isaiah 27–31

I HAVE MANY stories from Bible college about sleep. Every semester, like clockwork, I slept through my first class or two at some point. It happened just once per semester, but it happened every semester. I guess it doesn't matter how loud or obnoxious your alarm is when you reach complete exhaustion. One thing that drove me crazy about college roommates was those who constantly slept through their classes. I'm not talking about sickness or an occasional period of exhaustion, but as a constant, sometimes daily, occurrence. I did not want to waste my time and money by having to retake classes because I simply couldn't wake up in time to attend.

In the short time we have been given on this earth, many Christians are asleep spiritually. Isaiah 29:10 speaks of the deep sleep that God's people were in spiritually, unaware of their current state and oblivious to their foolish decisions. They were blind to the realities around them. This state of spiritual slumber is a dangerous place in the Christian life.

When you are spiritually asleep, you are not productive. Nothing gets done. Like the employee that sleeps on the job, the Christian lies idle while souls are going to hell, the next generation lacks godly teachers, and the truths of God's Word grow quiet. Spiritual slumber causes Christians to miss those opportunities, and you will never have another chance to reclaim the times you missed to please the Lord.

On the other hand, much gets done while Christians are asleep spiritually. Satan goes into overdrive, like a power play for a hockey team; he sees his mismatch and takes advantage of the opportunity.

—— Today's Truth ——

God's people need a wakeup call. Too much needs to be done for God, and Satan is going full throttle. We must get serious about this life, while taking every opportunity to make a difference for eternity.

Facing Your Fears

Read Isaiah 32–37

MUCH OF ISAIAH's prophecy centers around Judah's fall to the Assyrians. Chapters 36 and 37 give the history behind the attack and God's deliverance to the people in this time. Sennacherib, king of Assyria, had already conquered Israel (the northern kingdom), and now he was going through Judah (the southern kingdom), which led him to the capital, Jerusalem. His army now stood at the door of Jerusalem, threatening those in the city with the same fate. The leaders who spoke with the Assyrian general told him to speak in his own language instead of speaking in the language of the Jews, probably fearing that his threatening and taunting words would cause a panic among the Jewish people if they heard him.

Fear is a powerfully motivating tool of the enemy. President Roosevelt spoke in the middle of Great Depression and made the famous statement: "The only thing we have to fear is fear itself." At the end of the day, God kept Jerusalem safe and the Assyrian army was found dead outside of the city walls. God's people learned that there was no reason to be afraid after all, because the Lord was there to take care of them.

Learning to overcome your fear doesn't mean that life will always go your way, but rather that regardless of the circumstances, you have nothing to fear in this life. If you let fear guide you, you'd never go to work because of the fear of getting into a car accident. You'd never attempt to accomplish anything because of the fear of failing. Fear will control your life if you let it, and that's exactly what the enemy was trying to do in Isaiah 36. As the army general questioned, mocked, and threatened the Jews, he tried to use fear as a tool to get them to quit without a fight. Fear didn't win in that situation, and it doesn't have to win with you.

——Today's Truth——

Fears abound, but you don't have to give in to the fear.

A Message of Comfort

Read Isaiah 38–42

THE BOOK OF Isaiah is like a little Bible. It has sixty-six chapters like the Bible has sixty-six books, and its themes are divided much like the Bible as a whole. Chapters one to thirty-nine are predominately messages of judgment, ending with the prophecy of Babylon overtaking Judah. Similarly, the Bible has thirty-nine books in the Old Testament and a similar message of judgment. The final twenty-seven chapters of Isaiah are focused on the Messiah. They are messages of hope and comfort, similar to the like the message of hope and comfort of salvation through Jesus that is presented in the twenty-seven books of the New Testament.

Whenever I present the gospel, I always begin with the bad news. No one is perfect (Romans 3:10). We are all sinners (Romans 3:23). Sin deserves a punishment (Romans 6:23a). The payment for our sins is hell (Revelation 20:14–15). Then comes the good news! I will often say at this point, "Now, if I left today, I've only discouraged you. I've told you how bad you are and you can do nothing to right your wrongs except go to hell forever. But…here's the good news. This is where Jesus comes in (Romans 6:23b; Romans 5:8; Romans 10:9, 13)."

God told Isaiah to preach a message of comfort to His people. Isaiah 40:1 says, *"Comfort ye, comfort ye my people, saith your God."* The message of comfort doesn't sound like this: "Everything's going to work itself out," "It's going to be fine," "good things happen to good people." The message of comfort is the message of Jesus!

I once heard about a man who stopped to watch a Little League baseball game. He asked one of the youngsters what the score was. "We're losing 18-0," was the answer. "Well," said the man. "I must say you don't look discouraged." "Discouraged?" the boy replied, puzzled. "Why should we be discouraged? We haven't been up to bat yet."

—— Today's Truth ——

Discouragement and depression is all around us, and the message of the comfort of Jesus must be proclaimed. Share it today!

ONE GREAT TRUTH FOR YOUR DAILY WALK | 233

AUGUST 9

You Don't Have to Be Afraid

Read Isaiah 43–46

PEOPLE DO CRAZY stuff when they're afraid. A grown man will scream like a girl. People will wipe out the toilet paper in stores. When you're afraid, you do things you wouldn't normally do because fear kicks in and the survival instinct we all possess cares about nothing except getting past what we fear. What keeps you up at night? Is it the thought that your days are numbered and life is ending sooner than you'd hoped? Is it the stress of failure? Is it a person or a problem? God's message to Isaiah in chapter 43 and verse 1 was simple: *"Fear not."* But God didn't just tell Isaiah to "Suck it up, buttercup." He gave Isaiah good reasons for why he didn't have to live in fear. In Isaiah 41:10, God gave Isaiah five reasons to overcome fear.

"I am with thee." God was with Daniel in the lion's den. God was with the Israelites as they marched around Jericho. God was with David as he faced Goliath. God was with Abraham when he left his home. When you live in God's will, you live in God's presence, and you will face nothing that God won't stay by your side as you endure it.

"I am thy God." Your companion isn't a crutch or just a body to keep you company. Your companionship is with God Almighty! He's not a god, He's the only true God, and He's the reason you don't have to live in fear.

"I will strengthen thee." At times, you will feel your strength is not enough. This is where God's strength comes in. God won't do the work for you, but He will give you the strength you need to make it through.

"I will help thee." Whatever the need, God is there to help. Help can vary based on the need, and God has every resource at His disposal to help you overcome.

"I will uphold thee." He will hold you up, sustain you, and support you. To put it simply, God will take care of you.

—— Today's Truth ——

For all the reasons you may be afraid of your circumstances, God has the solution for you to escape living a life of fear.

Glory Goes to God

Read Isaiah 47–51

IF YOU COULD earn your salvation, then you could glory in the fact that you earned it. If God allowed sin to lead to a blessed life, then sin would get the glory for your prosperity. Only one deserves to receive the glory for anything good that happens in life, for God is the reason that any good thing happens in life. God declares in Isaiah 48:11, *"I will not give my glory unto another."* To give glory speaks of acknowledging His greatness and giving Him honor through worship and praise. It is right, it is fair, and it is true.

We are created for His glory. Revelation 4:11 states, *"Thou art worthy, O Lord, to receive glory and honour and power: for thou hast created all things, and for thy pleasure they are and were created."* Imagine inventing something that doesn't do what you want it to do, tells people that someone else made it, and that it was created for a different purpose—yet that is what humans often do to God. We are alive today for God's glory!

We are commanded to give Him glory. I Chronicles 16:28 says, *"give unto the Lord glory and strength."* We sing to give Him glory. We serve to give Him glory. Everything with our lives and with our lips should be directed to give glory to the Father.

We are cautioned to not give glory to another. The text verse makes it clear that God will not tolerate anyone or anything stealing His glory. No false god, no person, and no temporal pleasure should take away from His glory. It is blasphemous for anyone to think they deserve to receive glory. Not LeBron James, not Beyoncé, not Jeff Bezos…no one, no matter what they've accomplished, has the right to receive God's glory.

Jonathan Edwards said it this way, "From time to time [in Scripture], embracing and practicing true religion, and repenting of sin, and turning to holiness, is expressed by glorifying God, as though that were the sum and end of the whole matter."

—— Today's Truth ——

Do not allow anyone else to receive glory, but direct all glory in your life to the Lord, for He alone deserves it!

Little Wrath

Read Isaiah 52–57

ONE OF TWO things will happen if you choose to live a life away from God, a life sold out to sin. Either you will wake up on your own, turn to God, repent and ask forgiveness, or God will have to get your attention. In Isaiah 54:7, the Lord says, *"For a small moment have I forsaken thee...."* God is ready and waiting for us when we return, but while we're living it up in the world, He will remove Himself from us so that we do not feel His presence anymore.

The Bible is filled with stories of people like Saul, Lot, Absalom, and Judas whose lives were taken because they were too prideful to wake up and get right with God. Then there are those like Peter, Jonah, Paul, and David who made great mistakes, endured hard seasons without God's presence, but changed their course, got right with God, and received His mercy.

Isaiah 54:8 tells us, *"In a little wrath I hid my face from thee for a moment...."* You must understand that if God wanted to pour out His wrath on you, there would be no second chances. You would be consumed like we read about in Revelation concerning the Great Tribulation. It is "little wrath," because it's just enough to get you to feel the heat, understand the severity of the situation, and wake up before you're consumed by your own foolishness. The little wrath is your wake-up call to get right while you still can.

The latter part of that verse continues, *"but with everlasting kindness will I have mercy on thee, saith the LORD thy Redeemer."* Better to endure the little wrath and get right so you can experience His glorious mercy than to continue in your foolish ways and forever miss out on God's goodness.

—— Today's Truth ——

God may show a little wrath to get your attention, but it is only because He desires to give you everlasting mercy.

The Darker the Night, the Brighter the Light

Read Isaiah 58–63

THE WORLD IS not getting better as a whole. People are still getting saved and will continue to get saved until Jesus returns and even during the tribulation. However, the world as a whole is getting worse and worse, not better and better. The situation appears to be bleak, but there is still cause to press on and live for God.

Isaiah 60:1 says, *"Arise, shine; for thy light is come, and the glory of the LORD is risen upon thee."* One cannot shine until he has light personally. Jesus is the Light, and everyone must accept His sacrifice on the cross for their eternal payment in order to receive Him as their Saviour. A result of being saved is that Jesus shines His light through you, but you cannot have the light without the source. A light bulb is worthless without electricity. Likewise, a human being is useless without Jesus Christ, and the only alternative to light is darkness. The reason for the darkness in our world today is the lack of Jesus Christ in people's hearts. That is the source of the problem.

After salvation, we are commanded to allow the light of Jesus to shine through our lives in every way that we can. I will never forget an occasion like this while my wife and I were dating in college. We were out to eat with family, and an older woman came over and said something like, "I just had to come by and compliment your beautiful girls (speaking of my girlfriend and her cousins). It's not often you see such beautiful girls, and on top of that they are all dressed appropriately and modestly." It's amazing to me how modesty is such a hot topic in churches. People don't want to be told how to dress, but this is just another area where the light of Jesus can shine through you.

—— Today's Truth ——

By simply dressing right, talking right, and conducting your life in a godly manner, the light of Jesus will shine and those around you will notice.

Filthy Rags

Read Isaiah 64–66

GOD COMMANDS US to do good works. All throughout Scripture you will find "do's" and "don'ts" from the Lord. Living according to the Bible means you do what God commands, like attending church, tithing, witnessing, praying, reading the Bible, and loving your neighbor. It also means you don't do what God has forbidden, like abstain from drugs, alcohol, fornication, adultery, lust, and other sins. The result of following God's commands is receiving God's blessing because God is pleased with you. God blesses obedient and faithful believers because it brings Him pleasure to watch us follow His leading and will.

Let me caution you in your thinking concerning your good works for the Lord. Just because God blessed you as a result of obeying Him doesn't mean that you deserved the reward. Our works may bring pleasure to the One who can meet all our needs, but it is only because God loves us that He meets our needs. If He didn't, we would still be lacking because we are nothing without Him.

Paul said it well in I Corinthians 15:10, *"But by the grace of God I am what I am…."* God's grace is the reason for any success and usefulness in our lives. It has nothing to do with our works. It has everything to do with His grace. Jeremiah states in Lamentations 3:22, *"It is of the LORD's mercies that we are not consumed, because his compassions fail not."* God's mercy is another reason that our head is kept above water. We think we've earned much by our works, and that is true. Our sinful works are just as real, and they are just as deserving of a "reward." We praise God for His mercy because we would be consumed if it weren't for His compassion.

—— Today's Truth ——

Isaiah 64:6 calls our righteousness "filthy rags." They are worthless and meaningless. Without God, our works mean nothing. We don't deserve the credit, but rather lean on His grace and mercy.

God's Perfect Plan for You

Read Jeremiah 1–3

MARK TWAIN SAID, "There are two days that are important in a man's life—the day he was born, and the day he finds out why." God has a plan for every life, and it should be the goal of every life to live according to that plan. God said in Jeremiah 1:5, *"Before I formed thee in the belly I knew thee; and before thou camest forth out of the womb I sanctified thee, and I ordained thee a prophet unto the nations."* The will of God predates your birth and postdates your death. Not only has God created all lives, but God has also created a perfect plan for every life to be used in the greatest way possible and to receive the greatest joy. You want God's plan for your life!

I always knew that God had a plan for my life, but I never knew what it was until April 8, 2008, when I surrendered to be a preacher at a Missions Conference at my home church under the preaching of Evangelist Rob Hicks. I will never forget that day that I said yes to God's plan for me. I still didn't know the details, but I knew that I wanted whatever God had prepared for me. You may not know everything about God's plan for you, but you can trust that He has a plan, and His plan is the best plan for you.

An amazing thing happens to those who surrender to God's will. God doesn't just show you the plan, but He also equips you to fulfill it. In the verse to follow, God tells Jeremiah how He will give him the words and He will be with him as he follows the plan for His life. I cannot do it in my own power, and I must look to Him to show me the plan and to fulfill it.

——Today's Truth——

Your life was created with a purpose. God gave you life to fulfill His perfect will, and it is your duty to submit yourself to His will and lean on His strength to guide you to fulfill the perfect plan He has prepared for you.

The Old Paths

Read Jeremiah 4–6

PEOPLE IN OUR society are bent on tearing down the heritage of our country. They find fault in people of the past (news flash: all people have faults), and they want to demonize these people by tearing down their statues, removing them from textbooks so they won't be talked about, and do what they can to erase their history. People like this have no appreciation for what has been handed down from men and women of the past. Everything in our day is about a "new way."

Jeremiah 6:16 says, *"Thus saith the LORD, Stand ye in the ways, and see, and ask for the old paths, where is the good way, and walk therein, and ye shall find rest for your souls. But they said, We will not walk therein."* In our modern era of churches, a similar trend is taking place. The baton has been passed down to younger preachers, and many are trying to reinvent the wheel. Soul winning is being replaced with social causes. Music style is changing, and as a result, the atmosphere for the service is changing drastically too. Churches are now dark concert halls. Attire is becoming more and more casual in an attempt not to "intimidate" visitors. The bus ministry is becoming a thing of the past because it's too inconvenient. Preaching is all about love with little being said about holiness and sanctification.

I will be the first to admit that some of what we do is tradition, but a reason we learn and love the work of those in the past is because they paved a way to continue doing God's work in a great way. I don't apologize for being proud of the old paths that were set before me!

——Today's Truth ——

The old paths are times to learn from, sacrifices to appreciate, and strengths to carry on for future generations.

Cut Off Your Hair

Read Jeremiah 7–10

As you read the Bible, you will find that parts of the Bible seemingly don't make sense. Remember, if you don't understand something, it's either because God didn't make that thing clear enough because you don't need to really understand it all, or it just requires some study to find out what He's talking about. Parts of Revelation are left up to conjecture. God makes some things clear like the gospel, the church, the family, etc. However, other subjects are not so clear.

God's judgment is preached to Judah by Jeremiah in much of this book. In the midst of the message in Jeremiah 7, God commands in verse 29, *"Cut off thine hair, O Jerusalem…."* This seems like an odd request, but there is reason for this command. The Lord makes it clear that He is done playing games, and it is time for judgment. In verse 16, the Lord doubles down, *"Therefore pray not thou for this people, neither lift up cry nor prayer for them, neither make intercession to me: for I will not hear thee."* God's wrath is going to be poured out to this people, and cutting the hair was a sign of God's favor being removed from His people.

First is the Nazarite's vow not to cut their hair (Numbers 6:5). The long hair was a sign of God's favor on them. When Samson's hair was cut, God's favor was removed from Him. The cutting of hair or the pulling of a man's beard was also a symbol of mourning. In Jeremiah 7:29, God continues, *"and cast it away, and take up a lamentation on high places; for the LORD hath rejected and forsaken the generation of his wrath."* He wanted them to make it known that their time was over, and judgment day was coming.

—— Today's Truth ——

While we serve the God of second chances, we must not assume God's willingness to forgive means that His wrath won't come. Israel was playing games with God, and Christians must learn to not play around with sin. Get it right, and forsake it.

Leadership

Read Jeremiah 11–14

IT HAS BEEN said, "Everything rises and falls on leadership." If the home isn't right, it's not the child's fault; it is the parents' responsibility as the leaders of the home. Leaders have to accept their position of leadership and take sole responsibility for their duties.

Jeremiah 12:10 says, *"Many pastors have destroyed my vineyard, they have trodden my portion under foot, they have made my pleasant portion a desolate wilderness."* Jeremiah 2:8 says in similar fashion, *"the pastors transgressed against me."* While the people had their faults, God doesn't hold back on calling out the pastors who failed to keep to the right paths.

I understand the great responsibility that I have as a pastor. I will answer to God for the way that I lead Regency Baptist Church. Even though people come and go, it is my responsibility to be a godly leader. What area of leadership do you hold? It may be a class, your home, workers you have been set over, etc. If nothing else, you have responsibility over your own life, and God will hold you accountable for that.

I read of a little boy who asked his mother, "Can I go outside and help Daddy put snow chains on the car? I know all the words."

People are watching you, but people are also dependent upon you. You may not understand the weight of the responsibility that you hold, but one day when God holds you responsible, it may be too late to wake up.

—— Today's Truth ——

God gives leadership in different forms, and it is every person's duty to fulfill that God-given role and to conduct your life and lead those who follow you in a godly manner. More is at stake than you may realize.

Going Backwards

Read Jeremiah 15–18

A MAN WAS watching the news one night when it was reported that a car was going the wrong direction on the freeway. The man knew his wife was on that freeway and became very concerned, so he called her cell phone. When she answered, he warned, "Dear, there's one car going in the wrong direction on the freeway." She exclaimed, "One car? There's hundreds of them!"

Many Christians are going the wrong way on their journey through this life. Instead of going forward for the Lord, they are going backwards. Jeremiah 15:6 says, *"Thou hast forsaken me, saith the LORD, thou art gone backward...."*

The only healthy direction in the Christian life is to go forward. Throughout the book of Jeremiah, the preacher pleads with the people to turn back and return to the Lord, yet they remained in their backwards state. J. Vernon McGee gives this example about backslidden and backwards Christians: "When I was a boy, I helped a rancher load heifers in a wagon. We'd try to get the little old fellow up the ramp, and he'd stiffen his front feet and brace himself so you couldn't move him up. Usually he'd slip back. That's backsliding in the Bible. It means to refuse to go God's way—refusing to listen to Him. Pretty soon, you'll start moving backwards and get farther and farther from God. God asked Israel to return to Him and they wouldn't. As a result, they went into captivity."

In Jeremiah 15:6, the Lord continues, *"therefore will I stretch out my hand against thee, and destroy thee; I am weary with repenting."* God is tired of disciplining His children who are going backwards. He would much rather bless your life and give you favor. However, God will not allow His name to be dragged through the filth of sin.

—— Today's Truth ——

Get your life headed in a direction where you are growing in grace and moving forward in your walk with the Lord.

Tingled or Tickled?

Read Jeremiah 19–22

PREACHING IS NOT motivational speaking. Preaching is not a pat on the back as you continue on your path. Preaching is not a discussion time. Preaching is not for casual listening. Preaching is not noise in the background. Preaching is God's message given to God's people by God's man. Preaching is powerful. Preaching changes people. Preaching convicts the heart. Preaching calls out sin. Preaching encourages the Christian to live for God. Preaching lifts up the true God and tears down false gods. Preaching is centered around Jesus.

Preaching isn't given to tickle your ears like a dog seeks from his master. I Timothy 4:3 tells us, *"For the time will come when they will not endure sound doctrine; but after their own lusts shall they heap to themselves teachers, having itching ears; And they shall turn away their ears from the truth, and shall be turned unto fables."* The flesh likes preaching that is soft, preaching that doesn't touch sin, and preaching that soothes. It is the lusts of men that like this kind of preaching, but it's not the preaching our world needs or the preaching you need.

God told Jeremiah 19:4, *"Thus saith the LORD of hosts, the God of Israel; Behold, I will bring evil upon this place, the which whosoever heareth, his ears shall tingle."* Preaching isn't supposed to be comfortable; it is supposed to be helpful. What Israel needed wasn't a time of sharing, but the man of God to stand up and let it rip! You don't see change from a soft message. Change comes with a Bible message that pricks the heart and causes the ears to the tingle instead of being tickled. Every Christian should love hard, meat-filled, Bible-based, confrontational, convicting, and Spirit-filled preaching! You should crave it and receive it when it is given.

—— Today's Truth ——

Preaching that helps is preaching that convicts. Open your heart to receive this kind of preaching, as long as it is biblically sound, and allow it to change your heart and affect your life.

Two Baskets of Figs

Read Jeremiah 23–25

I HAVE LIVED in California my whole life. I have been part of a great church, attended Bible college, and immediately went into the ministry. I love what God has given me in California, and I remember praying often asking the Lord if it was His will to keep me in California because I really didn't want to go anywhere else. I was willing to, but if it was up to me, I'd stay in this state. However, if you talk to someone from the Midwest, they think people from California are just all fruits and nuts. That's not all that's in California, though. You can find great churches and godly Christians in this state.

God recognized that not all of Israel turned against Him. In Jeremiah 24, God gives Jeremiah a parable of two baskets of figs. One basket had good figs, the other had bad figs. One was ripe and ready to be used. One was so bad that it was useless. In this passage, God gives His twofold purpose for Israel's captivity. For the good figs, the believers who had not left the Lord, would have God's presence and help in their captivity. They would grow and be used. God would teach them and build them in this process. There was hope for them, and they were able to be used. The bad figs would be destroyed, forgotten, and deemed worthless.

You may live in the darkness of the world around you, but if you choose to live a life surrendered to God, then He will use the darkness for your good. You will feel His presence, you will grow in times of pressure, and you will have a heart to know Him. You don't have to give up just because the world seems lost all around you.

—— Today's Truth ——

God deals with everyone as individuals. You are not punished because your neighbors live in sin. God will deal with you based on your decisions and whether you draw nigh to God or whether you leave God in exchange for this world.

AUGUST 21

The Message of a Martyr

Read Jeremiah 26–28

MISSIONARY JIM ELIOT gives us one of the great examples of preaching the good news of the gospel to the ends of the earth, regardless of the consequences. He believed so deeply that all people needed to hear the saving message of Jesus Christ that he left his home in American and flew to Ecuador in South America. For three years, Jim and a handful of others prepared to reach people in their native language and hopefully see their lives transformed. However, God placed another tribe, the Aucas, on Jim Eliot's heart. They were a violent people. They killed many of the Quichuas, but Eliot's team believed the killing would stop if the Aucas had Jesus in their lives. They carefully and slowly attempted to make gradual contact by bringing gifts and building a tree house near the shore. They met a man that they tried to use as a mediator to gain access to the people of the Auca tribe. However, shortly after their arrival, they were met on the beach one day by Aucas who killed all five missionaries. Mrs. Eliot, her daughter, and the sister of one of the other martyrs went back to the Auca people, and God opened the door for them to reach many of them with the gospel.

Jeremiah 26 ends with a prophet, Urijah, who died for the message that he preached. He gave God's message regardless of the consequences to his own life. Some would say his life was taken, but God's Word makes it clear that his life, and the lives of others like Jim Eliot, are not wasted when they make the ultimate sacrifice for the Word of God to be preached. Jim Eliot made the statement, "He is no fool who gives up what he cannot keep to gain that which he cannot lose." We know little of this kind of persecution in America, but even if we faced this kind of response, nothing should be worthy of quieting the voices of God's people!

—— Today's Truth ——

No matter how people respond, you can be sure that God will bless those who are faithful to obey His command.

An Expected End

Read Jeremiah 29–31

IN JEREMIAH 29, GOD gives a message to the remnant that has been faithful as they prepare for captivity. God reminds them that He has a plan for them, and just because they are going to be taken does not mean that they are forgotten. Jeremiah 29:10–11 says, *"For thus saith the LORD, That after seventy years be accomplished at Babylon I will visit you, and perform my good word toward you, in causing you to return to this place. For I know the thoughts that I think toward you, saith the LORD, thoughts of peace, and not of evil, to give you an expected end."* After the seventy years of captivity in Babylon, there is hope for Israel as we see Zerubbabel and Ezra lead the rebuilding of the temple and Nehemiah lead the rebuilding of the wall around Jerusalem. However, while in Babylon, little hope can be seen. It appears that nothing but discouragement is waiting for them. They will be under the wicked rule of sin all around them, but God gives them hope of the "expected end" that He has promised them.

Like everything else, God gives this assurance that no matter what hardship you may be facing, it will pass. God promises restoration for His people—some in this life, and some in eternity. This "expected end" speaks of the assurance we have as Christians that defeat is never a possibility, enemies will never prevail, and you don't have to be afraid. David Gibbs, Jr., said it this way, "Following the plan that God has for your life will not always be easy, but contentment, peace, fulfillment, and purpose will be the end result if you do."

—— Today's Truth ——

Though you may feel that you are experiencing a never-ending season as a captive to pain and discouragement, remember that God has not forgotten about you. He sees where you are, and He has a plan for your future.

AUGUST 23

Investing in God's Real Estate

Read Jeremiah 32–33

NOTHING ABOUT REAL estate is simple. The housing market and the transaction of purchasing or selling property is about as complicated and as unpredictable as it can get. When my wife and I rented our first apartment, we signed our names on a few lines, and that was it. When we were able to purchase our first home, we signed more pages and documents than I ever expected. And for all I know, we could have signed our lives away, but there was no way I was going to read every word or study every page. I remember the biggest fear that I had was whether or not we were making the right decision. Would our home increase in value over time? Would maintenance and emergencies that come with being a homeowner be too much to bear?

Jeremiah was offered a piece of land by his cousin, Hanameel. Read the twenty-fifth chapter of Leviticus, and you'll find how land is transferred to family first and what is entailed in the process. It is quite detailed. However, this property is about to be worthless in a short time because Babylon is in the process of invading Judah, camped on the property in Anathoth that Jeremiah is about to buy. Jeremiah is imprisoned, and his message is a promise of Jerusalem's destruction. This doesn't sound like a very wise or logical decision to buy property at this point, but the Lord told Jeremiah to do it; so that's exactly what Jeremiah did. This may seem like a waste of money to some, but not to God.

God's commands may not always make sense to you, but something is waiting in the future that you will not witness if you don't listen. God promised to restore Jerusalem and His people, and this could be the sign that He would do so. Whatever His reason, Jeremiah had faith that God had purpose in this command.

——Today's Truth——

Following God's leading when you see no logic in the command requires faith that God has a plan. Investing in God's market will always pay off.

The Indestructability of the Bible

Read Jeremiah 34–36

KING JEHOIAKIM ATTEMPTED an impossible feat. Because he didn't like what God's Word said that was given through Jeremiah, he attempted to burn the Bible and destroy God's Word. Jesus said in Matthew 5:18, *"For verily I say unto you, Till heaven and earth pass, one jot or one tittle shall in no wise pass from the law, till all be fulfilled."* Since the beginning of time, Satan has attacked the Word of God. In fact, Satan's first recorded words in Scripture were an attack on God's Word, *"Yea, hath God said..."* (Genesis 3:1).

In the first three centuries following the resurrection, Christians faced especially severe persecution from Roman Emperors. Diocletian had also attempted the impossible feat of wiping out Christians. He killed so many Christians and destroyed so many Bibles that he actually thought he had been successful when he heard nothing from Christians or found any evidence of a remnant of God's Word for a season. He boasted in himself and had a medal inscribed with the words, "The Christian religion is destroyed and the worship of gods restored." He, of course, soon found that he had failed.

After the Roman Catholic church was in full strength, the Bible was forbidden; those found with a copy in their possession was tortured and persecuted. Though I don't agree with his Calvinist theology, Arthur W. Pink stated, "Books are like men—dying creatures. A very small percentage of books survive more than twenty years, a yet smaller percentage last a hundred years and only a very insignificant fraction represent those which have lived a thousand years. Amid the wreck and ruin of ancient literature, the Holy Scriptures stand out like the last survivor of an otherwise extinct race, and the very fact of the Bible's continued existence is an indication that, like its Author, it is indestructible."

—— Today's Truth ——

No matter the opposition, God's Word will stand!

Calling 9-1-1

Read Jeremiah 37–40

IF THERE IS a problem, it is usually the worst-case scenario when you have to call 9-1-1. That is who you call when the situation is out of your hands or you don't know what to do or you're not capable of doing what needs to be done. That call is the last resort. Jeremiah 37 shows King Zedekiah making his emergency call to Jeremiah to pray to God for help. This king might not have been as wicked as his predecessors, but he was no godly leader. God's response was that Egypt's aid would not come in time, nor would God deliver them from the hand of the Chaldeans (King Nebuchadnezzar and Babylon). The problem wasn't that Zedekiah went to ask God for help, but the fact that he looked to God as his last resort instead of his first option.

Ask yourself this: "Is prayer your steering wheel or your spare tire?" God is not just there for a lifeline when nothing else seems to work itself out. He is there for support every step of the way. Even when there's not an emergency, you still need to be on your knees seeking wisdom, power of the Holy Spirit, direction for your day, and His presence in everything you do.

Isn't it true that all of the emergencies that draw us to God are selfish? Only when the emergency affects us in some way do we go to the Lord as our last resort. There is an urgency every day to go to God in prayer, even if it's not an emergency that you notice. God deserves more from us than to be treated like a 9-1-1 operator that you talk to once every blue moon.

—— Today's Truth ——

God wants to be in your life for more than just your emergencies. Make prayer your first option in every situation, and you will see God bless you because you put Him first.

Move Slowly

Read Jeremiah 41–44

W E LIVE IN a fast-paced society. We like our cars to get us from point A to point B as quickly as possible. We expect packages to arrive promptly within twenty-four hours of purchase, because who actually pays for shipping these days? However, our culture shouldn't always translate into our spiritual lives and the decisions we make.

After the desecration at Mizpah in chapter 41, the leaders and people came to Jeremiah unlike they had done in many years. They came to seek direction from the Lord. They had reached their end and, without any hope in sight, they sought an answer. It takes hitting rock bottom before some will come humbly before the Lord to seek His face.

Jeremiah responds in 42:4, *"Then Jeremiah the prophet said unto them, I have heard you; behold, I will pray unto the LORD your God according to your words; and it shall come to pass, that whatsoever thing the LORD shall answer you, I will declare it unto you; I will keep nothing back from you."* Jeremiah didn't answer them the way that he saw fit. He did not want to give them direction until he received clarity from the Lord.

I believe this principle must apply to every area of life. We are on the move way too much as Americans, and we make decisions in haste. Move slowly when making life decisions. Do not move your family for a job that pays better. That is never the right reason to move. Move slowly, seek His face, and make sure that job is from the Lord, that the move is His will. We have so few who have been serving in areas of ministry for over a decade because they can't stay in one place long enough to reach that milestone. Moving isn't always bad, but without the Lord behind it, you can be sure it won't turn out how you expect.

—— Today's Truth ——

Move slowly to make decisions in life. Take time to pray, seek counsel, and seek direction in God's Word. Move only when God makes the path clear.

I Brought You In, I Can Take You Out

Read Jeremiah 45–48

Y ou've heard the saying, "If momma ain't happy, ain't no-body happy." We attribute a lot of sayings to fathers and mothers. One that I find humorous that we've all heard is when a mother tells her children, "I brought you into this world, and I can take you out." That saying is exclusive to mothers, because every dad knows that all women deserve a gold star in Heaven for enduring child birth. The Lord makes a similar point in this passage. Jeremiah 45:4 says, *"Thus shalt thou say unto him, The LORD saith thus; Behold, that which I have built will I break down, and that which I have planted I will pluck up, even this whole land."*

This realization should remind every believer about the power and authority of God. This is why it bothers me to hear people take God's name in vain because they stubbed their toe or refer to God as something as irreverent as "the Man upstairs." He is to be praised, obeyed, prayed to, and worshipped because He possesses all authority and all power.

With this understanding, we also turn our dependence upon His strength and not our own. Verse 5 continues, *"And seekest thou great things for thyself? seek them not: for, behold, I will bring evil upon all flesh, saith the LORD...."* People will fail you, and your strength will fail you too. It is God and God alone who has the ability you need. Imagine a glove in your hand. Without the hand, the glove is useless, but with the hand in the glove, the glove is able to do many things. It is the hand that acts and the hand that uses the glove, but the glove has purpose only when the hand fills the glove. Friend, you are the glove, and God is the hand. Without Him, your life is useless. You don't have the power to create life, nor do you have the power to create a great life. You must fill yourself with His Spirit in your life and rely upon Him to do great things through you.

—— Today's Truth ——

All power and authority belong to God. If you want to see real purpose in your life, you must rely upon His strength.

Dwell Deep

Read Jeremiah 49–50

I F YOU'VE EVER visited the ocean, you find that many beachgoers have something in common. Most of the people like to stay in the shallow water. They know the depths of the ocean hold great mysteries, and it takes a lot of effort and courage to reach the deepest parts of the ocean. Jeremiah 49:8 says, *"Flee ye, turn back, dwell deep, O inhabitants of Dedan; for I will bring the calamity of Esau upon him, the time that I will visit him."* F. B. Meyer said of this truth, "As originally spoken, these words summoned the people of Edom to seek the shadows of impenetrable forests, and retire into the secrecy of the caves and the dens of the rocks. The deeper their hiding place, the better it would be when the storm of invasion swept across the land." The shallows is common ground, but few will understand the peace, security, and strength of dwelling deep in the presence of God. Meyer gave the follow three thoughts as application to this truth:

Dwell deep in the peace of God. The people of Dedan would be destroyed when judgment came to Edom if they didn't dwell deep. Separating themselves from the evil and going to the place of God's instruction gave them peace.

Dwell deep in communion with God. Everything we do, we do to get close to God. Your motive shouldn't be what you get, but that you get to be close to God. James 4:8 says, "Draw nigh to God, and he will draw nigh to you."

Dwell deep in stillness of soul. Our busyness leads us to destruction if we do not take time to be still. Calm your spirit. Don't fret about it, but have faith through every problem you face.

—— Today's Truth ——

Wonderful blessings are found for Christians who learn to dwell deep with God. The world has too many shallow Christians who know nothing about being close to God. Determine to dwell deep.

God's Battle Axe

Read Jeremiah 51–52

A SOLDIER IS not prepared without weapons, and the weapons may differ depending on the skill set or duties of the soldier. Some may use a sniper rifle from afar, while others may use a weapon for closer combat; but when the battle comes, soldiers must have a weapon. No warrior goes to battle without one.

We are in a spiritual battle today, and God is a warrior for us in this fight. Ephesians 6:12 reminds us of this invisible war we are facing: *"For we wrestle not against flesh and blood, but against principalities, against powers, against the rulers of the darkness of this world, against spiritual wickedness in high places."* Like a warrior in battle, God has a weapon, and that weapon is you! Jeremiah 51:20 says, *"Thou art my battle axe and weapons of war: for with thee will I break in pieces the nations, and with thee will I destroy kingdoms."* The following several verses tell of what God will do "with thee" (His chosen weapon of war). You are His battle axe, and God wants to use you in this fight!

Perform an assessment of yourself and what kind of weapon you have presented yourself to be for the Lord's use? Are you sharp, constantly doing the work to sharpen the dull and weak areas of your life? Are you willing to be used, jumping at every opportunity to be used by the mighty hand of God? Or have you been content to sit on the shelf, collecting dust or even rust, or allowing yourself to remain dull in your spiritual walk? The Lord conveys to the people in this passage what He can do with them, and He can do the same with you! You can either be used of the Lord or under judgment from the Lord. You are the battle axe with which God has the ability to do great things, if only you willingly yield yourself to Him and allow Him to work in your life.

——Today's Truth ——

God has weapons in the battle we are in, and you are the weapon He uses often to do His powerful works. Present your life to Him as a willing soldier in this vital war!

A Funeral for a Nation

Read Lamentations 1–2

ONE OF MY least favorite gatherings is funerals. Some are very special, remembering the influence and meaning of a life. However, I don't enjoy the sorrow. It pains me to think of loved ones I'll never see again, and also to see families go through that same pain. Each one has been different in its own way, and all have had different circumstances surrounding the death of the individual. Still, these funerals were also all the same in some ways. They all involved great sorrow.

Lamentations is written as a funeral message for the nation of Israel. Lamentations 1:1 says, *"How doth the city sit solitary, that was full of people!"* The city of Jerusalem was once a city full of life, full of people, full of work, and full of prosperity. Now, it is a shell of what it used to be. Nothing looks the same. The prophet mourns as he thinks of what God created through His people and what He had to do because of their betrayal to His name. When you look back over a life, you think of how things used to be. Some look back and see more bad than good.

Everything good in this first chapter of Lamentations was a part of the past, and not the present. The excitement was gone, leaving behind only a memory of how things use to be. They are a walking shell of what they used to be. I know our church would be many times its size today if everyone who was once living for God was still living for God, but many have allowed themselves to die spiritually. They are a walking funeral in this walk with the Lord.

—— Today's Truth ——

The work of the Lord in a life brings you closer to God daily and creates growth in your life until the day you die. Continue in the grace of God daily so that you don't become a living funeral of a "has-been" Christian.

Is There Any Hope?

Read Lamentations 3–5

Y EARS AGO, AN S-4 submarine was rammed by a ship off the coast of Massachusetts. It sank immediately. The entire crew was trapped in a prison of death. Every effort was made to rescue the crew, but each effort ultimately failed. Near the end of the ordeal, a deep-sea diver, who was doing everything in his power to find a way to achieve the crew's release, thought he heard a tapping on the steel wall of the sunken sub. He placed his helmet up against the side of the vessel and realized it was Morse Code. He attached himself to the side and spelled out in his mind the message being tapped from within, over and over again. The question was: "Is - there - any - hope?"

It has been said that we can live forty days without food, eight days without water, four minutes without oxygen, but only a few minutes without hope. Lamentation describes a brokenhearted prophet who lost his hope, but in chapter 3, we see that hope renewed. Verse 21 reads, *"This I recall to my mind, therefore have I hope."* Our hope is based on what we think about. When you recall the truths about the Lord, your hope can be renewed, regardless of your circumstances.

God is the object of our hope. To have real hope requires something in which to have hope. Jeremiah is reminded of the mercy of God (v. 22), the goodness of God (v. 25), the longsuffering of God (v. 31), and a list of the many reasons to have hope. People, positions of power, and worldly prosperity cannot give hope. Your hope must rest in the Lord! It has been said, "There are no hopeless situations; there are only people who have grown hopeless about them."

——Today's Truth ——

Your hope will be challenged. It is when you remind yourself of your God who is above your problem that you will see there is always hope.

You Are What You Eat

Read Ezekiel 1–4

MOST COOKS WILL taste test their food before they distribute it. Because if they don't like it, then others probably aren't going to like it either. If it is something the cook considers delicious, then he will gladly share it so that others can experience the same satisfaction.

Now that you're hungry, apply the same principle when it comes to the Word of God. In the first three chapters of Ezekiel, we see the call of God upon Ezekiel to be a prophet. In chapter one, Ezekiel paints a great picture of the glory of the Lord. In Ezekiel 3:1–2, the Lord says, *"Moreover he said unto me, Son of man, eat that thou findest; eat this roll, and go speak unto the house of Israel. So I opened my mouth, and he caused me to eat that roll."* Before Ezekiel was going to share God's Word with others, he had to receive it for himself.

You cannot expect others to receive the message of Jesus from God's Word and the transformation of a changed life that comes as a result if you have not received it yourself. As a preacher, I preach each message I prepare to myself personally before I stand behind our pulpit. However, I allow that truth to get into my heart and convict me where I need it before I tell others to do the same. If my heart isn't moved by the truth, then I can't expect anybody else's to be. Moreover, if my heart has received the Word, then I can be a better help to others as I preach it. How foolish it is for parents to teach their kids to surrender and sell out for God when they won't do the same! It's no wonder that the majority of church kids that graduate from high school end up out of church or in some kind of night club church. You can't expect somebody to take you seriously if you're not living the message you're giving.

—— Today's Truth ——

Before you share the truths of God's Word, you have to receive those truths for yourself.

God's Broken Heart

Read Ezekiel 5–9

MAN WAS MADE in the image of God. This fact helps us to understand and relate to the Lord in how He deals with man throughout Scripture. As a parent, I fear the thought of our children one day walking out of our lives. It is because of that potential that we are training our children in the nurture and admonition of the Lord. Some have experienced that heartache, and there is no simple way of expressing the brokenness that comes as a result.

Divorce happens all the time. There are times where a committed spouse is left in the dust by their mate. This reminds me of a story my pastor would tell of a family in the church at one point in his ministry. While the husband was away, the wife left a note that she was leaving. When he got home, the note told him that she had packed her things, the kids were asleep, fed and changed, and she would not be coming back.

The heartbreak we experience from those we love is the same heartbreak God feels when His children whom He loves turn their back on Him. Ezekiel 6:8–10 tells of the remnant that God will allow to survive their destruction. He has a purpose for those that are spared, but in this explanation, He says in verse 9, *"because I am broken with their whorish heart…."* The people who once loved and worshipped His name had given their hearts to other gods.

You must understand the hurt that you can bring by turning your heart away from the Lord. Have you considered what it does to Him when you live for the world or neglect your relationship with Him? Not only does it anger Him, but it also causes Him great hurt to see the people He created, loves, and has a plan for their life turn their heart to the things of the world.

—— Today's Truth ——

Consider the heartbreak you bring to the Lord before you give your heart to the world or reject His fellowship in your life.

Foolish Prophets

Read Ezekiel 10–13

For the most part, I believe in the "mind your own business" philosophy as it pertains to ministry and life in general. However, false information needs to be "called out" at times. God addresses this in Ezekiel's day when He says in Ezekiel 13:1–3, *"And the word of the LORD came unto me, saying, Son of man, prophesy against the prophets of Israel that prophesy, and say thou unto them that prophesy out of their own hearts, Hear ye the word of the LORD; Thus saith the Lord GOD; Woe unto the foolish prophets, that follow their own spirit, and have seen nothing!"* Where there is truth, there will always be an opposition to that truth, and in some cases, a twisting of the truth.

We will exhaust ourselves to address every foolish new article, social media clip, or YouTube preacher. However, there is a time and a place when certain issues need to be addressed. Recently, the propaganda of racism has spread in our country to the point that every police officer and every white person should supposedly apologize for what some other person did in how they mistreated a person of another color. I am baffled when I see a white man apologizing for being white. That is completely absurd. So, I preached an entire message in our midweek service on what the Bible says about racism. Rarely do I do this, but every now and then, issues need to be addressed.

I pass several churches on my way to our church. I have very rarely mentioned a church by name during a sermon, but I am not afraid to preach on the false doctrine taught by the Catholic church, the dangerous philosophy of the hipster churches, or the complete misunderstanding of the gospel portrayed by famous television preachers. Not every foolish teacher needs to be pointed out, but we should not be afraid to point out the foolishness in order to teach the truth and to warn of false doctrine.

—— Today's Truth ——

Preaching the truth will always require an understanding of what is false. Do not be overly cautious to point out foolish teaching.

Unsatiable

Read Ezekiel 14–16

T HE WORLD IS constantly on the hunt, searching for new things to satisfy their wants and desires. Their search is chaotic, ever-changing, and unpredictable. Have you ever gone to the pantry or fridge late at night with a hungry appetite, but nothing looks good? If you're like me, you probably go back to the fridge a second or third time, just in case you missed something and what you really wanted just suddenly appeared in your refrigerator.

That feeling is also the result when your desires are directed to the things of this world. As God's judgment came upon Israel, he mentions in Ezekiel 16:28, *"Thou hast played the whore also with the Assyrians, because thou wast unsatiable; yea, thou hast played the harlot with them, and yet couldest not be satisfied."* The definition for *unsatiable* is "incapable of being satisfied" *(Merriam Webster's Dictionary)*. Everyone has a thirst for happiness and a hunger to have the satisfaction that your life means something. That void will never be filled with the sin of the world.

You can plead and warn young people about the dangers of drugs and alcohol, but some just have to find out the hard way that cheap thrills aren't all that fun after all. You can teach a child to wait until their wedding day to give themselves physically to another person, but some will learn personally how filthy it feels to be used by someone who doesn't love you. It has been said, "Jesus died *for* sin. Believers die *to* sin. Unbelievers die *in* sin." If you decide to live in sin, you will die in that sin. Your happiness will die. Your relationships will perish. Your heart for God will vanish. The pleasures the world has to offer will not give you what you are seeking. Instead, sin will take what you do have.

—— Today's Truth ——

Jesus alone can satisfy. We're all searching for something. You must realize that the answers aren't found in the world, but in a genuine and lasting relationship with the Lord.

Life or Death

Read Ezekiel 17–19

LIFE IS SHORT. As we look into the future, life seems like a long journey. As we look back into the past, we see life as the vapor it is described by God to be. In Ezekiel 18, life and death are set before Israel by the Lord. *Live* or *alive* occur thirteen times in this chapter. *Die, dieth,* or *death* occur fourteen times. At the end of the day, those are the options. You are either alive or dead. You have either died or you are living. Some are in the process of death, while others are enjoying the fullness of life. After this life, the same is true. Heaven is described as *"everlasting life"* (John 3:16). Hell, on the other hand, is described as *"the second death"* (Revelation 20:15).

Nobody can create a life. God is the giver of life. The creation story in Genesis is the foundation for everything we know and believe as Christians. All that God offers, He does because He is the One that created it. God gave you life if you are reading this, and He can also take away that life. It is not your duty to decide when your life is over. Life and death are in God's control. The great news is that God desires for all to live full, meaningful, and happy lives. More importantly, though, God's desire is for you to have eternal life with Him in Heaven.

Though God is the giver and taker of life, your actions and the decisions of your heart can also determine this. God promises His comfort, ability to meet your needs, and power to make a difference in life to all who obey and trust in Him. On the other hand, death will come to all who reject Jesus as their Saviour in a horrible place prepared for Satan and his angels. Death is also the term used to describe those who reap the benefits of sin (James 1:15). How you determine what you'll do with the life God has given you will play a large part in determining your life and death.

—— Today's Truth ——

Life and death can be a scary subject, but you can have peace knowing that you're in His care if you put yourself in His good pleasure.

Christian Pollution

Read Ezekiel 20–21

A s you read through the major and minor prophets, the Lord speaks much on judgment. The time of captivity falls in these passages, and Israel was experiencing this turmoil due to their own bad choices. This horrible time for God's people was for a reason. Ezekiel 14:23 says, *"ye shall know that I have not done without cause all that I have done in it, saith the Lord God."* God doesn't work by chance or without cause. In Ezekiel 20, God reminds Ezekiel what led Him to this point with Israel. This story begins with God's promise to make them a nation and when He fulfilled that promise by delivering them out of Egypt. As the story goes on, the Lord makes it known that while He was trying to give them a land and bless them, they continually held to their abominations and disobeyed the Lord.

As a Christian, you represent the Lord. What you do reflects the Lord's name. The reason that God had to judge Israel is because He would not allow His name to be dragged through the mud as they lived their wicked lifestyles. Ezekiel 20:9 says, *"But I wrought for my name's sake, that it should not be polluted before the heathen, among whom they were, in whose sight I made myself known unto them, in bringing them forth out of the land of Egypt."*

Consider the things that you allow in your life and ask yourself what that does to the name of Jesus. Churches are becoming more and more tolerant with alcohol, and it is weakening and polluting God's name. Christians are becoming looser with immodest dress, and it is polluting God's name. So-called Christian music is mirroring the world's style and sound more and more, and the result is a polluted name. God's will not allow His name to be polluted. His work in your life is how God spreads His name to the world.

—— Today's Truth ——

Your life is a representation of Jesus' name. We must be careful to keep His name pure and not polluted through our lifestyle.

No More Chances

Read Ezekiel 22–24

THE LORD MAKES it clear at this point in Ezekiel that He will follow through on His promise to allow Israel to be consumed. Ezekiel 24 gives a picture of a pot with boiling water and bones. Ezekiel 24:14 says, *"I the LORD have spoken it: it shall come to pass, and I will do it; I will not go back, neither will I spare, neither will I repent; according to thy ways, and according to thy doings, shall they judge thee, saith the Lord GOD."* There was no turning back at this point. The people had sown their wicked seeds, and the harvest of their actions was coming.

It is difficult to say exactly what it takes to get to this point in the Christian life. It's like when a parent tells a child, "You're getting a spanking" and the child apologizes and pleads for mercy. Still, the parent says, "Thank you for apologizing, but you're still getting spanked because you did wrong." This is why I am so weary of the Catholic practice of the confessional booth. Confession is good for the soul, but confessing your sins to man has no merit. Unless you have to get yourself right with a person that you have wronged, the Lord is the only one you have to bring your sins to in order to receive mercy. However, people can think sometimes that as long as they go to that booth and confess to their priest, they can live how they want and just repeat the process. This kind of living will reach a point where God's mercy has been exhausted, and that's exactly where Israel found themselves.

Playing with sin is a dangerous thing. Going back to your rap music, viewing garbage on your phone, gossiping about the dirty laundry that doesn't concern you, and other transgressions will test God's mercy. No one has the authority to tell you when God's mercy has been exhausted. All I know is that I never want to get close to that point.

—— Today's Truth ——

Confess your sins daily and keep a close relationship with God. Don't allow yourself to get to the place where you are so far gone that God has to deal with you according to your sin.

Men at Best

Read Ezekiel 25–28

EZEKIEL 25 BEGINS THE section of Ezekiel where God's focus shifts from Israel to the surrounding nations. This passage that you read today is directed toward Tyre, the great commercial harbor city of the Phoenicians (north of Israel).

Ezekiel 28:1–2 says, *"The word of the LORD came again unto me, saying, Son of man, say unto the prince of Tyrus, Thus saith the Lord GOD; Because thine heart is lifted up, and thou hast said, I am a God, I sit in the seat of God, in the midst of the seas; yet thou art a man, and not God, though thou set thine heart as the heart of God."* The prince of Tyre boasted in himself that his wisdom, power, and possessions had clouded his understanding that he was still just a man. I'm reminded of the statement, "The best of men are men at best."

The New York Times reported the following story: "Just five days after accepting the position as head coach of the Notre Dame Fighting Irish football team in December of 2001, George O'Leary resigned in disgrace. An investigation had revealed that more than twenty years before he had included false claims on his resume, including saying that he had lettered in football when he was not even on the team and that he had a master's degree which he had not earned. The lies had not been discovered at any of his previous coaching jobs, but the high profile accorded the position of coach at Notre Dame led to his exposure. In a statement O'Leary said: 'Due to a selfish and thoughtless act many years ago, I have personally embarrassed Notre Dame, its alumni, and fans. With that in mind, I will resign my position as head football coach.'"

—— Today's Truth ——

When we view ourselves as anything more than flawed, sinful, and finite men, we are deceiving ourselves. There is only one God, and all that God uses us to accomplish in life is a credit to His power, and not our own.

The Higher the Rise, the Greater the Fall

Read Ezekiel 29–32

Israel's last hope was Egypt. They were to be an aid for them against Babylon, but they failed to follow through, and God deals with Egypt in this passage. Egypt always has a negative effect in Scripture. This place pictures the world, and like the world, they failed to live up to expectations. It amazes me how many will leave the will of God and find out the hard way that the world never lives up to expectations. Alcohol isn't as fun as the Budweiser commercials make it seem. Drugs aren't as fulfilling as the fun stories you may hear. Loose living with the opposite sex isn't all it's hyped up to be. The world never come through.

Ezekiel 31:10–11 says, *"Therefore thus saith the Lord God; Because thou hast lifted up thyself in height, and he hath shot up his top among the thick boughs, and his heart is lifted up in his height; I have therefore delivered him into the hand of the mighty one of the heathen; he shall surely deal with him: I have driven him out for his wickedness."* Egypt had boasted themselves to be mighty in their heart, and the Lord was there to remind them that He is still God and sin always leads to destruction.

Saul lifted up himself and eventually was stripped of his position. Solomon neglected to keep his heart tender, and the nation was ruined. Nebuchadnezzar boasted in his heart, and God turned him into a wild beast. When you lift up your heart in pride, the result will always be the same. The greater the pride, the greater the fall will be. John 3:30 says, *"He must increase, but I must decrease."* This is the only way to avoid great falls and humiliating failure in your walk. Humble yourself before the Lord has to humble you and pride leads you to the end of its destructive path.

—— Today's Truth ——

Lift up yourself, and you will fall. Humble yourself and let God lift you up, and you will be used for His glory in great fashion.

The Warning of the Watchman

Read Ezekiel 33–36

A THEATRE MANAGER was interviewing candidates for being an usher. When he asked a young man what he would do if a fire broke out, he quickly replied, "Don't worry about me. I'd get out okay." Although Ezekiel was a priest, he was performing the duty of a prophet. God's call was evidently upon him, and throughout the book, we find the phrase *"the hand of the Lord."* Remember that who God calls, God also equips. Ezekiel is described in chapter 33 as a watchman. Notice a few truths about this task.

Judgment is coming. Hebrews 9:27 tells us that judgment comes after death. Hell is waiting for the Christ-less lives unless somebody warns them. Ezekiel 33:2 says, *"When I bring the sword upon a land…."* Not if, but when. The timing is uncertain, but the event is definite.

The watchman has a unique vantage point. He can see what others can't. The people below him are ignorant of what lies ahead. Verse 3 says, *"If when he seeth the sword come upon the land…."* It is our duty to preach the gospel, because sin has blinded the world from seeing their condition and its consequences.

Verse 3 continues, *"blow the trumpet, and warn the people."* As loudly as you can, get the message out with urgency and make it unmistakable to understand. We can't water down the gospel or quietly go about our Pharisaical lives. We must boldly proclaim that Jesus died as the ultimate sacrifice and rose from the grave so that hell can be conquered for every man.

The responsibility of a watchman is over the people. Verse 6 says of the watchman that warns not the people, *"his blood will I require at the watchman's hand."* Share the good news.

—— Today's Truth ——

Every Christian is a watchman. You have the call and the sight to share the truth of the gospel to a world that is on the brink of judgment.

Dead, Dry Bones

Read Ezekiel 37–39

IN ENGLAND IN the 1700s, a cobbler kept a map of the world on a wall of his workshop so that he could pray for the nations of the world, and he became burdened for the people of the world. He shared his burden at a preacher's meeting and was told by an older preacher, "Young man, sit down. When God wants to convert the heathen, He will do it without your help or mine." But William Carey did not let the fire of his enthusiasm be dampened by such a response, and eventually he left the shores of England for those of India, where he engaged in pioneer missionary work, doing exploits for God. He saw the spiritual death that needs the life that only the Lord can give.

Ezekiel 37 tells the vision that God gave Ezekiel of the dead bones. Verse 11 says, *"Then he said unto me, Son of man, these bones are the whole house of Israel: behold, they say, Our bones are dried, and our hope is lost...."* In a sense, Israel wasn't alive in captivity; they were merely existing. They were a dead nation.

Since the end World War II, the island of Saipan has continued to be searched for the bodies of the 40,000 to 50,000 Japanese soldiers who died there. They have discovered approximately half of their remains. Future missions will continue this search. Our world today has a similar spiritual state—with spiritual death all around us, and like Ezekiel, we must look around and see the death that surrounds our homes and churches. John 6:63 tells us, *"It is the spirit that quickeneth; the flesh profiteth nothing: the words that I speak unto you, they are spirit, and they are life."* The only way for spiritual life to be renewed is by Jesus Christ. Soul winning is more important than ever. Christians living the light of the gospel through their lives is more imperative than any other time.

—— Today's Truth ——

The world's spiritual pulse has flatlined, and God's children have a duty to give the life of the Spirit to others in need.

The Millennial Temple

Read Ezekiel 40–42

THIS LAST VISION given to Ezekiel in the final chapters of this book strike much debate among Bible students. The most fitting interpretation would be that the temple described in great detail in chapters 40–42 speak of a temple that will be set in Jerusalem during the Millennium.

Temples are places of worship. The tabernacle was a type of temple, then there is Solomon's Temple, and the temple built by Zerubbabel in Ezra. In the New Testament, Jesus Christ calls His body a temple (John 2:19), and all born-again Christians are described as the temple of God (I Corinthians 6:10) as Paul wrote to the church at Corinth. Although times have changed and will change drastically after Jesus returns, He gives the future hope of a great and grand temple that He will erect during His reign.

God will one day restore His people. All who are saved, although many have strayed during their time in this life, will be restored with God in eternity. This message was given in Ezekiel 40:4 to *"declare all that thou seest to the house of Israel."*

The vision and prophecies of the future for God's children is a message of comfort and hope. One day, Jesus will return, and we will forever be united in His presence in a way unlike we have ever known. George Sweeting writes in *Your Future*: "Of the 260 chapters in the New Testament, there are more than 300 references to the Lord's return—one out of every thirty verses. Twenty-three of the twenty-seven New Testament books refer to this great event. For every prophecy on the first coming of Christ, there are eight on Christ's second coming."

—— Today's Truth ——

You may not understand the details of the things to come, but the hope of the plans that lie ahead should bring joy and comfort to all God's children.

Abominations in God's House

Read Ezekiel 43–45

I THINK A MAJOR reason that we see so much worldliness in the church today is because we forget to whom that place and those people belong. I am the earthly leader of our church, but that doesn't make it *my* church. A biblical church belongs to Jesus. God has entrusted me with the privilege of being the pastor, and I do not take that lightly. However, I have no ownership over the church.

Our world in 2020 is becoming increasingly filled with churches that are more focused on their coffee corner and subwoofers than they are on their Bible message. Immodest dress is accepted even for singing or speaking on stage. While you're speaking, whatever Bible you choose is supposedly fine, since they basically say the same thing, after all. Just don't call for reading in unison because that could turn Pentecostal real quick. This is the place where men can boast their curly locks, women can share their feminist ideology masked as equality, and everyone can join together in "worship."

Forgive me while I take a moment to keep my food down after writing that paragraph that describes the modern-day "Christian" church. In Ezekiel 44:6–7, God says, *"And thou shalt say to the rebellious, even to the house of Israel, Thus saith the Lord God; O ye house of Israel, let it suffice you of all your abominations, In that ye have brought into my sanctuary strangers, uncircumcised in heart, and uncircumcised in flesh, to be in my sanctuary, to pollute it, even my house, when ye offer my bread, the fat and the blood, and they have broken my covenant because of all your abominations."* God speaks of the unsaved that were mixed in with his people, and it is the sins of the world that entered the people as a result.

—— Today's Truth ——

The church is God's house. We must be careful to look to Him for how He wants His church to worship His name.

The River of God

Read Ezekiel 46–48

SINCE 1850, OVER 5,000 BODIES have been recovered from Niagara Falls. Water can make for a beautiful setting, and it can also be a destructive force. I'll never forget almost drowning in the ocean as a preteen. As I tried to swim to shore, the waves pushed me out farther and farther. I was losing strength, but thankfully the lifeguard came to my rescue. When I got to shore, people on the beach cheered. I was thankful, but as a young boy trying to prove himself a man, I was also quite embarrassed.

These final chapters of Ezekiel conclude this future vision from the Lord. In chapter 47, God shows Him a river flowing from the temple. This river is a heavenly picture with many spiritual applications. This river is a representation of God's power, goodness, and the opportunity for you to be blessed from it. Notice that this river has no feeder streams. The Mississippi River is less than three feet wide where it begins, but leading into the Gulf of Mexico it is over a mile wide due to the many water sources that flow into it. Water is a symbol of blessing in the Bible, and the river flowing from the temple is a symbol of God's favor coming from God's house. This water healed, produced fruit and brought to life everything it touched (vv. 8–12).

Ezekiel was led into the water. First, to his ankles. Next, to his knees, and then to his waist. Finally, Ezekiel got in so deep that he could only swim to stay afloat. I believe the spiritual application here is similar to Peter's experience. Getting in the water can be scary, but that's where God shows up. Many stand at the shore of the water or just deep enough to feel it; but they never fully jump in. The power of the water of God can be experienced for every Christian.

—— Today's Truth ——

This future promise for God to restore His people admonishes us to see the blessings God can bring and the power He possesses. God wants that for your life if you'll have faith to get all the way into His river!

Conquering Compromise

Read Daniel 1–3

To be compromised in war is to be vulnerable to the attacks from the enemy. We are living with spiritual warfare all around us, and the enemy wants to find your weak points and hurt you so it will hurt the Lord. Daniel 1 tells of the captives that were taken and how their captors systematically planned to change these Jews and turn them into Chaldeans.

Their Procedure. The first thing that changed for these captives were their surroundings. They gave them a new home with wickedness all around them. Next, they changed their education. They taught them their ways and beliefs. Then came the new diet. They now wanted them to participate in their way of life. Finally, they changed their names. These were the steps they took, and these are the similar steps that the devil takes to change God's children.

Your Purpose. Although they changed everything around them, the only thing the captives could control in a foreign land was their personal decisions. They could move them, teach them, and call them different names, but they could not force them to participate. Their purpose was determined by their heart for God. They stayed true and committed to their purpose.

His Promotion. Resisting the adversary is no easy feat. However, God blesses those who stand tall in the face of opposition. Daniel graciously requested the freedom to exercise his decision to honor God, and God blessed them in this contest between them and the king's servants. It has been said, "There is no softer pillow than a clear conscience." Not only because you did the right thing, but also because you know that God's hand will be on your life if you remain true during opposition.

—— Today's Truth ——

Satan is looking for those that he can compromise. If you stay true to your purpose, God will reward you for putting Him first.

Time to Learn a Lesson

Read Daniel 4–6

GALATIANS 6:7 STATES, *"BE not deceived; God is not mocked...."* Regardless of how the wicked in the world stand tall in their pride, the Lord will not allow them to get the last laugh. Daniel 4 continues the story of Nebuchadnezzar's reign in Babylon while Daniel and other choice captives were his servants. This king had a hard lesson to learn. Nebuchadnezzar conquered nations, built a great statue for himself, and boasted in his heart of all the accomplishments he had successfully achieved. Verse 30 says, *"The king spake, and said, Is not this great Babylon, that I have built for the house of the kingdom...."* The next verse shows how God interrupted this boastful parade the king was having in his heart and, in that moment, God turned the prideful king into a filthy beast for seven years. Why did God do this?

God is supreme. Every ruler must realize that though men answer to them, they still must answer to God. God is supreme. The point that God was teaching is found in verse 32: *"until thou know that the most High ruleth in the kingdom of men, and giveth it to whomsoever he will."* No matter the promotion, never forget your place.

God promotes. Any success you have gained is not due to your efforts, but God's grace. Your hard work is possible only because of the mind God gave you to know what to do, the health to be able to apply yourself to a goal, and the fruit that was gained as a result. .

God uses humble men. Many verses clearly declare that God hates pride. Either you can humble yourself, or God will have to humble you the hard way.

—— Today's Truth ——

This king had to be taught through chastisement, but you can learn through God's Word these timeless truths and apply them to your life.

Visions and Dreams

Read Daniel 7–9

The first half of Daniel is the part of Daniel that you probably learned in Sunday school as a child. However, chapter
seven changes the focus to prophecy and begins with quite a descriptive vision of a lion with eagle's wings. This represents the rise of Babylon. In Daniel's vision, the winged lion's feathers were plucked and it
was made to stand like a man, which likely refers to Nebuchadnezzar's
punishment and restoration.

Next, Daniel sees a bear raised on one side. This speaks of the Medo-
Persian empire, and the raising up of one side likely symbolizes the su-
periority of the Persians. The three ribs in the bear's mouth allude to the
nations they had to defeat to come to power—Babylon, Egypt, and Lydia.

Next, he sees a leopard with four heads and four wings that symbolizes Greece. Alexander the Great was swift in his conquest as a very
young man. The wings and heads refer to his division of the kingdom
under four generals.

Last of all, Daniel sees a *"dreadful and terrible"* beast with iron
teeth and ten horns; his description was that *"it was diverse from all
the beasts that were before it"* (v. 7). This was the vision of Rome. The
ten horns match the description of the feet of the statue in chapter two
with ten toes. Both refer to Rome. More focus is put on this beast than
the previous three. The "little horn" is believed to have been Antiochus
Epiphanes.

The final aspect of this vision ends with the *"Ancient of days"* (v.
9) and the *"Son of man"* (v. 13), emphasizing the end more than the
beginning. None of it is that important, other than the fact that it leads
us to Jesus.

——Today's Truth ——

*It builds your faith to realize that God has a plan, and though
wicked rulers rise and pagan kingdoms rule, He is still in control
and works all things according to His conclusion of the matter.*

Spiritual Warfare

Read Daniel 10–12

THE VISION BEGINNING in chapter 10 extends to the end of the book of Daniel. This vision took a physical toll on Daniel as he fasted for three weeks during this time period. However, a struggle hindered Daniel in receiving this vision from the Lord. The spiritual warfare is described in verse 13: *"But the prince of the kingdom of Persia withstood me one and twenty days: but, lo, Michael, one of the chief princes, came to help me; and I remained there with the kings of Persia."*

The unseen war all around us is a startling reality. It doesn't involve atomic bombs, fighter jets, or tanks. This is the battle between the angels of the Lord and the minions of Satan. It is the battle between the flesh and the Spirit. Just because you can't see it doesn't mean it is not taking place.

This spiritual war that we're often caught in the middle of cannot be won with man's weaponry. It must only be fought with spiritual weapons. Daniel fasted, prayed, and yielded his spirit to the Lord. He fought on his knees, and he enlisted the help of the Holy Spirit. Daniel was so exasperated by this experience that he became speechless after the encounter. Then, verses 18 and 19 state, *"Then there came again and touched me one like the appearance of a man, and he strengthened me, And said, O man greatly beloved, fear not: peace be unto thee, be strong, yea, be strong. And when he had spoken unto me, I was strengthened, and said, Let my lord speak; for thou hast strengthened me."* God strengthen Daniel for the battle and from the battle.

—— Today's Truth ——

Make no attempt to fight spiritual battles with man's strength. Fervently seek the Lord to win the battle you can't see. He will give you what you need to overcome and to move forward from the fight.

Unfaithful

Read Hosea 1–6

MARRIAGE IS A sacred bond between two people. Vows are a lifelong commitment to an individual. Sadly, many will make their vows with every intention of upholding their sacred pact, yet fall somewhere down the road. *The New York Times* said in an article in 2018, "According to the American Association for Marriage and Family Therapy, national surveys indicate that 15 percent of married women and 25 percent of married men have had extramarital affairs.

The story of Hosea centers around the picture of infidelity. God said in Hosea 2:5, *"For their mother hath played the harlot…."* The sacred bond that knit the Lord to His people had been broken. He wasn't the one who had changed; it was the people of Israel. Everyone wants to point fingers in times like this, yet many times both parties have a part of the blame. Not in this scenario. If there is a problem between you and the Lord, it's not because He broke His vow to love you, protect you, give you purpose, provide for your needs, fulfill His promise of a home in Heaven, or remain close to you. It is you and I who fail Him.

I believe one of the most difficult wounds to heal is when a spouse has committed adultery. Forgiveness and healing is possible, which has been proven by many people. However, adultery is no small matter. It's serious business when you shun the Lord and give yourself to what you deem to be more important than He is in your life. We create false gods in our lives by how we consume ourselves and give ourselves to certain areas, and without even being aware of what is taking place, we have completely forsaken our vow to the Lord and given ourselves to something else. This is as serious to Him as breaking vows spoken at a wedding altar.

—— Today's Truth ——

God wants you to commit yourself to Him, but He also expects you to remain faithful to your commitments.

Do You Know God?

Read Hosea 7–14

HAVE YOU EVER been in a situation where you thought you knew more about something than you actually did? My wife and I have times where we both think that we are right about something. She thinks she is right, and I think I am right. Oftentimes, Google is the one to settle the matter. Unfortunately, I've been put in my place more times than I'd like to admit, realizing that I knew less than I thought I did. In Hosea 8, God says to set the trumpets against Israel. Trumpets were a way to gather the troops for battle. However, this time, it was the Assyrians that were assembled by God to overtake Israel.

God gives their response when they are faced with ruin. Hosea 8:2 says, *"Israel shall cry unto me, My God, we know thee."* I remember a time when I was preaching at a church when a man and his wife came to greet my wife and me. He said something like, "Good to see you! It's been a long time." Then, he quickly realized that I did not even know who he was. I was embarrassed that I had forgotten his name. He claimed to know me, but I did not remember him.

I wonder how many Christians claim they "know God" while God looks out and says, "No, you don't." Israel was being punished for their transgressions, and verse 3 says, *"Israel hath cast off the thing that is good…."* They claimed to know God in their mind, but they failed to truly know Him in their hearts and lives. Knowing God is more than just believing in Him. You know Him by doing the things that draw you closer to Him. You know Him the more you're in His church. You know Him more by being in His Word and in your prayer closet with Him. You know Him by telling lost sinners about His saving grace. Knowing God shouldn't be an empty statement that gives you the label of being a Christian. Instead, it is a daily dedication to have that personal relationship.

—— Today's Truth ——

To know God, you must do the work that draws you close to God.

The Day of the Lord

Read Joel 1–3

THE THEME OF the book of Joel is *"the day of the Lord."* This phrase refers to the end when Jesus returns to judge the nations of the world. Whether we are ready or caught off guard, Jesus is coming back again. This could be a good day or a bad day for you, but this "day" is coming.

Joel 2:1 states, *"Blow ye the trumpet in Zion, and sound an alarm in my holy mountain: let all the inhabitants of the land tremble: for the day of the LORD cometh, for it is nigh at hand."* We should not be silent about this day. As the prophets spoke of the day at hand, so must we in our day speak of the day of the Lord that is coming. We are not told to try to predict that day, but to simply and boldly warn others of that day. We must be looking for that day, but we must also be working toward that day.

My pastor, Stephen Ray Nichols, would tell the story about his dad who made this statement: "God has a scoreboard in Heaven, and it always shows the right score." When Jesus returns, there will be no contest or debate about who is the true king. In our day, there are different opinions, all kinds of belief systems, and mankind is absolutely divided in their thinking. However, that will all be settled when Jesus returns. He will make it known for the world to see. I don't want people to find out the hard way, but like it or not, they will find out that Jesus is King! Revelation 1:7–8 says of the Second Coming, *"Behold, he cometh with clouds; and every eye shall see him, and they also which pierced him: and all kindreds of the earth shall wail because of him. Even so, Amen. I am Alpha and Omega, the beginning and the ending, saith the Lord, which is, and which was, and which is to come, the Almighty."*

—— Today's Truth ——

We must live with the end in mind. It is for our lives and for the sake of others that we watch for His return and warn all the people we can so they can be saved from the judgment to come.

Walking in Unison

Read Amos 1–5

I DISTINCTLY REMEMBER a preacher giving the following story very bluntly in a service. The preacher named a fairly well-known preacher that he had preached for many times. He received a call asking him to come preach again, as he had many times before; and the host pastor said something like, "Now, I did want to let you know that we decided to remove the name 'Baptist' from our church name. Will that be a problem with you coming still?" He replied, "Well, yes, that will be a problem. I don't believe that I can preach for you anymore." From his side of the story, he declined graciously, yet sternly, and I believe it is for the reason found in Amos 3:3. The verse read, *"Can two walk together, except they be agreed?"*

If you are walking with somebody, then you are headed in the same direction as that individual. You may argue that no two people are alike, but you're going to have to draw the line somewhere regarding who you walk with. I'm not going to walk with people of other denominations. I've been invited to many gatherings in our area by local religious leaders of various denominations for prayer breakfasts and other "unifying" events. I am sure that they are generally decent people, but we are not headed in the same direction. I will be friendly to all people, but I cannot walk with them as close friends.

Who you walk with will determine who you become. Walk with people that help and strengthen you, and you will grow closer to God. Walk with people you are discipling, and you will help the cause of Christ. But if you walk with those who openly know what is right and knowingly live in sin, you are determining your future by your relationship together.

—— Today's Truth ——

Determine where you draw the line with those you walk with. Walk with those that walk in the steps of Jesus and seek to live like Him.

The Easy Life

Read Amos 6–9 and Obadiah

THE MAJORITY OF America lives very comfortable lives. They wake up each day to a hot cup of coffee, and not the cheap stuff either; it's probably prepared by a barista with a green apron or made from a specialty grind delivered in a day to your front door by Amazon. Then comes breakfast, which is freshly delivered from the farm. Work begins, and we complain because it's Monday, or Tuesday, or any day other than Friday. We get paid enough to cover our dozens of subscriptions, because no person can really live without at least five streaming services, a clothing line delivered monthly, plus a few that you've forgotten about, but that you definitely need. Driving in traffic stinks, but you have podcasts and music hooked up to your Bluetooth, cool air pouring from the vents, and hundred-dollar shades shielding your eyes from the sun. Each night, we look for the game of the night, a TV series, or a movie to completely knock our socks off. We can cook our dinner, as long as it's organic food delivered in a box containing the exact ingredients we need for the meal. Finally, we sleep on soft sheets in our favorite pajamas, covered by comfy blankets with the thermostat set precisely as we like it.

Amos 6:4 describes a similar lifestyle of the people of that day: *"That lie upon beds of ivory, and stretch themselves upon their couches, and eat the lambs out of the flock, and the calves out of the midst of the stall."* In verse 1, God says of the people, *"Woe to them that are at ease in Zion, and trust in the mountain of Samaria...."* Living with some luxuries is not sinful, but allowing those luxuries to affect your heart is a dangerous temptation. You may have possessions, but you still need God's help every day.

—— Today's Truth ——

Guard your heart from being swayed by the luxury you enjoy in life, and keep your edge for the things of God that cause you to grow spiritually.

You Missed It!

Read Jonah 1–4

M Y FAVORITE SPORT as a child was basketball, and my favorite
team was the Sacramento Kings. We went to a few games
each year, and I shouted as loudly as I could, waved my towel, and
cheered our team. One game I'll never forget was against the San An-
tonio Spurs, and both teams had championship potential. As the game
neared the end, it looked like the other team would win, so we left with
a few minutes to spare to avoid being stuck in endless traffic after the
game. As we drove away, listening to the game on the radio, the Kings
tied the game at the buzzer and put it into overtime. We were kicking
ourselves for not staying until the end in a close game.

Many view Bible examples with the attitude that they would never
do something like the men and women about whom they are reading,
but what we see in Jonah is very relatable to many believers. His will
was different than God's will for his life. He eventually repented, but he
had to learn the hard way. Finally, after he listened to God's command,
we read of one of the greatest revivals among some of the most wicked
people in Scripture. Then, the final chapter begins in verse one, *"But it
displeased Jonah exceedingly, and he was very angry."* Verse three continues, *"Therefore now, O LORD, take, I beseech thee, my life from me; for it is
better for me to die than to live."* How does this make sense? God called
Jonah, showed mercy toward Jonah when he deserved death, accepted
his repentance, gave him a second chance, and used him in an unprec-
edented way; yet Jonah's response was anger and discouragement.

The truth is that we allow ourselves to be distracted so easily from
the great works God is doing because of our selfishness and pride.
People get saved on Sunday, and others leave church angry because
someone didn't compliment their new haircut. However God works in
your life, don't miss the exciting blessings He gives all around you!

—— Today's Truth ——

God is doing a great work if you'll only stay long enough to notice.

280 | STEVEN BECKER

No Restrictions

Read Micah 1–7

WHEN YOU ENTER an elevator, weight restrictions are posted. On a jump house, restrictions are given for age limits, number of children, or total weight of those inside. Cars have restrictions oil, gas, and the list goes on. Everything in life has restrictions or limits. If you fail to adhere to those restrictions, you risk ruin.

As God's people were facing His judgment, they did what so many of us do when our back is up against a wall. They started pointing fingers. Few will take honest responsibility for their actions in life. We can always point to some person or situation if we want to pass the blame, but it is never helpful. This went so far that God's people aimed their complaint at God. Micah 2:7 says, *"O thou that art named the house of Jacob, is the spirit of the LORD straitened? are these his doings? do not my words do good to him that walketh uprightly?"* It wasn't God's fault that they had failed as a nation or that they had lost their independence.

God has zero limitations. Man has many. It is when we realize that we are nothing without Him that we turn to Him in desperation for His presence in our lives. A humble evaluation of yourself will lead you to a proper evaluation of your need for God's help. If God doesn't come through, just know it's not because He can't, but maybe that you have put restrictions on His ability to bless. Charles Spurgeon said, "Do you not think, again, that we very much act as if the Spirit of the Lord were straitened when we only look for little blessings? I am very glad to see three hundred or four hundred persons in a year converted and added to this church, and this has long been the case; but if I ever imbibed the idea that this was all that might be done, I should be straitening the Spirit of God."

—— Today's Truth ——

God is not restricted in what He can do. However, you can restrict what God will do based on how you live your life. Nobody deserves blame besides you, and nobody can take credit except for God.

Troubled Days

Read Nahum 1–3 and Habakkuk 1–3

I T'S BEEN SAID that you're either going into a trial, currently in a trial, or coming out of a trial. I once heard of a young preacher asking an older preacher how to make it to the finish line in the ministry. The seasoned man of God replied, "You just have to make it through the quitting times." Nahum 1:7 is a familiar passage that gives helpful guidance for the believer during times of trouble.

"The Lord is good." No matter what you're facing, God is still good. You may be in the bleakest season you've ever faced, but God is still good. If God wasn't good, He wouldn't be God. You may not see the good because you're too focused on the bad. Cast your burdens before the Lord, but direct your focus on the goodness of the Lord in your life today. A preacher who was stricken with cancer made this statement while I was in Bible college: "Your problems will always outweigh your blessings, but they'll never out number them."

"a strong hold in the day of trouble." A boat anchor has a simple, yet important job. When the water rages strong against the boat and when the winds fiercely blow, the anchor keeps the boat secure. Nothing in life will secure you in times of trouble like the Lord.

"and he knoweth them that trust in him." God draws close to those who put their trust in Him during troubling times. It's easy to say you trust Him when the waters are calm, but when you are tested and you still trust Him, God will become close to you; and that is a blessing unlike any other you can receive.

——Today's Truth ——

Jesus told us that man's days are full of trouble. Life is great, but life is hard at times; still, God is good, He can anchor you when you feel afraid for your life, and He will draw close to you if you continue to put your trust in Him.

The Prophet of Love

Read Zephaniah 1–3 and Haggai 1–2

Is there no other way, oh God,
Except through sorrow, pain and loss?
To stamp Christ's likeness on my soul,
No other way except the cross?
And then a voice stills all my soul,
That stilled the waves of Galilee,
Canst thou not bear the furnace,
If midst the flames I walk with thee?
I bore the cross, I know its weight,
I drank the cup I hold for thee.
Canst thou not follow where I lead?
I'll give thee strength, lean hard on Me!
—Author Unknown

God gets glory in judgment just as much as in blessing. Zephaniah is known as the prophet of love, like John is known as the apostle of love. Zephaniah is not a popular book like John, but its message is not inferior. I can't say that I've ever heard a sermon preached from this book, although I could be wrong. Many know John 3:16, but few know Zephaniah 3:17, which says, *"The Lord thy God in the midst of thee is mighty; he will save, he will rejoice over thee with joy; he will rest in his love, he will joy over thee with singing."* Zephaniah refers to *"the day of the Lord"* more than any other prophet. Although this will be a dreadful day for some, this future event gives hope to believers.

—— Today's Truth ——

Both God's justice and love represent who He is. God sent prophets because of His love for people, warning of impending judgment that could be avoided. He is a great and mighty God, and we can rejoice in Him.

Sweating the Small Stuff

Read Zechariah 1–7

I RECALL HEARING a seasoned preacher say, "The ministry is not about big days. The ministry is about every day." Zechariah 4:10 says, *"For who hath despised the day of small things?"* Life is about the day-to-day grind of doing what you're responsible for.

I love the song, "Little Is Much When God Is in It." Truth be told, there are no small tasks in God's work. Although you may not be front and center in church or the center of attention at a celebration, remember that God notices all work that is done for Him. I believe everyone at times looks at what they do for the Lord and is tempted to compare it with what others are doing. There are more small jobs that need to be done than what we'd consider big tasks. However, the small things quite possibly make a bigger difference over time than the few big things one can do. Never think of your work as small if it is what you can do for the work of the Lord.

Be diligent in the small stuff. Everything you do should be done with all your heart. How would an athlete perform if he slacked off in practice and decided to try hard only during a game? Allen Iverson is famous for his press conference rant, "Practice. We talkin' about practice. Not a game, not a game. Practice." Iverson was considered a great player, but many players don't reach their potential because they're not interested in putting in the small work during practice when no one is watching. Sweat the small stuff in life as well as the big stuff. It's not our job to rank the importance of our work. It's our job to do the work and to finish it.

——Today's Truth——

Count it a privilege that you get to be involved in God's work. Whether you consider your task big or small, it's important in God's eyes, and God notices no matter the size of the task.

A Reason to Rejoice

Read Zechariah 8–14

ZECHARIAH 9:9 BEGINS, *"REJOICE greatly…shout."* God's message brings a heavenly joy with which this earth cannot compete. R. A. Torrey said, "There is more joy in Jesus in 24 hours than there is in the world in 365 days. I have tried them both."

Verse 9 says, *"O daughter of Zion…shout, O daughter of Jerusalem."* This is a term of endearment. God's heart is still tender toward His people, even though they are in captivity in Babylon. People ask if God still loves sinners who aren't doing right. I believe it is true to state that God loves sinners even though He hates the sin.

This rejoicing is not for the strangers in the land (the lost), but for God's children. Verse 9 also says, *"behold, thy King cometh."* The thought of being united forever with Jesus brings rejoicing to the saved. This isn't just a king, but our King. If He's your King, then you have reason to shout for joy.

Lastly, we see Him *"lowly, and riding upon an ass, and upon a colt the foal of an ass."* This shows His intentions. Although Jesus will bring an end to the contest from Satan and the nations of the world that will rise up against Jerusalem in the last days, the donkey is a symbol showing that He came to bring peace the first time He came. Warriors ride horses, but that wasn't His purpose. This prophecy is fulfilled in Matthew 21:5 when Jesus made His entry into Jerusalem presenting Himself as the Messiah. Jesus didn't come with a sword, but with the purpose to give His life for the salvation of all who come to Him by faith.

—— Today's Truth ——

Jesus came once, and He will come again. We rejoice that He came and died to offer the free gift of eternal life. Now, we have joy that He will come again and bring us into perfect fellowship with Him for eternity.

The Only Applause That Matters

Read Malachi 1–4

IT WAS A memorable experience recently when earlier this year, at the Pastors' Conference at North Valley Baptist Church in Santa Clara, California, my former school principal (who was also the youth pastor and assistant pastor), Meredith Sears, put his arm around me in the middle of a service and said with great sincerity, "Steven, I am so very proud of you." It was such a wonderful moment to hear that the actions in my life have been pleasing to someone that I look up to.

Malachi 1 begins with stating God's unwavering love for Israel, but along with that love was great displeasure. Verse 10 says, *"Who is there even among you that would shut the doors for nought? neither do ye kindle fire on mine altar for nought. I have no pleasure in you, saith the* LORD *of hosts, neither will I accept an offering at your hand."* God said it was better for them to shut the doors of the church and halt their service than to continue in their polluted worship.

After a concert pianist finished his performance for a premiere event he had prepared to play for several months, the audience began to cheer. They stood to their feet and gave him a standing ovation. However, he exited the stage. His manager told him to go back out and play another piece. "They love you," he said. The man replied, "Not all," while pointing to a white-haired man in the balcony who was neither standing nor applauding. "That's one old man. So what?" he replied. The pianist said, "That's not one old man. That's my teacher." You can have the applause and recognition from the world, but it's all in vain if the God of Heaven is not pleased with you. When the day is over, the applause of One is all that really matters.

——Today's Truth——

You should constantly ask yourself, "Is God pleased with me?" Do not get sidetracked with the applause of the world and neglect what pleases Him.

What's in a Name?

Read Matthew 1–4

T HE WHOLE BIBLE could be summarized with just one word, or one name really. That name is Jesus! In our modern culture, names aren't given the way they used to be given. The beginning of Matthew records the beginning of the coming of the Messiah to earth and the names He was called. His names have both purpose and meaning.

Christ *(chosen one, anointed one)*. This is the equivalent to the Old Testament name Messiah. God's Son was chosen for a purpose. I Peter 1:20 says, *"Who verily was foreordained before the foundation of the world, but was manifest in these last times for you."* He was chosen and anointed to come and die for the sins of the world, and He surrendered Himself to that purpose. In Luke 2:49, He answers His earthly parents: *"And he said unto them, How is it that ye sought me? wist ye not that I must be about my Father's business?"*

Jesus *(Saviour)*. Rothschild is a potent name in the commercial world; Cuvier is well-known in the scientific realm; Irving is a powerful name in the literary world; Washington, an influential name in the political world; Wellington, a mighty name in the military world. But tell me any name in all the earth so potent to awe and lift and thrill and rouse and agitate and bless as this name of Jesus! That name means more than Victoria in England, Emperor William in Germany, Carnot in France, or Humbert or Garibaldi in Italy.

Emmanuel *(father, friend)*. Matthew 1:23 gives the definition as *"God with us"* to this name. This is a name not of power and strength, but of endearment. The gospel isn't just about what God can do for your life, but what Jesus can do with you in this life. He desires to have a relationship with you.

—— Today's Truth ——

The precious and powerful names of our Lord help us to understand more of who He is and what He desires to do with our lives.

OCTOBER 2

Why You Must Reconcile

Read Matthew 5–6

Matthew 5 begins what we know as the "Sermon on the Mount." This is the Great Manifesto given to the disciples. It is important to remember that this was not preached to lost sinners to draw them to the Saviour, but to followers of Christ to develop into mature Christians. Context is key when studying Scripture. This passage does not preach a social gospel or a works-based salvation.

One truth that Jesus brings to light is that your relationship with people directly affects your relationship with God. To take it a step further, your relationships with others can hinder and harm your relationship with God. Matthew 5:23–24 says, *"Therefore if thou bring thy gift to the altar, and there rememberest that thy brother hath ought against thee; Leave there thy gift before the altar, and go thy way; first be reconciled to thy brother, and then come and offer thy gift."* Giving yourself and the gifts that God has given you back to Him with a surrendered will is a good thing for you to do. However, Jesus emphasizes that if you come to Him and have a problem with somebody else, then you need to leave your gift on the altar and immediately go to restore your relationship with that person.

Maybe you do not have a perfect and close relationship with everyone in your life. You don't have the time to be close to everyone, and you may not be best friends with everyone, but there should not be a person on this planet that you cannot be in the same room with without bitterness and anger. Is there someone you need to forgive? Not every situation will work out like a book, but you can do your part. It is imperative that you do this, for Jesus makes it clear that your horizontal relationships can affect your vertical relationship.

——Today's Truth ——

It is important to put God first, but it is also vital to reconcile your relationships with others so that they do not come between you and the Lord.

When Jesus Marvels

Read Matthew 7–9

THE LONGER YOU live and the more you see in life, the less you are truly astonished by anything. The moments that make your jaw drop become more seldom and, through life experience, you are less surprised by people and situations. Now, put yourself in Jesus' shoes. He is the One who has always existed, has witnessed every world event, and has perfect recollection of it all. Yet, in Matthew 8:10, we read of Jesus, *"he marvelled…."*

In this passage, we read of a centurion that came to Jesus and pled with Him to heal his servant that was *"sick of the palsy, grievously tormented"* (v. 6). Keep in mind that this Roman soldier was a Gentile. Jesus offered to come to his home, but he refused saying that he was unworthy to have Jesus, a Jew, come to his house. His response is what caused Jesus to marvel. In verse 7, he says, *"but speak the word only, and my servant shall be healed."* He knew that Jesus didn't need to be there in person. He believe if Jesus would simply speak, it would be so. He believed in His power, and he believed in His authority over all.

I wonder how many Christians Jesus looks at and marvels. Have you ever showed such great faith that you would cause the Saviour to marvel at how much you believe in Him? This kind of example calls for a radical faith, a faith that goes beyond the normal prayers and vague requests. It is the type of faith that truly moves mountains. I am reminded of the song that says,

> *If Jesus said it I believe it. His Word cannot lie.*
> *If it's written in the Bible, I'll believe it 'til I die.*
> *Though the mountains be removed and cast into the sea,*
> *God's Word will last forever, throughout eternity*

—— Today's Truth ——

Jesus notices your faith in Him. So many have such little faith in what He is capable of. We must strive to show great faith that would cause Jesus to marvel.

Shake Off the Dust

Read Matthew 10–11

WHEN MY WIFE and I came to First Baptist Church of Loomis in 2013, one of the first things I wanted to do was begin the soul winning ministry. We met once a month for the first year and called it "The Fisherman's Club." My wife went with a group of ladies, and for many of them it was their first time ever going door to door to share the gospel. Like all who go out for their first time, they were nervous. My wife did most of the door knocking, but she challenged them all to knock on at least one door. One of the women knocked on a door, had a great conversation, and the next day that woman and her son came to church. I'll never forget that.

If you've ever gone soul winning, you know that it takes many doors, many tracts, many hours, and many conversations before you see someone get saved, and even more of the same to see someone come to church.

Matthew 10 tells of the instructions that Jesus gave to the disciples as they went out to be a witness to the lost. In verse 14, Jesus said, *"And whosoever shall not receive you, nor hear your words, when ye depart out of that house or city, shake off the dust of your feet."* In other words, when you have an unpleasant conversation, just move on to the next door and talk to the next person.

It is helpful to remember that God didn't command you to win souls, but to warn them. We call this time that we go door knocking "soul winning," but it might be better called "soul warning." Winning souls is the goal, but warning souls is the task at hand.

——Today's Truth ——

Don't let the results and fruit of your time out soul winning dictate whether or not you warn souls.

The Unpardonable Sin

Read Matthew 12

ALL OF THE Bible was written for your benefit. Parts of the Bible were not written directly *to* you, but all of the Bible is given *for* you. Every page contains something for you. While you study God's Word, you will come across passages, verses, or phrases that you don't understand. These "problem passages" are not a problem with God's Word, but a problem with us as human beings. I pray that if this happens (and if you read your Bible faithfully, it certainly will), you will not doubt that God's Word is still perfect in the KJV, but that you will study to understand and pray for God to teach you the meaning of that passage in its context and in comparison with other Scripture.

An example of what some consider a "problem passage" is Matthew 12:31, which says, *"but the blasphemy against the Holy Ghost shall not be forgiven unto men."* Some interpret this verse to mean that, even after salvation, you will not be forgiven and can lose your salvation. The problem with this is that the Bible teaches that once you get saved, you can never lose your salvation. How then do you explain the meaning of what is known as "the unpardonable sin"?

The primary ministry of the Holy Spirit is to testify of Jesus (John 15:26). Therefore, to blaspheme the Holy Spirit is to deny the work of the Holy Spirit and to reject Jesus. This passage shows people that were trying to catch Jesus in sin, rather than to accept Him as the Messiah. When you reject Jesus as the Son of God, you are calling the Holy Ghost a liar, and the result for the lost soul is an eternity in hell.

—— Today's Truth ——

To receive the Holy Spirit is to receive Jesus. To reject and blaspheme the Holy Spirit is to reject and blaspheme Jesus.

OCTOBER 6

Wheat or Weed?

Read Matthew 13–14

MATTHEW 13 IS THE "parable chapter" of the Bible. Jesus gave eight different parables in this passage. Parables are earthly illustrations with heavenly meanings. In the middle of Jesus' messages, the disciples asked him about one of the parables. In fact, this was the only parable they asked Him to explain in this passage. Verse 36 says, *"his disciples came unto him, saying, Declare unto us the parable of the tares of the field."* Here, Jesus makes this parable clear.

Tares are like weeds that look like wheat in the early stages. They go by the name "bearded darnel." Imagine a farmer that looks out among his crop. He sees a full harvest on the horizon. He gets excited. However, his servants notice a problem. When wheat matures, the kernels that form at the top cause it to bend toward the ground. The tares grow tall, straight, and proud. So, at this point when they're grown, they are easily distinguished from each other. The roots have intertwined over time, and if they pull the tares, it will affect the wheat.

The wheat are the children of God and the tares are phony Christians. Sadly, I believe churches all across the world are full of tares. They look saved, talk like they are saved, and many even think they're born again; but they are tares. I believe a few truths that we learn from this are: we do not truly know who is really saved, nor is it our duty to distinguish between the tares and wheat. When Jesus returns, He will sort out the saved and the lost and all will be settled in the end; we live amongst tares, and we aren't here to destroy them but to win them while we live together.

—— Today's Truth ——

Jesus owns the field, and when He determines that it is harvest time, the wheat will be gathered to the Master while the tares are burned.

What It Means to Take Up Your Cross

Read Matthew 15–17

REAL CHRISTIANITY IS needed today. The definition of a Christian is to be "like Christ." In our hyper-tolerant society, the term Christian has been diluted, but it is still a Bible word. The world is not to blame for polluting the meaning of that title; the children of God are. I believe that if one verse could describe what real Christianity looks like, it is Matthew 16:24 which states, *"Then said Jesus unto his disciples, If any man will come after me, let him deny himself, and take up his cross, and follow me."* So what does it mean then to "take up your cross"?

Taking Up Your Cross Demands Humility. Simon of Cyrene was pulled out from the crowd to help our beaten, bloody, and bruised Saviour carry His cross. Romans soldiers weren't going to touch that cross because carrying your cross was a symbol of shame. Pride has no place in Christianity. What the world views as shame, God's people should receive with humility. To truly follow Jesus, you must put aside your pride.

Taking Up Your Cross Demonstrates Honor. People will scoff at you while you give your tithe and then on top of that give toward missions, building programs, and more. They will tell you that you are a part of a cult that is just out to steal your time away from your family because you go soul winning and serve in the ministries of the church.

Taking Up Your Cross Denotes Hope. The cross is and always will be a symbol of hope. For a moment, the world viewed it as a time of defeat when the body of Jesus was nailed to the cross and He died, but three days later He fulfilled His promise and brought salvation to all who will receive Him. I don't care for jewelry and statutes that have Jesus' body on the cross because He's not on the cross anymore. The empty tomb and bare cross give us hope as we remember we serve a risen Saviour!

—— Today's Truth ——

Real Christianity is when believers follow Jesus, turning from their flesh, and realize the importance of taking up their cross.

Never Grow Up

Read Matthew 18–20

I'VE LEARNED MUCH since becoming a father. Some of that is from others that have given wisdom or an example to follow, but some of what I've learned has come from my children. In Matthew 18, Jesus turned to a child and gave this lesson to His disciples in verses 3 and 4: *"And said, Verily I say unto you, Except ye be converted, and become as little children, ye shall not enter into the kingdom of heaven. Whosoever therefore shall humble himself as this little child, the same is greatest in the kingdom of heaven."*

Children are humble. You can hurt a child's feelings, but it's hard to hurt their ego. There isn't much there. When church begins, I'll see all of the beautiful families walking onto the property with their boys in pressed shirts, clean shoes, and slicked down hair. Their girls have pretty dresses with bows and ribbons in their hair to go with their clean church shoes. By the time we leave, it's a different story. Kids don't care about their appearance.

Children are teachable. Parents tell their children about Santa Claus, the Easter bunny, the tooth fairy, and other mythical characters. Their response isn't to question whether or not they're real or to see if this is some big joke to make them look foolish. Instead, they believe in them wholeheartedly. When we tell our children about Jesus, they accept Him as being real, powerful, and Someone we talk to without hesitation. They may not understand it all at first, but since Mom and Dad told them He's real, then He must be real. Our experience in life can create pride. As a result of the bumps and bruises caused by the hard knocks of life, we think we have it all figured out.

—— Today's Truth ——

We grow out of some immature traits as we age, but we should never grow up when it comes to emulating a child's faith as Jesus pointed out.

Loving God and Loving People

Read Matthew 21–22

IF I COULD use one phrase to lead our church to be a truly biblical church, it would be this motto: "Loving God and Loving People." When I became a pastor at the age of twenty-two, I felt incredibly overwhelmed. I felt like a toddler trying on his dad's shoes and walking awkwardly around the house. The position felt too big for me, and I was scared to death that I would not live up to the call. I didn't know what to say if someone asked for counsel. I didn't know how to organize, delegate, and lead programs. I didn't know how I would truly help a marriage, a backslidden Christian, or a new believer to live for God and be changed by the gospel. In that first year, God struck me with this truth. My focus was not on having the administrative skills in order. My desire was to love God and to love people the way Jesus commanded.

Matthew 22:36–40 says, *"Master, which is the great commandment in the law? Jesus said unto him, Thou shalt love the Lord thy God with all thy heart, and with all thy soul, and with all thy mind. This is the first and great commandment. And the second is like unto it, Thou shalt love thy neighbour as thyself. On these two commandments hang all the law and the prophets."* Jesus didn't just say that they were important. He said that all of the law and prophets hung on these two commands. In other words, everything you do should trace back to the fact that your actions are a result of a love for God and love for people.

We can become easily distracted from what's most important. The world doesn't need better programs, more elaborate organizations, or impressive talent. The world needs God's children to love Him more and love people more. Loving something will cause you to give your life to it. If you love God, you'll serve God. If you love people, you'll serve people.

—— Today's Truth ——

Loving God and loving people is the very definition of your purpose.

Beware of Being a Pharisee

Read Matthew 23–24

O NE OF THE hottest sermons that Jesus preached is found in Matthew 23. This fiery message was directed toward the hypocritical Pharisees of the day. Verse 3 sums up what Jesus thinks of this type of "believers": *"All therefore whatsoever they bid you observe, that observe and do; but do not ye after their works: for they say, and do not."* I believe one of the traits that Jesus hates the most is hypocrisy and pride, and those characteristics most adequately describe the marks of the Pharisees.

More than anything, I want to be real. It isn't hard to notice when someone is genuine, or if they are simply performing for the applause of others. We can dissect much in this passage that Jesus rebukes. I'd encourage you to study and reread this passage and ask yourself, "Is there anything in my life in the work of the Lord that resembles the character traits of a Pharisee?"

Their motives are clear. They sought the admiration of men (vv. 1–5). Positions were important to them (v. 6). They loved to be worshipped and praised by men (vv. 7–12). The result of their motives then showed up in their actions. Their message became a polluted gospel (v. 13). Their prayers were more about men seeing their spirituality than talking with the God of Heaven, and their prayers became useless (v. 14). Their fruit, their converts, was proof of the fact that their work wasn't producing real disciples, but more fakes and phonies (v. 15). Because of their distorted motives, their principles and priorities were completely misplaced (vv. 16–22). Finally, in verses 25–26, Jesus points out that they are so focused on their outward show that they have become hallow and empty inside.

—— Today's Truth ——

Genuine disciples allow God to work on their lives from the inside to the outside. Your service is not about you, but about God and others. Beware of becoming a Pharisee.

The Horrors of Hell

Read Matthew 25–26

ONE DAY WHILE I was soul winning by myself, I knocked on the door of a woman who was a Jehovah's Witness. I tried to give her the gospel, but her own beliefs based on that religion seemed to conflict which much of what I was trying to express. The biggest problem she had with the gospel as I gave it to her was on the subject of hell. She, like many, would not accept that God would create a place of eternal fire and punishment for those that reject Jesus Christ.

Hell is real. Matthew 25:41 describes that there will be those at the judgment whom God will cast into everlasting judgment in this place. The separation takes place for those who reject His Son, Jesus Christ.

Hell is separation from God. Verse 41 says, *"Depart from me...."* This is the Lord speaking. The worst part about hell is that it is complete and eternal separation from the Lord and the possibility of ever having a relationship with Him.

Hell is forever. There is no hope, no second chances, and no mercy given. The word *"everlasting"* in this verse makes it clear that this is no temporary judgment.

Hell is torment. The lake of fire that Jesus describes gives no details of people throwing a party or having a fun time like some may joke. Every description of hell is torment. It is terrible in every way.

Hell is not for you. Notice the last phrase of this verse: *"prepared for the devil and his angels."* Jesus said He is going to prepare your mansion in Heaven if you are saved, but hell was never made for you. Satan deceived Eve into falling into sin because Satan is a recruiter.

—— Today's Truth ——

These insights into this place draw us to Jesus and move us to tell others about how they can be saved.

A Job that Everyone Can Do

Read Matthew 27–28

MANY YEARS AGO a young man went to China as a missionary with an income of $2,500 annually. A company decided that they wanted this young man to work for them and offered him a position with a $5,000 salary. He declined the offer, and it was raised to $7,000 and then to $10,000, but he still declined. The company asked him if the salary was his sticking point, to which he replied, "Oh, the salary is big enough, but the job isn't." The work that Jesus declared to the disciples to end this passage is found in each of the Gospels. We know it as the Great Commission.

You can't spell gospel without the word *go*. The hardest part about the Great Commission for many disciples is that first step. It is making the decision to knock on the first door, strike up a spiritual conversation with a family member, coworker, or complete stranger, and obeying the impulse of the Holy Spirit to be a witness for the Lord.

Jesus noted in Matthew 9:36–37, *"Then saith he unto his disciples, The harvest truly is plenteous, but the labourers are few; Pray ye therefore the Lord of the harvest, that he will send forth labourers into his harvest."* Will you be a laborer for the gospel? There is too much work and not enough workers for the task at hand. It has been said that it is typically 10% of the people who do 90% of the work.

Think of the souls you've won to Jesus in your life. Lord willing, you've seen a number of people get saved. If not, start today. Take that first step. I promise you that you will not fail, because Jesus promised *"lo, I go with you…."* Someone made the statement that "the 'lo' is for those that 'go.'" We've got work to do.

——Today's Truth ——

The work of the Great Commission is nearest to the heart of God. To please Him and be used of Him, you must be a witness for Him.

Jesus Goes Viral

Read Mark 1–3

THANKS TO YOUTUBE, fame is not attained by great inventions, entrepreneurship, or noble accomplishments. Instead, you can become famous by making a fool of yourself and posting the video online. One of the most iconic viral videos is the "Charlie Bit Me" video of two brothers. Since 2007, that video has been viewed over 800 million times on YouTube with over 2 million likes. It has held the title as the most viewed video on the platform for a time and remains one of the most viewed, most liked, and most discussed videos to go viral.

Imagine if Jesus went viral today. Not as just entertainment, but rather that His name went viral because Christians shared His message to the world around them. Mark 2:1 shows that the name of Jesus began to spread in His day: *"And again he entered into Capernaum after some days; and **it was noised that he was in the house.**"*

The work of Christ in our lives does something so miraculous that it should be something that we are not able to keep to ourselves. If every Christian just talked about the transformation that took place because they got saved, our conversations wouldn't be all about sports, politics, or gossip, but about the Saviour of the world. We then see the response of Jesus going viral in verse 2: *"And straightway many were gathered together, insomuch that there was no room to receive them, no, not so much as about the door: and he preached the word unto them."* Instead of having to beg and bribe the people to come to church, they packed the place out because they had to see who they were talking about and the message He gave.

—— Today's Truth ——

You can have a part in making the name of Jesus heard around the world. Share Him with someone today!

How Faith Is Measured

Read Mark 4–5

THERE IS A long list of various instruments that are used to measure. An odometer measures distance travelled; a galvanometer measures electricity; a creepmeter measures the slow surface displacement of an active geologic fault in the earth (not the creepy neighbor you may try to avoid), and the list goes on. To measure something reveals the truth or facts regarding the answer you are looking for. Our faith can be measured by how it is revealed in our lives. Jesus rebuked the disciples in Mark 4:30 after it was revealed that they had no faith: *"And he said unto them, Why are ye so fearful? how is it that ye have no faith?"* How does your faith measure up and how is it measured?

Faith is measured by your actions. If you go to church, you are practicing your faith. It takes faith to believe that you will receive help by preaching. You can say you have faith all you want, but if it's not seen in your actions by what you practice, then the measurement is going to reveal that your faith is very small, if not completely nonexistent.

Faith is also measured through times of testing. It was on the sea when the disciples feared for their lives that Jesus rebuked them in this passage. The best of people can say and do the most foolish things when their faith is gone. How you respond in times of trouble shows how deep your relationship with God really is. People who trust God for their eternity have trouble trusting Him when their health fails them. Testing is never easy, and everyone has had moments of weakness and even failure, but we must learn to have faith in our earthly needs on top of our eternal needs.

——Today's Truth ——

Whatever state we are in concerning your faith, we must strive to continually increase our faith so that when it is tested and proven, we may be used of the Lord to draw close to Him and make a difference in this world.

Not Welcome Home

Read Mark 6–7

MARK 6 GIVES THE first account of Jesus' return home during His earthly ministry. Returning home is generally a happy occasion. When I was in Bible college, I was always excited when I was able to return home for the holidays or other special occasions. One day, I asked another student on my floor if he was going home for the holidays, and I'll never forget his answer. He said, "No. When I left to come to Bible college, my mom told me not to come back home." I quickly realized how fortunate I was to have a home, parents, a church, and people to look forward to coming back to.

If you have experienced a similar situation, then you can relate to this passage. Mark 6 begins with Jesus' return to His hometown. Nazareth was a small and lowly village. Historians estimate that there were somewhere around 500 people in this town. This was a place where everyone knew each other's names. It is probably safe to assume that a small town like this wasn't too accepting of new ideas and teaching, and it showed when Jesus came home.

Returning with disciples showed that Jesus revealed Himself as a leader. Mark 6:5–6 says, *"And he could there do no mighty work, save that he laid his hands upon a few sick folk, and healed them. And he marvelled because of their unbelief."* People who knew his parents and home would not accept His message. This was undoubtedly a heartbreaking experience for Jesus and for His family as well. Facing rejection from those you know and love can be difficult to bear, but it must not take you off course. Putting God first means that nobody's approval is more important than His. This experience hits home for too many people, and it can be one of the more difficult faces of rejection you can experience.

—— Today's Truth ——

If you face rejection from people you know and love, you must determine to continue in God's work with or without the acceptance of others.

A Bargaining Buffoon

Read Mark 8–9

A THIEF AND his girlfriend were walking down Main Street when she spotted a beautiful diamond ring in a jewelry store window. "Wow, I'd sure love to have that!" she said. "No problem, baby," the thief says, throwing a brick through the glass and grabbing the ring. A few blocks later, his girlfriend was admiring a leather jacket in another shop window. "What I'd give to own that!" she exclaimed. "Sure thing, darling," the guy responds again, throwing another brick through the window and snatching the coat. Finally, turning for home, they pass a Mercedes car dealership. "Boy, I'd do anything for one of those!" she cooed to her boyfriend. "Forget that!" the guy moans. "Do you think I'm made of bricks or something!?" Window shopping can be a dangerous game.

Jesus asked the question in Mark 8:36–37, *"For what shall it profit a man, if he shall gain the whole world, and lose his own soul? Or what shall a man give in exchange for his soul?"* It's humorous to think of all the deals we think we're getting because a price tag or sign said something was 50% off when the clear marketing strategy is to raise the price and just stick a big "ON SALE" sign on it. It's like the businesses with signs that say "Going Out of Business. Everything Must Go!"

Nothing in this world is worth the price of your soul. As a child of God, you've already been paid for by the blood of Christ. However, many give themselves to the world in exchange for cheap thrills, a night of fun, riches, fame, or other temporal rewards. Instead of looking around at what the world has to offer, why not look at what you have in the Lord and realize Satan can give you no better deal than what God has already given and can give if you'll follow Him?

—— Today's Truth ——

Stop yourself from coveting the items of pleasure that Satan has on display. Nothing is better than what you have and can get through Jesus Christ.

The Ministry Is About...

Read Mark 10–11

WHEN I WAS in Bible college, Pastor's Trieber's class that I took every semester on church education was a practical insight into his ministry and his heart for what is done in ministry and why it's done. He would make a few statements over and over that have come to characterize his example. He would often say with a spirit of enthusiasm, "The ministry is GREAT!" Another statement that stuck out that he often repeated was, "The ministry is about people." I had the opportunity to see this firsthand, not only in the classroom, but in real life situations. I remember a time when I was struggling with a major decision. I felt awkward asking for his time to receive counsel and wanted to wait for a good opportunity that would not interfere with his schedule. I went to men's prayer meeting on Saturday evening at 8:00pm. After it was over, I asked if I could talk with him for a moment. We went directly into the side "ready room" and he spent about twenty minutes talking with me. Looking back, this was probably the worst time to ask for a moment. However, I will never forget how gracious and kind he was whenever I asked for help.

We have many great examples in this life, but there is none greater than our Saviour. Mark 10:45 says, *"For even the Son of man came not to be ministered unto, but to minister, and to give his life a ransom for many."* Jesus should be magnified and lifted up in our world, in our hearts, for everyone to see. Yet, He came with a heart to serve. The word *ministry* is a form of the word minister. A definition of this word in *Webster's 1828 Dictionary* is, "to attend and serve; to perform service in any office." Therefore, our focus should be on how we can serve and attend to the needs of others.

—— Today's Truth ——

If one sentence could encompass the reason for your life, would it be to be served by others or to be a servant to others? Jesus came to minister, to serve, and our purpose should seek to mirror this pattern.

OCTOBER 18

The Poor Widow's Offering

Read Mark 12–13

AMY CARMICHAEL MADE one of my favorite statements on giving: "You can give without loving, but you cannot love without giving." While giving is one of my least favorite subjects to preach on in church, it is absolutely an essential aspect of our Christian lives.

At the close of Mark 12, Jesus makes much of a poor widow woman who gave. She did not write the biggest check in the church. Her name wasn't put on a building because of her riches. In fact, she possessed little to nothing. In Mark 12:43, Jesus says, *"Verily I say unto you, That this poor widow hath cast more in, than all they which have cast into the treasury."* From this widow's example, we see that Jesus cares about how we give, how much we give, and that He wants to bless us in return.

We are to give *proportionately*. Jesus saw her heart, but He also saw the amount. Make no mistake, we have an amount we are commanded to give. The tithe is still ten percent of your income (yes, that means before taxes).

We are to give *properly*. Donating to the commercial that pulls on your heart strings may not be a bad thing to do, but our giving must first be done in God's house. You can give to people outside the church, but you cannot tithe outside of the church.

We are to give *perpetually*. This isn't about one-time donations. Giving has to be a part of our lives. As God continually gives to us, we are to continually give to Him. Notice that by this account, no one has the excuse, "I just can't afford to give right now." Jesus stopped to notice this woman who had less money than all, but her sacrifice was unmatched. Make the commitment to give from every check, every increase, and every time you're in God's house.

——Today's Truth——

God doesn't need your money, but He commands it because if He can get you to give your things, then He knows you are willing to give yourself.

She Hath Done What She Could

Read Mark 14–16

ALL MEN ARE created equal. In the eyes of God, we are similar in this single foundational fact. Every person was created by God in His image. It is through this fact, I believe, that we are able to relate with God and understand who He is. God created me in His image as a man, a husband, a father, and a leader, and I am able to understand Him more because of being made in His likeness.

When we see people, we see facial features, body type, skin color or nationality, and other physical traits. In addition, when we're around a person long enough, we notice their personality, talents, and maybe even strengths and weaknesses. This can often lead to pride or discouragement if we are not careful.

By Heaven's standards, we're all humans created in God's image. By the world's standards, we are extraverts or introverts, smart or dumb, funny or rude, attractive or ugly, and the list goes on and on. The principle Jesus gave when Mary broke the alabaster box of spikenard on Jesus gives an important truth regarding this battle we face with comparison.

In Mark 14:8, Jesus said of Mary, *"She hath done what she could...."* You may not be able to achieve what others can, but God has created you with something to offer. Mary did what she could with what she had, and Jesus praised her for it. He didn't mention someone had a bigger box of ointment or that another church member's business was more successful, but He gave her the compliment for using what she had for His glory. Jesus isn't in Heaven with a scoreboard to see who has given the most money or won the most souls. He is simply looking for Christians to use what they have been given and to give themselves back to Him.

—— Today's Truth ——

God has given you something to give. Doing what you can with what you have is all He expects from us, but it is something He still expects.

The Dumb Doubting Dad

Read Luke 1

THE BOOK OF Luke is unique, and many are unaware of several striking facts about the book. For example, the book of Luke is the longest book in the New Testament. While the four Gospels each have similarities and parallel stories, about fifty percent of Luke is untold in other books with twenty-nine events in the life of Christ found only in this book. This book puts a greater focus on individuals than the other Gospels, including thirteen women not mentioned elsewhere. Luke begins chronologically before the other Gospels and breaks a 400-year silence. Also, Luke was a Gentile and presents the message of Jesus to non-Jews as well.

Malachi ends with a prophecy given about John the Baptist (Malachi 4:5–6). Luke 1 tells of the story of the birth of John the Baptist. However, after the angel Gabriel told Zacharias that he and his wife would have a son, he responded, *"Whereby shall I know this? for I am an old man, and my wife well stricken in years"* (Luke 1:18). Immediately after this future dad expressed his doubt, the angel told him that he would be dumb and not able to speak until the birth of his child.

As Mary and Elisabeth both were given the good news that they would have children promised and given by God, they rejoiced! God's Word is filled with promises that He has given, and He has kept His promises every time. The Bible contains many promises. One man claims to have counted 8,810 promises in the Bible. Psalm 37 has a promise for every verse. Isaiah, Jeremiah, and Ezekiel each contain over 1,000 promises each. Whenever God makes a promise, He has proven that He will keep His promise. One of the most encouraging reminders is to review the promises that God has given you throughout His Word. Doubting is an expression of the flesh, but God has given man no reason to doubt Him.

—— Today's Truth ——

God makes promises, and God keeps His promises. You should not speak words of doubt, but trust the promises He has given.

Where Is Jesus?

Read Luke 2–3

EVERY PARENT'S NIGHTMARE is to lose your child. Knowing some of the horrific people in the world, it can be a terrifying experience. So much so that I don't even like to recall small experiences we have had in a park or a store with our children.

In Luke 2, Mary and Joseph noticed that their son, Jesus, was missing. However, it wasn't until a full day had passed that they figured this out. This should make any parent feel a little better about themselves, even though He was not a child here, but a twelve-year-old boy. Finally, after three more days, they found their Son in the synagogue, astonishing the educated people with His understanding and answers.

While this is a situation to which parents can somewhat relate (except that we more likely will find our child into some mischief instead of talking about the Bible at church), we see an application here with Jesus in our lives. The presence of Jesus should be a part of life every day. Sadly, many go about their day, week, month, or even longer without stopping to consider whether they are close to the Son of God.

Do you notice God's presence in your life? The longer you wait to take notice and the longer you wait to seek Him, the farther apart you will drift and the longer it will take for you to find Him again. We so easily go about our day, consumed with work, errands, and lists, that we fail to take inventory of what is most important. Imagine a parent at Disneyland. I've seen parents put a leash on their kids at parks to make sure they don't get out of sight. They look every few seconds or don't even take their eyes off their children. I wonder what this kind of diligence would mean to a Christian who desires that much to have the presence of Christ in their life.

—— Today's Truth ——

Be diligent every day all throughout your day to ask yourself, "Where is Jesus in my life right now?" Is He close?

The Temptation of Jesus

Read Luke 4–5

OSCAR WILDE, A British playwright, said, "I can resist anything except temptation." Temptation raises its ugly head and dangles wrong decisions in front of us on our spiritual journey. Like all of us, Jesus faced temptation as well. He is our great example and shows us how we can overcome any temptation in life. We don't have to fall, no matter how great the temptation.

Temptation often comes after you set out to do something for God. Luke 4 presents Jesus full of the Holy Ghost as He gets ready to begin His earthly ministry. Much of what we read about in the Gospels takes place after His forty days of fasting in the wilderness. It seems after times when you decide to surrender yourself to the Lord, Satan comes knocking to get you off course. The devil isn't focused on the complacent, backslidden, out-of-commission Christians, but has his eyes set on those who are busy and fighting in the battle.

Temptation is conquered through the power of God's Word and the Holy Spirit. Jesus was full of the Holy Spirit and responded to temptation by quoting the Word of God. Psalm 119:11 says, *"Thy word have I hid in mine heart, that I might not sin against thee."* God's Word is the sword of the Spirit listed with the armor of God. You can't overcome temptation by your own strength, but God has the tools you need to give you victory. You don't have to be another casualty of Satan's tricks.

Temptation will cease, but will return. After Jesus resisted the devil, verse 13 says after the temptation ceased, *"he departed from him for a season."* Temptation won't last forever, but it won't stay away forever either. It is a continual battle we face in this life. Either it will overtake you, or you will overcome the temptation by following the Son of God's example.

—— Today's Truth ——

Though temptation is a part of our lives, it doesn't have to take your life. You can have victory as Jesus did when you are tempted by the devil.

Looking for a Fault

Read Luke 6–7

THE PREACHING OF George Whitefield was a key factor in bringing revival to England in the 1700s. One could easily praise a man like this for the accomplishments in his life and his surrender to the work of the gospel ministry. However, even amid all the good in his life, he was not without critics. After a letter containing a personal attack on his integrity, Whitefield responded, "I thank you heartily for your letter. As for what you and my other enemies are saying against me, I know worse things about myself than you will ever say about me."

Responding to criticism with the right spirit can be difficult. Jesus often faced personal attacks from people like the Pharisees. Instead of lashing out in anger, He either used the opportunity to teach a Biblical truth or even ignored their wicked plot to criticize Him altogether. Luke 6 begins with the Pharisees seeking to attack Him on His teaching concerning the sabbath.

Rebuking sin and resolving problems is very different than searching for faults in people to criticize. Problems will come and sin cannot be ignored, but praise, thankfulness, and other areas must be a part of your life if you are going to have joy as a Christian. Are you constantly pointing out people's faults? The answer to this is to live with the fulness of the Holy Spirit. Galatians 5:15–16 admonishes, *"But if ye bite and devour one another, take heed that ye be not consumed one of another. This I say then, Walk in the Spirit, and ye shall not fulfil the lust of the flesh."*

—— Today's Truth ——

God's desire is for you to live with joy. Only you can consume yourself with negative things that will steal your joy and hurt others.

Stormy Seas

Read Luke 8–9

S TORMS CAN CAUSE great disillusionment to those in the middle of them. The fear of the waves and the great power that leaves you helpless can make you lose all sense of the faith you thought you had. The disciples saw Jesus perform miracles with their own eyes, yet they still doubted Him when they were in the storm.

Remember, it was Jesus who led them into the storm. All of the storms that you will face in life are Father-filtered. He allows you to go through them and even leads you into the storm for a purpose. Your desire may be to get out of the storm, but God may keep you in that storm to grow you in a way that only He sees.

The separation felt real. The disciples felt alone. Jesus was on the ship, but He was asleep. He was quiet, and they couldn't feel His presence. They knew He was there, but they felt the same as if He had been on the shore or somewhere else completely. Sound familiar?

In reality, Jesus never left them, and He promises His presence to all who are saved. There are times when God feels quiet. There may even be times when He seems to be silent. Fear grows. Insecurity creeps in. You may doubt that He is there, but He has promised to never leave you.

Jesus was just a call away. They knew He was there, but until they came to ask for help, they were on their own. Jesus was ready to do the miracle, but He awaited their call. Prayer is a free resource that many don't use. They know God is available, but they stand alone on the ship and leave the Lord off to the side. Trusting God means leaving it in His hands after you've put it there. This is done through prayer.

——Today's Truth ——

Smooth sailing is never promised. Storms are a reality. The question is what you'll do in the storm. Have faith in God even when you feel alone, and run to Him when your flesh is weak and your faith is low.

The Needful Part

Read Luke 10–11

MEN AND WOMEN have distinct differences. Women are known by specific traits, and men the same. Women are generally more emotional than men. That has its advantages and disadvantages. Men are generally stronger. Because we have different strengths and weaknesses, we have different needs. A big issue in working through problems in marriages is due to a misunderstanding of the other person's needs. It's almost like speaking a foreign language when trying to explain yourself.

At the close of Luke 10, Jesus points out our greatest need. Martha was busy getting the house in order, because that's what people do when they have company. You clean rooms guests won't even go into just in case they open that door. Some will do this to the point that they won't even spend time with their guests because they are too busy "hosting" the whole time. This was Martha's problem. Mary wasn't much of a help to her sister, and Martha complained.

Jesus made it clear which of the two was most important to Him. Luke 10:41 says, *"Martha, Martha, thou art careful and troubled about many things: But one thing is needful: and Mary hath chosen that good part, which shall not be taken away from her."* Serving is good, but it's not needful. Spending time with Jesus is the needful part. Serving your family is good, but spending time with them is needful. Cleaning the church is good, but spending time with your church family and being in church is needful. Service can't replace the quality time that you spend with others. This is the needful part in our relationship with God and with others.

—— Today's Truth ——

Good parts are not always needful parts. God wants to have a relationship with you, and that is the part of your relationship you need the most.

Don't Worry

Read Luke 12–13

Howard Hughes was a big-time businessman who dabbled in oil, entertainment, and the aviation industry. These pursuits made him billions of dollars. The last twenty-five or so years of his life, Howard Hughes was the poster child for worry and anxiety. Overwhelmed by an unsubstantiated fear that people were out to get him, he spent his last decades living in hotels, where he would rent out whole floors. Those closest to him say he was so overwhelmed by worry and fear that he sat in a pitch-black room for long stretches of time, refusing to allow anyone to come in to see him. If you had to communicate with Mr. Hughes, specific instructions were provided. You had to take several tissues, cover the door knob with them, knock, and open the door ever so slightly. Hughes required this process because he was exceptionally fearful of germs. His worry led to severe stomach problems, causing him to sit in the bathroom for hours at a time. In fact, one aide notes that Hughes once sat in the bathroom for twenty-seven straight hours. On the rare occasion that Hughes would venture out of the hotel, he gave specific instructions to his driver: only smooth roads were to be taken, and the driver was never to exceed thirty-five miles per hour. On the chance that they had to cross railroad tracks or some uneven part of the road, the driver was to slow down to two miles per hour.

If you allow it, worry can dominate your life. Jesus said in Luke 12:24, *"Take no thought for your life…."* In layman's terms, don't worry about it! Worry can consume you, and that's not the way Jesus wants you to live. At the root of it, worry is me-centered. Verse 32 gives us this comfort, *"Fear not, little flock; for it is your Father's good pleasure to give you the kingdom."* God will take care of you, He has control, and He will work it out for good.

—— Today's Truth ——

Live your life by faith, not by worry. Don't let your worry consume your thoughts, but rather focus on God's goodness to you.

God's Lost and Found Department

Read Luke 14–16

JOHN 3:16 MAY BE unarguably the most famous verse in the Bible. *"For God so loved the world..."* is a statement that gives the fundamental context for the message of salvation and God's desire for all men to be saved. There is not a person in the world who has ever lived or will ever live in the future that God doesn't love and for whom God didn't die. Just as much as this is true, God also loves the individual.

In Luke 15, we see three parables that Jesus gives. All of these parables illustrate the same truth. God loves the world, but He also loves the individual. The parable of the lost sheep tells of a shepherd that leaves ninety-nine sheep in his flock to go find just one sheep that is lost. The parable of the lost coin tells of a woman who lost a coin and searches diligently until she finds it. The last parable may be the most familiar. The parable of the prodigal son speaks of a son that took his inheritance and wasted it. After he "came to himself," he returned home to find his father waiting for his return and ready to forgive and restore his son.

The result of every parable is the same. When just one person gets saved, there is rejoicing in Heaven. You may think that you are only one person in a sea of people, wondering how you could matter to God. Well, Jesus gives us three stories to illustrate that we do matter to Him.

For every person who gets saved and every backslidden believer who is restored, we must rejoice as Jesus does. Everyone wants to make a difference in as many lives as possible, but there is no magic number in the thousands or millions that should make you rejoice more than when any person, even just one person, gets saved or comes back to the Shepherd.

—— Today's Truth ——

God loves the whole world, but He also loves every individual person. He rejoices at each salvation and restored Christian.

A Life That Is Full of Troubles

Read Luke 17–18

I DON'T LIKE to think about negative things. If there's a problem, I'd rather not talk about it or think about it. However, ignoring the problem is a good way to multiply a problem. Luke 17:1 says, *"Then said he unto the disciples, It is impossible but that offences will come: but woe unto him, through whom they come!"* The Greek word used here for *offences* is *skandalon,* and it comes from the word for a bent-stick—the stick that springs the trap or sets the bait. It also was used for a stumbling block, something that people trip over. Some trip and fall, but others will be watchful and wise so they don't fall.

Expecting trouble prepares you so that you won't quit. If you know a fight is coming, you aren't going to live casually. If you ever played sports, your coach might have admonished you to "put your game face on." There is a seriousness to the battle that lies ahead and if you go into it with a lackadaisical spirit, then you will likely lose. You don't have to lose, but you can be prepared today so that you don't get knocked out by your problem.

Keep yourself from being the one to bring trouble. It is humorous at times when people complain about all the problems with people in their life. They act like the world is out to get them. The common denominator in their problems is themselves, but they are too prideful to realize that they're the one who is the most responsible for their troubles. If you have fires in life everywhere you go, you may be the culprit, not the victim. Instead of being a fire starter, be the one to put out the fires.

—— Today's Truth ——

Living by the Holy Spirit will give you victory over troubles, but it will not take away troubles. Life comes with problems. Seek to be one who solves problems, not the one who creates them.

The City of Peace

Read Luke 19–20

THE CITY OF Jerusalem has great significance in God's plan. Much can be said about this city regarding what has already happened there and what will happen in the last days. As Jesus came to the city of Jerusalem in Luke 19:41, the Bible says, *"And when he was come near, he beheld the city, and wept over it."* The name *Jerusalem* means "city of peace." This was God's design and desire for this city, but this is not what took place there after this point in Jesus' ministry.

Jesus gives five prophecies about Jerusalem in this passage: the building of an embankment, the surrounding of the city, the destruction of the city, the killing of the city's inhabitants, and the complete leveling of the city. Jesus wept as He looked over the city, knowing what their future held. Most of the Jews were looking for someone to save them in a political way. Because of this, many missed Jesus as their Messiah as He came to offer Himself as a sacrifice to save them eternally.

What Jesus will do in the last days reveals what His plan is for the city of Jerusalem, but also what His will is for His people. The city of peace was to be a beacon of light for God's people. They didn't have to face destruction, but because they missed His purpose, they missed the peace that came with knowing Jesus.

The end does not bring peace for nonbelievers. Those who have rejected Christ will see destruction as it is explained in the greater part of the book of Revelation. For the Christian, the end brings peace. We should weep to think of the destruction that will come to many, and we must also turn to Jesus for the peace that only He can truly give.

—— Today's Truth ——

Jesus wept because of the destruction that would come to Jerusalem. This wasn't His desire for Jerusalem, and it isn't His desire for your life either.

Not My Will, But Thine Be Done

Read Luke 21–22

FLORENCE NIGHTINGALE WROTE in her diary, "I am thirty years of age, the age at which Christ began His mission. Now no more childish things, now no more vain things, now Lord let me think only of Thy will." Jim Elliot, a missionary murdered in South America by the Auca Indians, wrote these words in his diary, "God, I pray Thee, light these idle sticks of my life. Consume my life, my God, for it is Thine, I seek not a long life but a full one like you, Lord Jesus." Miriam Booth, daughter of the founder of the Salvation Army, was a brilliant and cultured lady. Her ministry had begun with promise of great success for she was being wonderfully used of the Lord. In a short while, however, her health completely broke down; and she was brought to the point of death. A sympathetic friend spoke to her one day about the tragedy of being laid aside, and the fact that she was being prevented from doing the Lord's work. With a look of contentment on her face, Miriam Booth responded, "It is wonderful to do the Lord's work, but it is greater still to do the Lord's will."

In the hardest part of Jesus' ministry, the hour that He was to lay down His life on the cross, He prayed in Luke 22:42, "*Saying, Father, if thou be willing, remove this cup from me: nevertheless not my will, but thine, be done.*" Not your will, God's will. Not your desire, God's desire. This is the example that Jesus gave as He surrendered Himself to the will of the Father. The difficulty in doing this is the beauty in the act. You are putting your life in God's hands when you put your life in His will. He will see you through, He will give you strength, and He will use you for something beyond your understanding; but you must surrender your will for His will.

—— Today's Truth ——

This should be the daily prayer of every Christian: "Not my will, but thine be done." Seek God's will above your own today and for the rest of your life.

They Know Not What They Do

Read Luke 23–24

I f there is a part of the story of Calvary that grips my heart more than any other, it is found in one of the seven statements that Jesus made on the cross. Roman soldiers would normally expect resistance when they crucified a criminal. With the cross laid down flat on the ground, they would put the body on the cross; it normally took four men to secure a man to the cross, whether by rope or by nails. One man would grab each arm or a leg and fight to keep the criminal in place while they secured him to the cross. I always try to picture how this took place with Jesus. I don't expect that He fought them. After all, they didn't kill Jesus. Jesus gave Himself. I imagine that as the soldiers braced themselves for a fight, they were taken back by the fact that Jesus placed each arm on the posts and one foot on top of the other as they nailed Him to that old rugged cross. It is in times like this that I can't help but think those soldiers must have thought, "There's something different about this Man."

After Jesus was buffeted, scourged, spat on, and mocked; while He had a crown of thorns shoved into His skull and His beard plucked; and during all the other horrific acts of hatred His accusers imposed, Jesus responded in a way that was unthinkable. I believe it was at a time when tensions were high that He said, *"Father, forgive them; for they know not what they do"* (Luke 23:34). How could He forgive them after all they had done? Jesus' act of forgiveness here reminds us that He is ready to forgive us, even before we come to Him and confess our sins. His forgiveness is already decided.

—— Today's Truth ——

Whatever the offence, Jesus has a heart to forgive. Before you even ask, Jesus has already decided that He is willing and ready to forgive. Do not hesitate to receive His forgiveness.

I Am a Voice

Read John 1–3

DURING THE GREAT Awakening, George Whitefield preached across the colonies covering over 5,000 miles one year and preaching over 350 times. One of the most notable characteristics about Whitefield was his voice. He was known for his booming, powerful voice that could be heard by several thousand people—before microphones and other audio technology.

The book of John begins with the account of John. This is not the apostle John, but Jesus' earthly cousin, John the Baptist. By the way, isn't that a wonderful title that God gave him…"*The BAPTIST.*" It just has a nice ring to it. John was the forerunner of Jesus, preparing and preaching of Jesus' first advent. The people questioned who this man was. They thought he could possibly be the Messiah. I love John's response as they questioned him for information about himself. He said in John 1:23, "*I am the voice….*"

The description he gave of himself was a voice. Think of the way a microphone amplifies the sound of a person's voice. The microphone is nothing without the voice. Like a glove without a hand, a microphone cannot produce; it can only be used by something. It is an amplifier of a voice, but it is not the voice. John realized that he was not important, but what He was speaking of and Who his message was about was what the people needed to pay attention to.

Far too many Christians want to be the focal point instead of just being a voice. Are you allowing God's message to speak through you? As His Word enters your heart, His Word should make its way out of your lips as you tell others about Jesus. Be a voice. Not a showman, not an entertainer, not an influencer, not a star, but just a voice.

—— Today's Truth ——

The humble Christian understands that they are just a vessel for God to use for His glory and His message. Be a voice for Jesus today.

Wants vs. Needs

Read John 4–5

IF THERE IS one thing that I learned during the 2020 coronavirus shutdown, it was the difference between the things that I really needed in life versus the things that were nice to have but may not be considered a necessity. I remember driving down the road on Sundays to go to our church to do our livestream services. Those were difficult times, knowing that I'd walk into an empty church with just a handful of cars in the parking lot. As I passed by businesses, restaurants, gyms, stores, and other places, many were dark, empty, and had signs that they were closed. It was an odd feeling to see everything closed so quickly. However, in this time, I learned that I could live without things like Starbucks coffee and my favorite restaurants. On the other side of the coin, I realized the few things in life that were absolutely essential for me. Going to church is something I need. Being with my family is a need. Talking to people about Jesus is a need in my life. It's easy to get caught up in our modern society and to have the lines fade between needs and wants.

John 4 gives the account of Jesus' interaction with the Samaritan woman. That story is only possible because it was something Jesus felt He must do. John 4:4 says, *"And he must needs go through Samaria."* This wasn't an option for Him; it was a need. Talking to this lost woman and opening her eyes to the truth of eternal life through Him was absolutely imperative at that moment.

What do you have in your life that you can't live without? Hopefully your answer to that question isn't filled with selfish desires and temporal satisfaction. Wants aren't always bad, but we can't let our desires cloud our judgment on what is truly important every day.

—— Today's Truth ——

What you need should be determined by what God commands and desires. Be careful not to allow your wants to override what you truly need to do in life for God's glory.

The Bread of Life

Read John 6–8

J ESUS MAKES SEVEN statements in the Gospels that begin with *"I am…."* These are specific and declarative statements He uses to describe Himself as the Messiah and Saviour. People can believe what they want, but the truths about Jesus stand true whether scoffers believe them or not. There are no arguments, no debate, and no doubts about the facts about Jesus Christ. He is exactly who He said that He is, and He is the same yesterday, today, and forever.

In John 6, following the famed miracle of the feeding of the five thousand (the only miracle aside from the resurrection that appears in all four Gospels), Jesus says in verse 35, *"I am the bread of life: he that cometh to me shall never hunger…."* Jesus presented several applications to this example to give insight concerning Himself. Through this, the main point to understand is that Jesus wants you to know who He is and He wants to reveal Himself to you. By these statements and this one in particular, we are able to understand Him more.

Bread is common. One of the most common items at the dinner then, and even today, was bread. Bread was something that most people were able to have on a regular basis. Jesus presents Himself as the Bread because He came not for a select few, but for the whole world (John 3:16).

Bread is filling. There is reason for the bread that is served with most meals in some form. It satisfies hunger. Jesus makes it clear that when He fills your life, you will not be hungry again. He can satisfy your desire for life, joy, peace, purpose, and all the things you truly desire when you receive Him and follow His Word.

Bread is necessary for life. In Matthew 4:4, Jesus gives the example of bread that sustains your temporary life. For eternal life, all must come to Jesus. He is the Bread of Life, and He will give what no one else can.

—— Today's Truth ——

Jesus reveals Himself to us in many forms in His Word. He wants you to know Him, but more importantly, He wants you to receive Him.

What It Means to Be a Sheep

Read John 9–10

GROWING UP IN church, I can recall the song that says, "I don't want to be a Pharisee…I don't want to be a Sadducee…I just want to be a sheep." (Then everyone would say "baa" like a sheep.) Over and over in the Bible, we see the analogy given to us that God is our Shepherd, and we are His sheep.

First, we understand that we have a good Shepherd. John 10:11 says, "I am the good shepherd: the good shepherd giveth his life for the sheep." We are what we are as sheep because of the flock that we are in. The leading and care from the Shepherd determines what we obtain as sheep. There is no better place to be than to be a part of God's flock and to have Him as your personal Shepherd.

Sheep hear the voice of the shepherd. John 10:27 says, *"My sheep know my voice…."* If you're close to God, you know His voice. Moreover, you know when you're being spoken to by someone other than the voice of God. The closer you are to Him, the more you know the distinction between what is of Jesus and what is not.

Sheep are known of the shepherd. A shepherd's job is to care for his sheep. He has to know them in every way. He must know their strengths, weaknesses, what they need, and what they need to be protected from. Jesus knows His sheep. In fact, He knows you better than you know yourself.

Sheep follow their shepherd. Sheep that go astray get hurt, but they also aren't a part of the flock anymore. This doesn't mean you can lose your salvation, but you can lose fellowship, protection, and blessing from the Shepherd when you don't follow Him and decide to lead your own life.

—— Today's Truth ——

Being a sheep in Jesus' flock is a blessing. There are benefits to having Him as your Shepherd and being close to Him.

A Window of Light

Read John 11–12

Jesus is coming again! Four times in Revelation, Jesus says, *"I come quickly"* (Revelation 3:11; 22:7; 22:12; 22:20). To be honest, I have read these verses many times and thought to myself, "That was over two thousand years ago. That doesn't seem very quick to me." Perhaps you've had the same thoughts. In John 12, Jesus gives a message about the brevity of His time with the disciples that gives us purpose as we wait for the next phase of Jesus' timetable.

John 12:35–36 says, *"Then Jesus said unto them, Yet a little while is the light with you. Walk while ye have the light, lest darkness come upon you: for he that walketh in darkness knoweth not whither he goeth. While ye have light, believe in the light, that ye may be the children of light."* He reminded the disciples that they had a small window with Him before He departed. After He went to Heaven, He speaks of a small window before He comes back again.

The window is closing, the signs are getting clearer, and the events of the Bible are unfolding before our eyes. God has commissioned you and I to a work in this life, and we have just "a little while" to accomplish these tasks for His glory. We often live like we have all the time in the world to get to those things we've thought of doing. "One day, I'll start soul winning." "One of these years, I'll read through my Bible." "Eventually, I'll get serious about going to church faithfully." Procrastination can be a deadly disease that causes you to waste your time while you have opportunity to do something for the Lord. Before the light goes out, we have work to do. God's work can't be done when He is gone. Now is the day to get to work and walk in the light while we still have the opportunity.

—— Today's Truth ——

Nothing lasts forever. Your opportunities will fade. You can use your time in the light to work, or you can waste it.

Look to Your Right, Look to Your Left

Read John 13–16

WHILE UNDER PREACHING, you might have heard something like this, "Look to the person on your right. Now, look to the person on your left. Ten years from now, one of you won't even be in church anymore, much less doing anything for God." Statistics show that around two-thirds of teenagers drop out of church before the age of twenty-two after graduating from high school and leaving their home.

John, along with the other Gospels, ends with the same alarming story of Judas. At the Last Supper, Jesus told the disciples *"Verily, verily, I say unto you, that one of you shall betray me"* (John 13:21). The reality of the Christian life proves that the longer you stay, the more people you will see come and go, and betray the Lord Jesus. Judas was a wolf amidst sheep, and here he reveals his true colors.

Several different characters are seen in the crucifixion story. We see the betrayer, Judas. We see the denier, Peter. We see the doubter, Thomas. We see the faithful, John. While most of the disciples came back to their senses, Judas became a casualty. He couldn't blame Jesus or his fellow disciples, but he realized in his own time that he had made a horrible decision.

Nobody considers themselves to be in danger of being a casualty. Verse 22 says, *"Then the disciples looked one on another, doubting of whom he spake."* You might not think you will fall, but you must consider that you can fall. Determine not to be another illustration of someone who used to go to church, used to abstain from alcohol, used to go soul winning, etc. People will betray Jesus, but you don't have to.

——Today's Truth ——

Not everyone who follows Jesus will stay with Jesus. Will you be another casualty or will you be among the faithful until the end?

How Jesus Prays

Read John 17–18

PRAYER IS A lot less complicated than we make it out to be. I've had many people say to me as a pastor, "I just don't know how to pray." New Christians all have this fear that they need to possess eloquence or theological understanding in order to pray correctly. Prayer is just the word that describes how we talk to God. While prayer is not complicated, we see patterns for prayer throughout the Bible and commands concerning what we are to pray about. In John 17, we have possibly the best insight during Jesus' ministry of Him praying, and we can learn from His pattern.

Jesus prayed for Himself. Before I pray for my wife, I pray for myself. Before I pray for anybody, for that matter, I first pray and seek forgiveness, I thank the Lord for what He's given me, I yield myself to Him, and seek His help in various areas in my life. If I am going to be a help to anyone else, I must first receive help for myself. On an airplane, they tell you to put on your own oxygen mask first in case of an emergency. You aren't much help to anyone if you're unconscious because you didn't make sure you got the oxygen you needed. It isn't selfish to pray for yourself; it is taking responsibility over your life.

Jesus prayed for the saved. We should pray for many who are in this group, and I believe we start with those closest to us. Pray for your spouse, your children, your family, your church family, missionaries your church supports, and maybe others that God has laid on your heart. God's people need your prayers just as much as the lost.

Jesus prayed for the lost. The smallest section (vv. 25–26) is given to the lost. That is because there is only one prayer you should make for the lost, and that is for them to be saved. They have no greater need.

—— Today's Truth ——

We learn from Jesus' example that there is a pattern to our prayers and that we should be diligent to pray for various needs all around us.

Gone Fishing

Read John 19–21

I NEVER CARED for fishing until I went with someone who really knew what he was doing. My dad did many activities with me when I was a kid. We rented kayaks and canoes several times, went on bike trails in the mountains, shot guns, and played baseball; but fishing was one thing we didn't really do. For me, fishing isn't a big deal, but it was Peter's old way of life. It was something that he could easily fall back to if the disciple thing didn't really pan out.

After Jesus was crucified and buried, I believe the disciples were depressed. Everything they had believed and lived for over the last three years had been taken from them. John 21:3 says, *"Simon Peter saith unto them, I go a fishing."* This was Peter's way of throwing in the towel.

Quitting is never an option. God changes plans and alters your compass, but quitting should not even be in your vocabulary. When I went to Bible college, I knew that God had called me to the ministry. I didn't know where, but I knew it was His will for me to be somewhere in ministry. If you had asked me at the beginning of the second semester of my senior years about my plans, I would have shrugged my shoulders. Even then, I had no clue where I was going. Another thing I didn't have was a plan B. There was nothing to fall back on for me.

The result of Peter's decision gives truth to where that path will lead for those who take it. Verse 3 continues, *"They say unto him, We also go with thee. They went forth, and entered into a ship immediately; and that night they caught nothing."* Anything outside of God's best will always disappoint. Peter wasn't made to be a fisherman anymore, and I think this was just the confirmation he needed that his old life could no longer give the satisfaction he needed.

—— Today's Truth ——

Quitting should never be a discussion, a thought, or even an idea. God's way is best, even when it's hard. Have no fall back plan when it comes to the things of God in your life.

Needy People

Read Acts 1–3

Mᴏʀᴇ ᴛʜᴀɴ ᴀ quarter of the world's population lacks access to clean water. There is a water crisis in many countries, whether it is fear of a water shortage or access to clean water. This is just one need. As Peter and John went to the temple, they encountered a man with a need and God used them to meet his need.

All people have needs. Instead of wondering how your need will be met, realize that God may use you to meet someone else's need today.

Be careful not to make assumptions. Acts 3:2 says this man was lame from birth. Everyone has a different story, and God never called us to find out the story of everyone's past.

Needy people are still people. In verse 4, Peter said, *"Look on us."* It was common to beg with your head down. Peter wanted to talk eyeball to eyeball with this man.

People don't always know what they need. Peter sounds more like a Baptist preacher here than ever. He said in verse 6, *"Silver and gold have I none; but such as I have give I thee: In the name of Jesus Christ of Nazareth rise up and walk."*

God deserves the glory. The man stood up and went nuts for Jesus! Peter could have been hurt by the fact that he wasn't getting any praise, or he could realize that God was rightfully getting the glory He deserved. After all, people don't work miracles.

Helping people helps the cause of Christ. Verse 9 and 10 speak of those that noticed. People notice and are drawn to Christ when they see a life that is truly changed.

——Today's Truth ——

There are needs in the world that God may use you to fill. You can have a part in someone's life if you are willing to be a help.

A Couple of Nobodies

Read Acts 4–6

GOOD PARENTS WILL tell children that they are special to make them feel loved. However, the longer we live, the more we might feel like we aren't that special after all. Not every teacher, boss, or friend will think you are God's gift to humanity. Throughout life, the truth about ourselves becomes more apparent. None of us is special due to our own merit. Our talents, personal traits, and even our accomplishments will be lost and forgotten in history as the years pass. History will likely not promote our name or legacy. We came into this world as nobodies, and we will leave it the same way.

The truth of who we are is the beauty of Christ's work in our lives. Acts 4:13 says, *"Now when they saw the boldness of Peter and John, and perceived that they were unlearned and ignorant men, they marvelled; and they took knowledge of them, that they had been with Jesus."* When the people heard Peter and John, they weren't impressed with their social status, their past accomplishments, or any personal traits. They had no buildings named after them, no statues erected in their honor, and to this point, no books had been written on their story. Because of this, the people saw what was really special about these men. The verse ends by saying the people realized *"that they had been with Jesus."*

Instead of seeing your manmade glory, people should see the impression that Jesus has made in your life. When we are small, Jesus can be seen clearly. When we realize that truth about the fact that we are all nobodies, it helps us understand that we aren't the ones with whom people need to be impressed. Can it be said that when people see your life and hear you speak that there is evidence that you have been with Jesus? I heard a preacher once put it like this: "I am a nobody telling everybody about Somebody who can save anybody."

—— Today's Truth ——

Your nothingness is a clear path for people to see the greatness of Christ in you.

Don't Drink the Kool-Aid!

Read Acts 7–8

ACTS 8 BEGINS WITH persecution brought against the church once again. A common pattern seen in Acts and in church history is prayer, power, preaching, then persecution. After persecution comes, the resolve of the apostles is seen by their dedication to continue in the work of the Lord.

Not all attacks from Satan come by destruction. What Satan cannot accomplish by destruction, he seeks to accomplish by deception. This is the picture we have of him as a serpent. Acts 8:9 tells of a man, Simon, who was a sorcerer. The Bible tells us in verses 9–10 that he *"bewitched the people of Samaria, giving out that himself was some great one: To whom they all gave heed, from the least to the greatest, saying, This man is the great power of God."* To bewitch means "to fascinate; to gain an ascendancy over by charms or incantation; to deceive and mislead by tricks or imposter" *(Webster's 1828 Dictionary).*

God's people can usually point out persecution clearly, but the work of Satan that comes by deception may take more lives than the former. An extreme example is Jim Jones, founder of the People's Temple. A disturbing forty-five-minute audio recording shed light on the wicked deception he imposed on his followers. On November 18, 1978, in Jonestown, Guyana, he urged his followers to drink a Kool-Aid that contained cyanide and valium. This murder/suicide took 909 lives that day and was the greatest loss of American lives unrelated to a natural disaster until 9/11.

By the work of the Holy Spirit and the truth of God's Word, you don't have to fall to deception. Much of Satan's work isn't done in your face with great noise and boldness. It is done in the dark, little by little, so that he will deceive you without you realizing that you are under attack.

—— Today's Truth ——

Satan is a defeated enemy, and God can give you power to overcome his tricks and deception. The gospel is greater, and you can win!

One Lady with a Lasting Legacy

Read Acts 9–10

Throughout the Bible, we see how God uses just one person to impact countless people, sometimes even an entire nation. There is no telling what God can do with your life. You are just one person, but in God's hands, the potential of your life is limitless. The legacy of a godly lady is recorded in Acts 9:36–43. Tabitha of Joppa was just one lady, but her legacy made an enormous impact.

As seen in the beginning of the chapter with Saul (later changed to Paul), reputations stick with you wherever you go. In Tabitha's case, she had a godly reputation. She is called as a disciple. Her life went beyond her words and into her lifestyle. She was *"full of good works."* Notice that what she did wasn't detailed, but rather that she did something. Her life wasn't filled with her own selfish desires, but with good deeds. It is also noted that she gave alms, which was giving personally to others, which usually referred to the poor.

Tragedy struck when this godly lady became ill and died. Cancer and disease don't affect bad people more than good, and Tabitha died because of her illness. The people heard that Peter was near and called for him. The people were weeping when he arrived, but God used him to give her life again. Verse 42 states, *"And it was known throughout all Joppa; and many believed in the Lord."*

The whole city was impacted because of Tabitha's story. People were impacted by her life, people mourned her death, and many believed because of her resurrection. Her legacy goes beyond herself because she put herself in God's hands. Much of this story focuses on what God did to her rather than what she did for God.

—— Today's Truth ——

God can stretch the impact of your legacy beyond what you are capable of when you put yourself in His care.

I Am a C-H-R-I-S-T-I-A-N, Amen?!

Read Acts 11–13

IN A CHILDREN'S Sunday school class, I learned the song, "I am a C, I am a C-H, I am a C-H-R-I-S-T-I-A-N. Amen! And I have C-H-R-I-S-T in my H-E-A-R-T, and I will L-I-V-E E-T-E-R-N-A-L-L-Y." Each time we sang it, we went faster and faster each time. Acts 11:26 says, *"And the disciples were called Christians first in Antioch."* This is the first of three mentions of this word Christian in the Bible.

Christian refers to a "little Christ" or someone who was "like Christ." In other words, Christians were those who lived to emulate the works and teachings of Jesus Christ. While many call themselves Christians, few realize that this title is rightfully given to those who mirror what Jesus preached and practiced during His earthly life. You can't call yourself a Christian and live for the world and the devil. The reason this term has lost its meaning is because people call themselves Christians while they drink alcohol, strut around in immodest attire, mark their bodies with tattoos, and outwardly live no different than the world other than their time spent in "worship" for an hour on Sundays.

What is possibly the most important realization here is that these people in the book of Acts didn't call themselves Christians. Their lives so much resembled the life of Christ that others gave them this label. I heard a preacher put it this way: "If you were put on trial for being a Christian, would there be enough evidence to convict you?" If this term is ever going to have meaning again, it will be because believers get serious about their life in Christ and determine to live a life that looks like Jesus.

——Today's Truth ——

We may compare ourselves to others, but our standard is Jesus Christ. He is the goal we must strive to resemble to truly be called a Christian.

Follow Up

Read Acts 14–16

I WOULD SAY that one of the most difficult and frustrating aspects of our outreach is found in what we call "follow up." It is exciting to see people saved, to meet someone while soul winning who wants to attend church, or be told that someone has made a major decision. It should be noted that most of the time, I believe the best person to follow up and stay in contact with that individual is the person who led them to Christ, knocked on their door, or spoke to them about their decision. Paul followed up with the churches he started, and we see the purpose of that at the close of Acts 14. Derbe was the end of Paul's first missionary journey. When he returned, it would have been much easier to travel through his hometown (Tarsus), but following up with these churches was too important for him to neglect.

Confirming (v. 22) — You could say that Paul stopped by just to check up on the people to make sure they were still in church, hadn't quit on God, and were growing. A personal call, text, visit, email, or some form of contact goes a long way. It's important to pray, but we must be making contact in addition to our prayers.

Encouraging (v. 22) — His visit wasn't just to take a head count as he slipped out the back door. He took time to talk with them and encourage them in what they were doing and what they should be doing.

Ordaining (v. 23) — We see the authority that God gave Paul was used to set apart men that were fit for leadership, some as pastors. It has rightly been stated that "every creature needs a preacher." Titus 1:5 clarifies the goal that there are to be *"elders in every city."*

—— Today's Truth ——

After we reach people, we must continue ministering to their spiritual growth. Somebody helped you. Now you must continue the work.

The Work on the Inside

Read Acts 17–19

Although I am not a big fan of wearing jewelry (I take off my ring more than I care to admit), I love watches. If you've ever seen the inside of a watch, some parts in there work behind the scenes to give you the purpose of that watch—which is to tell time, and not to show you your heart is beating or how many steps you've taken. God was doing a work inside Paul's heart throughout his ministry, and while we focus much on what Paul did on the outside, these chapters give insight into what God was doing on the inside of this great missionary.

While Paul waited for Timothy and Silas at Athens, Acts 17:16 says, *"his spirit was **stirred** in him, when he saw the city wholly given to idolatry."* His eye impacted his spirit, and he was moved by what he saw. People often say how they want a burden like other Christians, but Christians are stirred because of what they see.

Acts 18:5 says, *"Paul was **pressed** in the spirit, and testified to the Jews that Jesus was Christ."* This wasn't just a feeling, but an impulse inside of Paul to act upon what God was doing inside of him. This was something he couldn't deny or sit by and watch. He was pressed to action!

Finally, Acts 19:21 says, *"Paul **purposed** in the spirit…to go to Jerusalem."* The work that God was doing behind the curtain of his flesh produced a dedication in his spirit to do what the Holy Spirit led him to do. This decision was made regardless of circumstances or consequences, but sown by the motivation to please God and glorify Him.

Is God doing a work in your spirit? Do you feel Him speak while you sit in church? Do your eyes stir up something inside of you? Before fruit shows on the outside, and even while work is accomplished in the light, God is working behind the scenes inside of you.

—— Today's Truth ——

What the Lord does inside of you will determine what you can do for Him. Allow God to move and mold your heart.

Ready to Die

Read Acts 20–22

Foxe's Book of Martyrs gives this account of the death of the martyr, John Philpot:

In 1555, as part of her campaign to re-establish the Catholic Church in England, Queen Mary, also known as Bloody Mary, arranged for John Philpot, one of the leading Protestant ministers of the day, to be burned at the stake. When his death sentence was pronounced, Philpot said, "I am ready; God grant me strength and a joyful resurrection." Philpot walked to the place of execution on his own, rather than having to be dragged to it, and when he reached it, he knelt and kissed the stake at which he would be burned.

What are you ready to die for? Acts 21:13 says, *"Then Paul answered, What mean ye to weep and to break mine heart? for I am ready not to be bound only, but also to die at Jerusalem for the name of the Lord Jesus."*

Another story from *Foxe's Book of Martyrs* tells us about Nicholas Ridley:

In 1555, Dr. Nicholas Ridley was sentenced to be burned at the stake in England because of his witness for Christ. On the night before Ridley's execution, his brother offered to remain with him in the prison chamber to be of assistance and comfort. Nicholas Ridley declined the offer saying, "I intend (God willing) to go to bed, and sleep as quietly tonight, as ever I did." Because he knew the peace of God, he could rest in the strength of the everlasting arms of his Lord to meet his need.

—— Today's Truth ——

Most will never face the reality of this question, but it's good for you to consider what you are ready to die for as it provides clarity on what you should live for.

A Good Conscience Before God

Read Acts 23–25

PAUL IS ON trial at the close of the book of Acts. This example should challenge you to realize that there is no worldly consequence that should cause you to stray from God's plan. While he was set before the council that was set to accuse him, Acts 23:1 says, *"And Paul, earnestly beholding the council, said, Men and brethren, I have lived in all good conscience before God until this day."* Paul had nothing to be ashamed of and no reason to fear the powerful men before him.

One day in Bible college, I was with a small group of young men who were having a discussion. The question came up, "Can anyone really say that they are *right with God?*" Without hesitation, I said, "No." In my mind, any honest person knows their heart and sinful nature. An upperclassman looked at me and said, "I know I'm *right with God.*" It was evident that he wasn't boasting or being prideful about it, but he truly believed that he was right with God. That conversation has stuck with me throughout the years, and I believe that was similar to Paul's spirit in this situation.

Conscience is defined as "internal or self-knowledge, or judgment of right and wrong…Conscience is called by some writers the moral sense, and considered as an original faculty of our nature" *(Webster's 1828 Dictionary).* The problem doesn't lie with how men perceive your life, but rather how God sees your life. Understanding that God sees all of your deeds, knows all of your thoughts and intentions and past, you must realize that nobody's opinion is greater than how you stand before God.

—— Today's Truth ——

When you have a good conscience before God, you should fear no man. When you have a good conscience before men only, you should fear God.

Shake It Off

Read Acts 26–28

THE FINAL CHAPTER in Acts begins with Paul and his fellow sailors shipwrecked on the island of Malta. This island is eighteen miles long, eight miles wide, and located about sixty miles south of Sicily. Greeted by friendly natives, they made a fire that night. However, Paul did not notice a snake among the branches and was bitten by the snake. The Bible mentions this was a venomous snake, and from the reaction of the spectators, it's obvious the snake should have made him very ill, if not even taken Paul's life. Calmly, Paul shook off the snake into the fire and continued on like nothing had happened. May I say…what a man! This was the ultimate macho move.

This story reminds me of a story that Pastor Stephen Nichols tells of his father. One day they were working in his shop and his father had accidently cut off part of his finger with a saw. He calmly told his son, "Well, you had better go get your mother." That's probably something our modern society would call "toxic masculinity."

Paul had reason to be calm. While they were faced with the storm in chapter 27, Paul testifies in verses 23–24, *"For there stood by me this night the angel of God, whose I am, and whom I serve, Saying, Fear not, Paul; thou must be brought before Caesar: and, lo, God hath given thee all them that sail with thee."* Paul knew this snake was just an obstacle, but he already had a promise from the Lord that he would make it to Caesar in Rome. Paul had a job to do, and he wasn't going to let a silly snake get in the way of his mission.

Every obstacle you face is a temptation to push you off course. Just like Paul shook off the snake, you must shake off any discouragement, opposition, and attacks that come your way lest they result in your defeat.

—— Today's Truth ——

People were amazed at how Paul shook off the snake, and your resilience can likewise be a testimony of your dedication to God's mission.

Without Excuse

Read Romans 1–3

A S A VERY young girl, Helen Keller was stricken by a disease that left her blind and deaf. A lady named Anne Sullivan worked tirelessly and selflessly to help Helen learn to communicate. Eventually, Helen learned to communicate through touch, and she even learned to talk! When Anne Sullivan tried to tell Helen Keller about God, the girl's response was that she already knew about Him, but that she just didn't know His name.

God has revealed Himself to man because He wants man to know Him. Romans 1:20 says, *"For the invisible things of him from the creation of the world are clearly seen, being understood by the things that are made, even his eternal power and Godhead; so that they are without excuse."* There are three primary ways that God has revealed Himself to mankind.

God reveals Himself by Creation (Romans 1:20). The world and the universe around us scream to us of a Creator. It was created by God Almighty.

God reveals Himself through the heart of man (Romans 2:15). All men were born with a knowledge of God in their hearts. They may not know who He is, but they know there is more to life than just what we see.

God reveals Himself through Jesus Christ (John 1:1, 14). God's Son, Jesus Christ, was God in the flesh on this earth. He was the icing on the cake of God's existence and master plan.

God reveals Himself through His Word (Genesis 1:1). The infallibility of Scripture gives weight to the truths about God and who He is. We know what we know about God largely because of what He has given us in His Word.

——Today's Truth ——

God wants man to know Him. He wants you to know Him and no person has an excuse to not know the God of Heaven.

Freedom in Slavery

Read Romans 4–7

I HEARD A story a long time ago about an old woman who was sold as a slave along with many others. Her countenance showed that he had lived a hard life, and the bitterness in her heart was very evident. When she approached the man who purchased her, she said, "I'll never be your slave." The man replied, "I didn't purchase you to be my slave. I purchased you so that you could live freely." Her countenance changed as she looked up and said, "Then I'll be your slave."

Slavery is a touchy subject, but it is also a very misunderstood subject as well. Everybody is a slave to someone. What it means to be a servant is to be a slave.

A slave is not forced to serve, but willingly yields to their master. Romans 6:16 says, *"Know ye not, that to whom ye yield yourselves servants to obey, his servants ye are to whom ye obey…."* As servants of the Lord Jesus, we are to be ready to answer His call and ready to obey His commands. You may think you are independent, but you are a slave to someone in this life.

Becoming a slave to God is not a life of bondage, but a life of freedom. The world views the life of a Christian and sees the rules, regulations, and restrictions. What they don't see is the freedom from the chains and heartache that come with sin. Romans 6:18 says, *"Being then made free from sin, ye became the servants of righteousness."* Slavery is not something to look down upon when it comes to God, but rather a state of mind that must permeate the heart of every child of God. Your purpose is for the Master, and if you don't yield yourself to Him, then you are giving your life to something that can never give you what the Father can give you in return.

—— Today's Truth ——

Are you a slave? The answer is yes. The real question is who you are a slave to and what will you gain as a result of your service to your master.

What We Know

Read Romans 8–10

WITH THE EXCEPTION of John 3:16, we find one of the most well-known and quoted verses in the New Testament in Romans 8:28, which says, *"And we know that all things work together for good to them that love God, to them who are the called according to his purpose."* In a life filled with uncertainty, we can know some things, and this verse, along with many others, gives us assurance of certain truths to which we can hold when facing uncertain times.

God doesn't say that everything in life will be a bed of roses because we're Christians, and any preacher or Christian who tells you otherwise has a shallow or skewed understanding of the Bible. Life can be hard, and often takes us through difficult seasons. The promise God gives is that it will all "work together for good." Baking is a good example. My wife decided to learn how to make the perfect homemade cookie. She had made cookies before, but she set out to find the ultimate recipe (given my hidden addiction to chocolate-chip-filled dough balls of heaven). Her recipe contains basic items like eggs, flour, and baking soda, among others. I would never dump a cup of uncooked flour in my mouth, and unless I'm training to become the next Rocky, I'm not going to crack open an egg into my mouth either. With cookies, the process isn't so grand, but the result is wonderful. This is the promise of Romans 8:28 that many misunderstand.

Another part of this verse that you must understand is that this process of working all things for good is *"to them that love God."* This isn't about loving God just in word, but in works as well. You live for God by proving your love for Him through your actions, and God will have His hand and favor on your life as a result. If you truly love God, there's nothing you won't do or give up for Him.

—— Today's Truth ——

It is "his purpose" that He wants to work for good in your life, and even if you can't see what the Master is doing, you can claim these promises that give confidence to every believer.

The Least You Can Do

Read Romans 11–13

MY DAD TAUGHT me something about work as a child that has stuck with me. He would give me a job, a chore of some sort, and then say, "When I get back, I don't want to tell you to fix something. I just want to be proud of the job that you did." He would also say, "You should be proud of the job you did. If you did your best, you'll be proud of the work you accomplished." Now, I'll be honest, that wasn't always my mentality. Often, I would think, "What is the easiest way that I can get this done with the least amount of time and effort?" The truth is that the easiest way was rarely the best way.

I watched this with his business. It drove me crazy sometimes how long we would be at a job when I went to work with him. My dad liked to work fast, but he was more concerned about doing the job right. If there was a problem, he was going to figure out how to make it work instead of just taking shortcuts and moving on to the next stop, crossing his fingers that it would all work out. As a kid, I just wanted to be done so I could get home and play. I watched all those times that he took the extra time to be proud of his work instead of taking the shortcut.

I say all of that to say this: God has expectations for your life. He lays out His commands and gives direction in Scripture. However, if you want to know what it is that is the very least you can do for God, it is found in Romans 12:1. It says, *"I beseech you therefore, brethren, by the mercies of God, that ye present your bodies a living sacrifice, holy, acceptable unto God, which is your reasonable service."* Most talk about what they're willing to die for, yet God gives us instruction on what we are to live for. A willing and surrendered life that is given to Him is quite literally the least that you can do. It is your "reasonable service."

—— Today's Truth ——

After all that God has done for you, the least you can do is give your life back to Him. In reality, that is where the Christian life truly begins after salvation.

Will You Pray for Me?

Read Romans 14–16

IT GRIEVES ME how many self-proclaimed Christians view church today. Attending church is not considered a command to be obeyed, but a suggestion to be left up to each individual. Those who skip church miss out on something, and one of the blessings of going to church is the support, love, and relationships you build with other Christians.

Not only as a pastor, but also just as another Christian in the church, I've been asked this question in some form, "Will you pray for me?" One of the joys that I have in the body of Christ in which I serve is knowing that if I have a prayer request, people are willing to pray for me and with me. At the close of chapter 15, Paul makes a similar request. Verse 30 says, *"Now I beseech you, brethren, for the Lord Jesus Christ's sake, and for the love of the Spirit, that ye strive together with me in your prayers to God for me."*

Before you give people your list of prayer requests, ask somebody how you can pray for them. I guarantee that your compassion for others can be revealed by how big your prayer list is for people other than yourself. Aside from your family, who do you pray for on a regular basis? Do you pray for the people with whom you serve in choir, nursery, a Sunday school class, or bus route? Do you pray for the elderly, youth, or newcomers in the church? Do you pray for the missionaries your church supports? Do you pray for other Christians outside of your region that God has laid on your heart to commit to pray for regularly? Do you pray for leaders over you in the secular world at work, in government, or people you see regularly?

——Today's Truth ——

Somebody out there needs a prayer warrior praying for them. You may not be able to pray for everybody, but you can pray for somebody.

Signs of the Carnal Christian

Read I Corinthians 1–4

THE FIRST LETTER that Paul wrote to the church at Corinth was a letter of rebuke. Paul didn't beat around the bush. This church needed a wake-up call, and Paul was God's man to give it. Instead of the church having an influence on their city, this church allowed their city to have an influence on the church. Paul addresses many problems in this epistle, but I believe you can sum up the problem with this church to be one of carnality. Carnality is a life driven by the flesh. In chapter 3, Paul hits the nail on the head, and from this, we can learn how to ensure that we are not carnal Christians.

Envying. Though many will say that they wish for the best in the lives of others, there are those that deep down do want good to happen to others, as long as their lives are either just as good or better. You should never root for someone to fail. Likewise, you should never despise someone because of the good they are experiencing.

Strife. When you have a personal agenda and when that agenda is not followed or put at risk, strife is inevitable. The fighting, backbiting, and quarreling that takes place in churches is not what God wants for the church or for the home. Your carnality shows when you allow things to affect your personally and lash out through your flesh.

Divisions. Not everyone in your church may be a best friend to you, but you shouldn't have a clique in the church. Your fellowship should branch out to the youth, the elderly, those that have common interests, and those who are completely different from you. It's okay to have close friends, but we must be very careful not to allow our close relationships to create divisions in the church when we are supposed to be one body, unified under the head, Jesus Christ.

—— Today's Truth ——

A constant battle rages between the carnal flesh and the spirit. We must be careful to not allow our flesh to take over and to purpose to live as a Spirit-filled people.

Eighteen Inches

Read I Corinthians 5–9

IT HAS BEEN said, "Some Christians grow, others just swell." Growth is commanded in the Christian life. It is also a natural process for a spiritual life to grow, just as it is natural for our physical bodies to grow. The problem lies with how this growth process takes place for each person. Paul addresses a common problem with this church, and it is a problem that we still see in our churches today.

When you got saved, you probably had to find the index page in your Bible when the preacher gave the text for his message. The more you read your Bible, went to church, and were around other mature Christians, the more knowledge you gained about the Bible and the Christian life. Here's the problem: some will grow in their knowledge about the Lord, but they will never grow in their love for the Lord. It has been said that some will miss salvation by eighteen inches (the average distance between the head and the heart). The same can be true about the Christian life. Some will learn to say all of the right things, do all the right works, and on the outside, they appear to have it all together. However, on the inside, they are unchanged.

I Corinthians 8:1 ends, *"Knowledge puffeth up, but charity edifieth."* This is not to say that knowledge is bad. The bottom line is this: a tender heart toward the Lord will affect your mind and drive you to learn more and gain knowledge; but knowledge alone will not always drive you to have a heart for God. The heart gives you motive for everything that you know is right. You can know all the Bible stories, but if you do not know God in your heart and develop a love for the information you've retained, you are no better than the Pharisees that Jesus so often rebuked.

——Today's Truth ——

One of the keys to Christian growth is to develop a sincere love for the Lord. Your knowledge will increase, but it should never exceed your heart for God.

Christian Charity

Read I Corinthians 10–13

PAUL PAUSES IN his epistle of rebuke and correction to dedicate an entire section to this church on charity. It's almost as if this chapter was meant for another book and somehow got mixed in the pages of this letter. In chapters 12 and 14, Paul is addressing the church on spiritual gifts. Although the placement and timing of it is an anomaly, it is an emphasis behind the spirit and heart of the Christian life.

Love is a deep word. John 21 is an example of different forms of love as Jesus referred to *agapé* love while Peter understood it as *phileo* love. Charity is a specific type of love. This isn't how you would describe the love between a husband and wife. It is a brotherly love between fellow Christians. It is the type of love that we are to have, not just to a select number in our family, but to all people.

Charity is supreme. Talent and skill will get you only so far. Leaders, co-laborers, and loved ones must understand the absolute necessity to have charity. You can survive with flaws in others areas, but you cannot be a successful Christian in any capacity without understanding the great importance of expressing charity to others.

Charity is spoken. Paul's example is seen by his letter. He loved this church, and because he cared too much to see them fall, he wrote this letter to give them the help they needed. He expresses his heart for this church. It's not enough to simply feel for others; people need to hear it from your tongue as well.

Charity is shown. Paul takes several verses to describe the action of charity. People need to know you care, and the greatest way you can express that is by your actions.

—— Today's Truth ——

It has been said, "People don't care how much you know until they know how much you care." You cannot succeed without having charity.

A Work Worth While

Read I Corinthians 14–16

THOUGH CHAPTER 16 IS the final chapter of the first letter written to the church at Corinth, chapter 15 is the close of the body of Paul's message, with the last chapter giving his farewell and parting words. I Corinthians 15 ends in verse 58 by saying, *"Therefore...."* My pastor always said, "Whenever you see the word *therefore*, you have to see what it's *there for."*

The work of God is not just for a season; it is a way of life. Verse 58 continues, *"Therefore, my beloved brethren, be ye stedfast, unmoveable, always abounding in the work of the Lord...."* After the decision is made to answer the call, follow the instruction, and trust the right path, you will eventually face the temptation to quit. *"Stedfast, unmoveable, always abounding"* speaks of not just the decision you make, but the resolve in your spirit that you make it with. If you've decided to follow God's plan for your life, decide now that you will not quit. Don't wait until the moment of temptation to commit to your path. Decide before the real decision actually comes. Plant your feet. Dig in deep. Resolve to never be moved, whether by yourself or any outside force.

Why must you not quit? The verse ends, *"forasmuch as ye know that your labour is not in vain in the Lord."* I love that song, "It's Not in Vain." Hollywood gives meaningless fruit, sports show nothing for those dedicated to a ball game, and riches can't ever fill the emptiness in a life. God's way is different. His work is a work worthwhile and a life worth living! You may be facing a moment where you question whether or not you're wasting your time living for God, but let me remind you, friend, it's not in vain!

—— Today's Truth ——

You can do no work that will give you the return like serving the Lord with your life. If you commit and stay with it long enough, you will see the fruit from your labor and realize there are no regrets on God's side.

Don't Lose Heart!

Read II Corinthians 1–4

ABRAHAM LINCOLN IS known for many reasons. Many know him by his reputation as "Honest Abe." Another trait about one of the key leaders in our nation's history was his perseverance. His unfailing spirit that would not let him quit led him down a challenging path that made him one of America's most honorable leaders. Here is his record: Failed in business at age 22, ran for Legislature and was defeated at age 23, failed again in business at age 24, elected to the legislature at age 25, his sweetheart died at age 26, had a nervous breakdown at age 27, defeated for speaker at age 29, defeated for elector at age 31, defeated for Congress at age 34, elected to Congress at age 37, defeated for Congress at age 39, defeated for Senate at age 46, defeated for Vice President at age 47, defeated for Senate at age 49, and then was elected to be the sixteenth President of the United States at the age of 51.

II Corinthians 4:16 says, *"For which cause we faint not...."* This phrase means to not lose heart. Some will quit on a business, a personal goal, marriage, or even their faith. An excuse can be, "My heart just isn't in it anymore." Now, this change of heart does not happen overnight. No, it is a gradual decline that has been neglected and left to die.

The truth is that your flesh has its limits. You can only will yourself to do so much. This is where God steps in. Verse 16 concludes, *"but though our outward man perish, yet the inward man is renewed day by day."* Your inward man is what needs daily refreshing. Your quiet time with the Lord is what is going to keep your heart in the things that you can't afford to quit.

—— Today's Truth ——

Quitting may be a temptation, but it is never an option. Renew yourself daily in God's strength so He can give you the heart to continue.

Unequally Yoked

Read II Corinthians 5–8

Contrary to the popular bumper sticker that reads, "Coexist" with its different symbols of various religions, some things just don't mix. Light and darkness cannot exist in the same place. It's either light or dark. The light shines only so far, and then the darkness takes over. Thus, it is true of a Christian living among the lost and even other believers that you wouldn't be able to tell that they're saved anyway because they act just like the world.

The command is clear in verse 17: *"Wherefore come out from among them, and be ye separate, saith the Lord…."* Call it "reaching out," "trying to be a friend," or "keeping the peace," but a saved person has to draw the line with who they fellowship with and what they want to be associated with. The problem lies in the fact that the line often shifts closer to the world and farther from the Lord in areas of question. Instead of taking the high road, we call ourselves tolerant, compassionate, and nonjudgmental for excusing sin, turning a blind eye to wickedness, and jumping in the mud with sinners. Living in the day of social media, you should give more thought to what people see from a picture of you. Call it whatever you want, but you are judged based on who you're with, where you are, and even what you "appear" to be doing.

The end of verse 17 is the key to the doctrine of separation. It says, *"and I will receive you."* God receives you, not for salvation, but with His favor and His fellowship when you choose Him over sin. There is a difference between being a friend to help someone and being close friends with someone while they're involved in a lifestyle that is contrary to Scripture.

—— Today's Truth ——

No one is perfect, but you have to choose who you want to yoke up with and what direction that will take you. When you're yoked together, your journey is set on the same path.

I Get to Do This!

Read II Corinthians 9–13

GOD'S WORD GIVES clear responsibilities that come with the Christian life. Because God has given you life with Him in Heaven for all eternity, He requires you to offer your temporal life as a sacrifice for His glory. You can look at the Bible two ways. You can read the do's and don'ts and say, "I have to do this" or "I get to do this."

My wife and I always have fun buying gifts for each other. It's not a competition, but we always try to outdo each other for birthdays, anniversary, Christmas, etc. Once I know what I want to get her, I can hardly contain myself. I'll say things like, "You're going to love your gift" or "I bet you can't guess what I got you," just to have fun with her. I really do enjoy getting her something that shows her I love her.

Now, imagine that someone gave you a gift for your birthday. Instead of being excited, they give it to you with a shrug as they grudgingly murmured with a sigh, "Here…happy birthday I guess." You can tell by their attitude that they don't really want to give you the gift. Maybe they don't like you. Maybe they felt obligated to get you something, but didn't really want to. Whatever the reason, it doesn't make you feel good about receiving their gift, and you would probably rather just give it back.

God delights in those who give to Him and are excited about the opportunity. II Corinthians 9:7 says, *"for God loveth a cheerful giver."* Yes, it is important to give out of obedience, but somewhere along the way in the Christian life, you should be able to serve God and say to yourself, "I GET TO DO THIS."

—— Today's Truth ——

It makes God happy to know that you are happy to give to Him. Your obedience can be right while your attitude is wrong. God cares about your doing the right thing, but He also cares about your doing it the right way.

A Slippery Slope

Read Galatians 1–3

A TOURIST ATTRACTION in Santa Cruz, California, is called "The Mystery Spot." It is an interesting place to go to, especially for science enthusiasts. Without pictures or illustrations, it's difficult to describe the uniqueness of the place. You'll find demonstrations like rolling a billiard ball on a plank. Normally, when you roll a ball down a hill, it starts out slow and then gains speed along the way. However, in the Mystery Spot, instead of rolling down the plank, the ball rolls up the plank, appearing to defy gravity.

When Paul wrote to the churches in Galatia (the only epistle written to several churches together), he finishes his introduction by saying in verse 6, *"I marvel…."* He was taken back by something about this church. What was it that caused Paul to marvel? Verse 6 continues, *"that ye are so soon removed from him that called you into the grace of Christ unto another gospel."* In Paul's eyes, these Christians had been infiltrated with false doctrine and were drifting from the truth at an alarming rate.

The initial impact that Satan has in a person's life is generally minimal. However, as time passes, people begin to change at a rate that increases rapidly. These people were "so soon removed." I have seen Christians who have "left the faith" who have turned into completely different people in a short amount of time. Satan wants you to gives excuses like, "It's just a small compromise," "It's just a minor sin," or "It's not that big of a deal." After a short amount of time passes, you'll be surprised where that small change will lead you.

—— Today's Truth ——

Cut off any opportunity for Satan to get a hold of your life. Don't allow yourself to start down a path that will change you more quickly than you can ever imagine.

The Law of Sowing and Reaping

Read Galatians 4–6

I SAAC NEWTON'S THIRD law of motion states that for every action in nature there is an equal and opposite reaction. If you
throw a ball up in the air, it will fall back down. Thus, the statement
came about, "what goes up must come down." Some laws in physics
and nature are concrete, though we see some exceptions of the supernatural events that God has allowed and performed. In some facets of
life, however, there are no exceptions to the law.

Galatians 6:6–9 is an example of this with the law of sowing and
reaping. We had a cherry tree on our property when I was growing up.
We would take a big bowl out and pick cherries off the tree, pluck the
stems off, and then rinse them off with water. Then, I'd eat so many my
stomach hurt. You know, I never went out to our cherry tree to find
candy canes growing instead of cherries. I never even saw another fruit
from that tree, like oranges or bananas. Cherry trees produce cherries.
That seed was planted, and that fruit was produced.

All throughout your life, you are planting seeds. Raising your kids
in church is planting seeds in their life to live for God and obey His
Word. Reading the Bible plants the seed of His instruction, wisdom,
and knowledge in your heart. Going soul winning plants seeds in your
life and in the lives of others to further spread the gospel. These seeds
are going to reap the kind of harvest God desires in your life.

On the other side, people plant the wrong seeds. They skip church,
drink their booze, curse God's name, never witness to anyone about
Jesus—they sow seeds to the flesh. The amazing thing about this is that
Christians who sow these kinds of seeds somehow expect God to give
them spiritual and blessed fruit when they're sowing to the flesh and
sin. God doesn't work this way. He never will.

—— Today's Truth ——

*To reap good fruit, you have to sow good seeds. You won't get one
without the other. Do your part, and God will do His. If you sow
the wrong seeds, don't be surprised when you reap the devil's fruit.*

The Branding of the Believer

Read Ephesians 1–3

ONE CHRISTMAS PRESENT stood out to me in my early childhood years, and I still remember to this day when I was given my first full-size basketball. It even had the logo of my favorite team on it (Sacramento Kings). Before long, my mom asked to have the ball. She took a sharpie and wrote my name in big letters so that I would always know that it was my ball. In the same way that a cow is branded with a branding iron, my ball was branded with my name.

Paul uses a similar analogy to branding to describe to the Christians at Ephesus, and to us as well, that Christ brands His children with the Holy Spirit at the moment of salvation. Ephesians 1:13–14 says, *"ye were sealed with the holy Spirit of promise, Which is the earnest of our inheritance...."* That word *earnest* is a powerful word for a believer to understand. This truth impacts the life of every believer in three important ways.

Ownership. In Bible times, different seals were used to signify ownership. Wax and clay were used with a seal by an owner to make it clear who owned an item. In the same way, when you receive the seal of the Holy Spirit, it shows you now belong to God.

Authority. Branding signified not only the owner, but also who was in charge of it. The owner is the boss, and the boss is the authority. Whether you accept this truth or not doesn't change the fact that God is your authority. He is our authority, and He is to be respected and obeyed.

Protection. Ownership also implies protection of what belongs to the owner. You have the blessings and benefits of being in God's protection because you're His. He protects His own, and His protection is the best form of defense you could ever hope to have. He is your rock, your shield, and your safety.

——— Today's Truth ———

This truth of ownership, authority, and protection helps you understand what to live for and listen to because you are branded by God.

Why You Are the Way You Are

Read Ephesians 4–6

NOT EVERYTHING IN life has a purpose. Have you ever pushed the "close door" button on an elevator and waited until the doors finally closed seconds later? I think the designer of the elevator put that button there just to mess with those in a hurry, since you're going to wait for the elevator to close regardless. While there may be things in this world without a clear purpose, you can rest assured that everything God does is on purpose and for a purpose.

Ephesians 4 speaks of the purpose of spiritual gifts. Everyone who is saved has a spiritual gift and maybe more than one. Spiritual gifts are different than talents. They describe who you are and how God has created you. Verse 11 lists a few gifts (see also Romans 12:6–8 and I Corinthians 12:7–11), and then verses 12–16 give the purpose for these gifts.

Spiritual gifts were not given for your benefit, but for you to be a blessing to others and to further the work of God. Many false teachers describe speaking in tongues as a spiritual gift, but no spiritual gift was given for your personal benefit alone. Verse 12 states that they are given *"For the perfecting of the saints, for the work of the ministry, for the edifying of the body of Christ:"*

If you aren't actively involved in your local church, presently helping others and working to further the gospel, then you are wasting your gift. God made you the way that you are so that you could use your gifts for His glory. Many will sit on the sidelines while they are perfectly capable of getting in the game. There is no limit to how many people can serve God. There's always room for more workers, and God has created you for a specific purpose.

—— Today's Truth ——

Your life was given to you on purpose. It is your duty to fulfill that purpose by giving your life to the work of God and exercising the gifts that God has given you.

Think on These Things

Read Philippians 1–4

ONE OF THE greatest battles in the Christian life is the battle that takes place in the mind. Before sin is manifested as an action, it starts with a thought. It is the victorious Christian who realizes they can conquer sin when it is just a thought, and thereby keep it from becoming a sinful action. In Philippians 4:8, God tells us through the apostle Paul to *"think on these things."*

You can control what you think. Your thought life is not a passive portal where thoughts come and go that you cannot control. Thoughts may come that you know you shouldn't think about, and you must purposefully fight to remove those sinful thoughts lest they grow into something bigger than just a bad thought. This battle is won by purposeful thinking.

Proverbs 23:7 states, *"For as he thinketh in his heart, so is he...."* It has been said, "You are not what you think you are, but what you think, you are." Your heart can be revealed by your thought life. God brought a worldwide flood on the earth because of the wickedness of man, but it was also because of their thoughts as well. Genesis 6:5 says, *"And God saw that the wickedness of man was great in the earth, and that every imagination of the thoughts of his heart was only evil continually."*

God sees what you are doing and He also knows what you are thinking. I Peter 1:13 tells us to *"gird up the lions of your mind...."* Take control of your mind and what you allow yourself to think. So much focus is placed on actions, but you must realize that God cares about what He sees on the inside and the outside. What does God see in your mind? Do your thoughts match your actions that you seek to accomplish for the Lord?

——Today's Truth ——

A battle is taking place within. Passive thinking can lead to immoral thoughts, but to actively "think of these things" that are laid out in Scripture is the secret to a victorious, joyful Christian life.

Do Your Part

Read Colossians 1–4

GOD CREATED ORDER in the world so that we can live in harmony. People in positions are not more important than others, but those positions are determined so that order can be achieved. Colossians 3 lists the duties of the roles of those in the home and in the workplace. In every role that you fill, you have a part. Without everyone doing their part, homes go from being a haven to a UFC octagon. What are the roles and how are they fulfilled?

Wives, submit to your husband. You are not God's leader for your home, but your role is still vital. As you submit to your husband, you will show your children firsthand what willing and joyful submission looks like. This doesn't mean you can't have an opinion. It doesn't mean you can't discuss things. It means that the man has the final authority and answers to God for how he directs your home.

Husbands, love your wife. Additionally, *"be not bitter against them"* (Colossians 3:19). Your tone, your spirit, and your demeanor can tear down a woman. Men are rougher around the edges. Women are more delicate. Your wife deserves to be treated with care, not the way you treated your younger brother growing up.

Children, obey your parents. This only direct command to children in the Bible is repeated several times. A child's first responsibility is toward Mom and Dad.

Fathers, don't provoke your children. Gentleness isn't weakness. It is power under control. Your strength can scare off your children if it goes unchecked. They're not your employees. They are children, and they are given to be in your care.

Servants, obey your earthly leaders, knowing that you are serving God by doing so. Submit to your leaders, and do it with a proper spirit and a good work ethic.

—— Today's Truth ——

You have a role to fill. God gives specific instructions for each role that you fill in life. This is your first duty.

A Testiphony or a Testimony?

Read I Thessalonians 1–5

W̲HEN YOU SAY or hear the name of a friend, a famous politician, or a successful business person, a few thoughts that generally pop into your head about that person. This is what we would call a "reputation." Some people would rather not have the reputation they have earned. Others are proud of what they are known for. It has been said, "What you are speaks so loudly that I cannot hear what you say." Actions do, in fact, speak louder than words. Therefore, the question you need to ask yourself is this: Do I have a testimony or a testiphony?

The birth of the church of Thessalonica is recorded in Acts 17. This church was primarily a Gentile church, yet we see Paul commend this body of believers for their godly testimony in the Lord. I Thessalonians 1:6–7 says, *"And ye became followers of us, and of the Lord, having received the word in much affliction, with joy of the Holy Ghost: So that ye were ensamples to all that believe in Macedonia and Achaia."* The word *ensample* means "an example; a pattern; a model for imitation."

What jumps out to me about this compliment to this church is the fact that they were not seasoned Christians. In fact, most of them had been saved only a short time before Paul wrote this letter after he saw them receive Christ. Anyone can have a powerful testimony and can serve as an example to others. People in this world are looking for somebody to follow. They search their social media feeds, notice people they admire at work, and watch others throughout their lives. Without even thinking about it, they think of that person as they try to emulate their example in a specific area. Christ-like believers who are mirroring God's Son need to live as an example to the next generation, to young Christians, to the lost, and to all people.

—— Today's Truth ——

People are watching you and they see your actions more than they hear your words. What kind of testimony are you to the people in your life?

Tradition

Read II Thessalonians 1–3

THE HOLIDAY SEASON is filled with traditions. We have general traditions like exchanging presents, family dinners, and putting up Christmas trees. Every Christmas, your family may have someone read from Luke 2 before opening presents. At Thanksgiving, you may all take time to name something for which you're thankful, though hopefully not while there is hot food on the table.

Traditions can be a two-way street. There can be good tradition, but there can also be bad traditions. An example of a bad tradition would be when tradition is followed above the Bible. Catholics follow tradition heavily, and they follow it to a fault. I've met very few Catholics whose beliefs are actually based on Scripture. Most of them that I've met are Catholics because that's what their parents practiced, rather than because of what they read in the Bible.

Traditions can also be good, and Paul speaks about that in this passage. II Thessalonians 2:15 says, *"Therefore, brethren, stand fast, and hold the traditions which ye have been taught, whether by word, or our epistle."* I'll be the first to admit that we have certain practices in our church because of a tradition. It's not necessarily a Bible doctrine, but something good that was passed down to us.

Traditions are good if they reinforce the doctrines and practices of the Bible. My in-laws passed down the tradition to our family to have an evening "Family Bible Time." My father-in-law wrote a chorus that their family sang every time they began "Bible Time." This is a good tradition for our family, and we have many more like this from our parents and family. Good traditions that strengthen your faith should be kept and preserved. Not only should you keep them, but you should also pass them down.

—— Today's Truth ——

Traditions should never take place of God's Word, but godly traditions must be practiced and passed down to the generations who follow you.

Praying for People

Read I Timothy 1–6

JOHN R. RICE IS known for his statement, "All failures are prayer failures." This statement contains great truth because a great need exists for Christians to become more dedicated to a life given to prayer. I Timothy 2 gives instruction for the prayer life, but more specifically how we can be better prayer warriors for others.

First, Paul notes the *people* for whom we are to pray. I Timothy 2:1–2 tells us that we are to pray *"for all men; For kings, and for all that are in authority."* While this verse is quoted often to remind us to pray for our leaders, it begins by noting that prayer must be made for all people. I'm so grateful for the people in my life who pray for me, and I owe it to others to be that blessing to them as well. Prayer is not about what you do for others, but rather moving the hand of God through your petitions to Him.

Prayer is not pointless. Paul makes it clear that a *product* is attained through praying for others. Verse 2 ends, *"that we may lead a quiet and peaceable life in all godliness and honesty."* This truth makes me believe that we would have much less strife in our churches if we would learn to pray for one another. Prayer gives a deeper burden for people and teaches us to have the heart of God as we think of the needs of others.

Why is praying for people so important? The *passion* behind our prayers is driven from the truth in verse 3, *"For this is good and acceptable in the sight of God our Saviour; Who will have all men to be saved, and to come unto the knowledge of the truth."* It is God's desire to work in the lives of people. When we pray, we are seeking God's working in the lives of others. This is pleasing to Him, and this is the greatest motive behind all our service for Him.

—— Today's Truth ——

People need your prayers, and God is pleased when you direct your prayers to the needs of others.

Preach It, Preacher!

Read II Timothy 1–4

THE LOCAL, NEW Testament church was founded on Bible preaching. The book of Acts mentions preaching thirty-seven times because the church was focused preaching. You can have a church without having a coffee shop, a spectacular Christmas light show, and big potlucks; but you cannot have a church without Bible preaching. In Paul's parting words to Timothy, a young preacher in training, he declares in II Timothy 4:2, *"Preach the word; be instant in season, out of season; reprove, rebuke, exhort with all longsuffering and doctrine."*

Sadly, many are drawn to a preacher's style instead of the substance of what is being preached. The command given is to preach the Word of God. No command is given concerning how long the sermon should be, what music should be sung beforehand, or the colorful lighting on the platform. As long as the Bible is being preached, then people can be helped. It is a shame that we focus more on what leads up to the preaching, what facilities surround the preacher, and all the amenities that go along with the "church experience." I'm not against making the church look first class, but we must be vigilant to give proper emphasis where it is needed.

In my years as a pastor, I've been asked much about our youth program, fellowship events, music, facilities, and other parts of our ministry that I'm very glad we have. However, very few have set their focus on the preaching to determine whether or not our church is the church for them. The modern church has become more of an entertainment business than a place where a man of God lifts his voice and heralds God's Word, regardless of the emotional climate of the crowd.

—— Today's Truth ——

Preaching is paramount for a church to be a church. You need preaching, and you should have a desire to hear God's Word being preached.

DECEMBER 11

What Grace Does

Read Titus 1–3, Philemon

A MOTHER ONCE prayed earnestly for her son to be used of God as a preacher. When the boy was young, however, his mother died. When he grew up, he followed his father's footsteps and joined the Royal Navy. However, he learned he wasn't too fond of the Navy and deserted the ship. He was found, flogged, and discharged. Later, he was in western Africa working for a slave trader who physically abused him. After about a year of this, he was rescued by a sea captain who knew his father. Soon, he became captain of his own ship. One day, he found himself in a brutal storm at sea. The storm was so bad that his crew strapped themselves to the ship so that they wouldn't be thrown overboard.

In the midst of that storm, this captain said, *"I thought I saw the hand of God displayed in our favour. I began to pray: I could not utter the prayer of faith; I could not draw near to a reconciled God, and call him Father...the comfortless principles of infidelity were deeply riveted...The great question now was, how to obtain faith."* This man cried out to God for mercy and received Jesus as his personal Saviour. As an 80-year-old man, looking back on this life-changing moment, he wrote in his diary, "March 21, 1805. Not well able to write. But I endeavor and observe the return of this day with humiliation, prayer, and praise." The man was John Newton who wrote what is possibly the most famous hymn ever written, "Amazing Grace."

Newton experienced what God's grace does to the life of those who receive it as Titus 2:11–14 describes. Grace enables us to be saved and works in us to sanctify; and the final completion of the work of grace is fulfilled with the change that takes place in eternity. Paul rightly stated in I Corinthians 15:10, *"By the grace God, I am what I am...."* Nothing good in your life can come to pass without God's grace.

——— Today's Truth ———

God's grace is given to all, received by some, and continues its purpose in the lives of few. Grace does much for those who receive it.

So Great Salvation

Read Hebrews 1–4

ONLY TWO KINDS of people will be recognized after death. In this life, a number of variables can separate and create distinct differences between people. However, in eternity, there are only one—the difference between saved and lost. Hebrews 2:3 uses the phrase, *"so great salvation."*

As great as salvation is, the opposite is equally true for those who are lost. Voltaire, the noted French infidel and one of the most fertile and talented writers of his time, used his pen to try to retard and demolish Christianity. Of Christ, Voltaire said, "Curse the wretch!" He once boasted, "In twenty years, Christianity will be no more. My single hand shall destroy the edifice it took twelve apostles to rear." Shortly after his death, the very house in which he printed his foul literature became the depot of the Geneva Bible Society. The nurse who attended Voltaire said, "For all the wealth in Europe, I would not see another infidel die." The physician, Trochim, waiting up with Voltaire at his death said that he cried out most desperately: "I am abandoned by God and man! I will give you half of what I am worth if you will give me six months' life. Then I shall go to hell; and you will go with me."

D. L. Moody was on his deathbed when he woke up and said, "Earth recedes. Heaven opens before me. If this is death, it is sweet! There is no valley here. God is calling me, and I must go." His son, who was standing by his bedside, said, "No, no, father, you are dreaming." "No," said Mr. Moody. "I am not dreaming: I have been within the gates: I have seen the children's faces…This is my triumph; this my coronation day! It is glorious!"

—— Today's Truth ——

Many stories like this can be told, and while I don't know what these men or others have seen or felt in those final moments, I do know that after their last breath, there will be either great salvation or great damnation.

Still Got Milk?

Read Hebrews 5–7

OUR SCHOOL COMPETED in a Fine Arts competition at another church each year. We were required to sign up for a certain number of events like basketball, physical fitness, vocal music, instrumental music, academic testing, and much more. I took piano lessons for much of my childhood. Unfortunately, it was never a passion of mine, and since piano is one of those things you can't do halfheartedly to excel, I eventually hit a plateau. I continued playing, but progressed very slowly. One year, I played for this competition. After I finished, one of the judges, a well-respected man I knew of, asked me, "How long have you been playing?" I said something like, "About seven years or so." I'll never forget his response. He said, "You should be better by now." My lack of growth was evident, and I knew it.

Some have been in church for many years, yet know very little about the Bible. They've led few to none to a saving knowledge of Jesus Christ. They've never read through their Bible. They've never developed a consistent prayer life. They should be much more mature than they are in their Christian walk.

Hebrews 5:12 says, *"For when for the time ye ought to be teachers, ye have need that one teach you again which be the first principles of the oracles of God; and are become such as have need of milk, and not of strong meat."* In other words, they should have been teachers by this point, but they were so stagnant in their growth, they still needed to be taught themselves.

Much like how an infant can digest only milk for a time, new Christians also need the basic milk of the Bible. However, eventually that baby will grow and eat whole foods, meats, and finally a wide variety of food. Christians are meant to grow..

——Today's Truth ——

Your journey should be one of growth. If you grow, God will teach you and use you. He will give you more to handle and more to understand.

Is Church Mandatory?

Read Hebrews 8–10

THIS TIME OF year, a Gallup Mental Health Study was done in 2020. After the novel coronavirus pandemic, shutdown of our economy, election circus, murder hornets, and all the other curveballs the year brought, it was found that the ONLY people group in America doing better at the end of the year than the previous year were those who go to church. However, this group wasn't just the casual Christmas and Easter church goers. This was the faithful believers who attended church weekly (https://news.gallup.com/poll/327311/americans-mental-health-ratings-sink-new-low.aspx).

God commands His people to attend church. I can't tell you how many times I've heard statements like "I can have a good relationship with God and not go to church." While that may be the cultural norm, it is certainly not a Biblical statement. Hebrews 10:25 says, *"Not forsaking the assembling of ourselves together, as the manner of some is...."* We are not to forsake the house of God. Your seat should be filled for Sunday school, Sunday morning, Sunday night, and the midweek service. Too many are skipping God's house like they would a second cousin's vegan-themed birthday party instead of making church a priority.

Not only does God command us to attend church, but to increase our opportunities to gather as His church. Verse 25 ends, *"but exhorting one another: and so much the more, as ye see the day approaching."* In many churches, Sunday evening services are a practice of the past. Midweek service has turned into small groups that meet at Starbucks on their own time. While I'm not opposed to a Bible study with a cup of coffee (I've certainly had my share of meetings over coffee), those methods should not be a replacement for church.

—— Today's Truth ——

You need to be in church, and your church needs you, too. It is high time for Christians to be serious about and dedicated to the local assembly of believers for which Christ died.

What's Weighing You Down?

Read Hebrews 11–13

WE HAD A swimming pool in my parent's backyard. Most summer days would include swimming, and we would try to come up with new games that we could play. One day, we had the bright idea to grab some rocks. The game was won by carrying a heavy rock under water. The winner was determined by who could walk the farthest under water while holding the rock until you had to let it sink to the bottom to come up for air. We thought this was great, but my dad wasn't as excited as we were, especially when he found a pile of rocks in the deep end of our pool!

If we were to hold on to that weight in our hands for too long, we would eventually drown. The only way to get the oxygen needed to sustain life, we had to let go of the weight. Hebrews 12:1 says, *"let us lay aside every weight."* To be a follower of Jesus, you have to let go of sin, harmful relationship, ungodly influences, and temptation that can weigh you down.

The battles you face may look different than the battles that others face. Still, everyone has a battle they must face. Satan knows your weaknesses, and he will use your weak points to tempt you so that he can weigh you down. After all, what can you accomplish when you are weighed down by sin? In order for you to move forward for God, you have to decide to lay down the things that are weighing you down. You know what your struggles are, and you must view them as the very thing that can cause you to drown if you continue to play around with sin.

—— Today's Truth ——

Sin has a weight on your usefulness. Sin has a way of removing your influence for God. Set aside the weights in your life so that you can be used for eternity.

Just Do It

Read James 1–4

GARY GILMORE WAS a criminal who had been convicted on two counts of murder in the state of Utah. He became internationally known for requesting capital punishment. He was the first death sentence in America in ten years and chose to be executed by a firing squad. When the armed officers, who stood behind a curtain with their rifles inserted into small holes, asked if Gary Gilmore had any last words, he replied, "Let's do it." This phrase is said to have been the origin for the famous Nike slogan, "Just do it." This campaign began a ten-year period that took Nike from just under a billion dollars in sales to nearly ten billion dollars. Their slogan has such a famed reputation, you probably immediately thought of the shoe company when you read the title of today's devotional.

The book of James was written to believers. It is important to know this because some will use the book of James to refute the fact that salvation is by *"grace through faith"* alone (Ephesians 2:8). However, in James, much is said about how the saved person is to live. James 1:22 admonishes, *"But be ye doers of the word, and not hearers only, deceiving your own selves."* In just 108 verses in the book of James, we find 54 commands. That means those who believe the Christian life is all about only how you feel and not also what you do obviously never opened this book, let alone other parts of the Bible.

So often, we complicate our lives. We look for shortcuts or easier avenues to receives God's blessing without having to put in the work. If you want to lose weight, you have to exercise and eat healthy. If you want to grow a business, you have to put in extra hours. Sometimes, the simplest answer is the just the right answer.

—— Today's Truth ——

If you know what needs to be done, stop looking for a secret method that's going to appear out of thin air. JUST DO IT!

The Fire Test

Read I Peter 1–2

FIRE HAS NO defined shape or substance. You can't taste it or smell it or hear it—though the effects of fire cause both a smell and a sound. You can't weigh it or measure it or examine it with instruments. You can never grasp it in its fullness because it never stands still. Yet the extraordinary power of fire is undeniable. The flickering candle that lights the old woman's way to bed is the same flame that sweeps through miles of forest like a galloping beast. The power of fire is able to devastate and utterly consume.

Though not literal flames, God will often take His children through the fire of hardships and obstacles in life. I Peter 1:7 says, *"That the trial of your faith, being much more precious than of gold that perisheth, though it be tried with fire, might be found unto praise and honour and glory at the appearing of Jesus Christ."* God will put you through the fire for one of two reasons: to teach you so that you may grow or to chastise you so that you will turn. Both are for your benefit. Neither are enjoyable in the middle of it, but if you endure to the end, you will be better for it.

Many of us pray, "God, take me out of this fire in my life" when it may be God's perfect plan to have you right in the middle of the fire you're facing. God may not answer your prayer to take you out of the fire, but He may give you the strength you need to get through the fire. You don't have to be consumed by it.

Fire purifies. When gold is heated, the dross rises and separates from the gold to purify it. Going through the fires of life does the same for the believer who turns to God in the middle of the flames. Your faith is increased, your trust is greater, your relationship is sweeter, sin doesn't look so appealing, and God is bigger to you than He's ever been before.

——Today's Truth ——

Going through the fire test isn't pleasant, but you will be thankful for it if you allow the Lord to work in you the way that He sees fit.

A Roaring Lion

Read I Peter 3–5

FOR EVERYTHING GOOD that God has to offer, Satan has a cheap counterfeit. As you read Isaiah 14, you see that Lucifer's desire was to take God's place. Jesus Christ is pictured as the great lion that came from the tribe of Judah. He is the supreme King of the land. The Bible likewise describes Satan as a lion. I Peter 5:8 says, *"Be sober, be vigilant; because your adversary the devil, as a roaring lion, walketh about, seeking whom he may devour."*

Lions are said to be fourteen to twenty-one times stronger than humans. Your opponent, the devil, is a might foe. One of the greatest mistakes made in sports or a fight is when one opponent underestimates the other. You are foolish to think that you are stronger than Satan on your own. With God by your side, you have no need to fear. However, we are sober and vigilant because our enemy has great force.

At one sitting, lions can consume about thirty percent of their own body weight. Lions don't just kill, they devour their prey. Satan isn't satisfied with one life turning from the Lord, nor is he fulfilled with just a small victory. He is out to kill, to devour, and to feast on all that he can.

Lions do most of their roaring at night. They say you can hear the roar of a lion from about five miles away. Lions do this to instill fear. Fear is one of the most powerful emotions. If you can get people to fear, they will divert from almost all logic or reason to respond to their fear.

I John 4:4 states, *"Ye are of God, little children, and have overcome them: because greater is he that is in you, than he that is in the world."* While you should have a healthy respect for your adversary, you must not fear Satan in any way. He is a defeated foe in the end!

—— Today's Truth ——

Whatever the opposition, Jesus is greater! Open your eyes to the enemy in the world and live in victory under the shadow of the Lord.

Take It to the Bank

Read II Peter 1–3

Rick Ezell wrote the following story in his newsletter *One-Minute Uplift*:

George Tulloch led an expedition to the spot where the *Titanic* sank in 1912. He and his crew recovered numerous artifacts. Before leaving the site, Tulloch's team set out to raise a twenty-ton piece of iron. They were successful in lifting it to the surface, but a storm blew in and the ropes broke, and the Atlantic reclaimed her treasure. Tulloch was forced to retreat and regroup. Before he left, he did something curious. He descended into the deep, and with the robotic arm of his submarine, attached a strip of metal to a section of the hull. On the metal he'd written these words, "I will come back, George Tulloch."

I Peter 3:8 says, *"But, beloved, be not ignorant of this one thing...."* Emphasis is placed on the truth that the Lord is about to state. Verses 8–10 continue, *"that one day is with the Lord as a thousand years, and a thousand years as one day. The Lord is not slack concerning his promise, as some men count slackness; but is longsuffering to us-ward, not willing that any should perish, but that all should come to repentance. But the day of the Lord will come as a thief in the night."* We hear preachers herald with confidence that Jesus is coming again, but this passage states that scoffers will cast doubt, mockers will make fun, and wicked ones will totally oppose the promise of Jesus' return.

The Bible reminds of this truth to give you confidence that you can take it to the bank, ***Jesus is coming again!*** We must not be ignorant of this. We must be watchful. We must have faith that He will come.

——Today's Truth ——

The Bible gives us confidence that what Jesus promised, He will fulfill. The rapture is no different. We must remember and prepare for His return.

Scriptural Fellowship

Read I John 1–3

PEOPLE WERE CREATED to be social. Fellowship is Biblical and practiced by the church in Acts as we see the apostles going from house to house, breaking bread. I worry about Christians who have no desire to spend time with God's people. The people who come to church late and leave as soon as the pastor says "amen" are missing a major benefit of being a part of a church. I also worry about those who have the wrong kind of fellowship in their lives. They allow themselves to be influenced by having a close companionship with someone headed in the wrong direction.

A major factor in friendship is having a common interest. Fellowship is described in I John 1 between Christians and between a believer and the Lord. The first three verses of chapter one make it clear that their common interests weren't related to work, hobbies, or personalities. It was the Lord that brought them together. Saved people should marry saved people, not lost people with the hopes that they'll get saved after marriage. The Lord must be the common factor in your relationships, especially the close ones.

Fellowship is both horizontal as well as vertical. Your relationships with people should draw you closer to God, and your relationship with God should draw you to people. Getting close to God helps you develop the heart of God. It'll create a desire in you to reach those who are lost to help them see their need for a Saviour. It will give you a longing for your closest relationships to be with godly people that sharpen and strengthen you. Fellowship is natural, but it must be nurtured in a way that is working according to God's Word in your horizontal and vertical relationships.

—— Today's Truth ——

It is good to have close fellowship with people in this life, but your most important relationship begins with God. It is this relationship, however, that should guide all fellowship in your life.

Perfect Love

Read I John 4–5

BART STARR WAS a Pro Bowl quarterback for the Green Bay Packers. Starr made a deal with his son, Bart, Jr. Every time Bart, Jr., brought home an "A," Starr gave him a dime. Starr came back from a rough game against St. Louis. He didn't play too well. He was beaten, tired, and discouraged. When he got to his bedroom, he saw two dimes taped to a note that said, "Dear Dad, I thought you played a great game. Love, Bart."

First John speaks about love, but in a special and specific kind of way. Verse 18 says, *"There is no fear in love; but perfect love casteth out fear: because fear hath torment. He that feareth is not made perfect in love."* I like how God puts it: perfect love. Love isn't something you only feel, it is an attribute that you attain. Love is something you put work into. The context of this passage is speaking about standing tall for the Lord and doing it out of a heart of love. When your love is great, fear cannot diminish its power. When you love in a big way, you aren't afraid of being rejected, mocked, or ridiculed.

It is this kind of a love that speaks of the maturity of a Christian. As children grow, they begin by receiving love from their parents. Although they may feel love in their heart as well, they don't reciprocate it much until they're older. As they grow, they give it back more and more. As verse 19 says, *"We love him, because he first loved us."* I know I didn't do much in exchange for the love my parents showed me as child, but as an adult, I've tried to express my love for them for the love that they have given to me. Loving God with a perfect love shows God that you are mature enough to understand what He's given to you and that you appreciate it in a way that drives you to give that love back to Him.

—— Today's Truth ——

Loving God is more than just a feeling. It is shown by your actions as proof of your heart of love. Strive to love God with a perfect love.

What Makes the Difference

Read II John, III John, and Jude

ONE DAY A man was walking along the beach when he noticed a boy picking up something and gently throwing it into the ocean. Approaching the boy, he asked, "What are you doing?" The boy replied as he threw another starfish back into the ocean, "The surf is up, and the tide is going out. If I don't throw them back, they'll die." "Son," the man said, "don't you realize there are miles and miles of beach and hundreds of starfish? You can't really make much of a difference!" After listening politely, the boy bent down, picked up another starfish, and threw it back into the surf. Then, smiling at the man, he said, "I made a difference for that one."

The aspiration of many people is to make a difference in this world with the life they've been given. One person's goal of making a difference by creating a revolutionary invention may be very different than the goal of another who invests in the lives of those in poverty. While God may use you in a different way than someone else, He can use you to make a difference in this world just like He can use anybody else.

When you survey history and read stories of people who made an impact in the world and did it God's way, they possess one common characteristic that was the driving force behind their impact—compassion. It is the reason for your actions that motivate you to go that extra mile, take that extra step, and push that last leg to the finish line. Jude 22 says, *"And of some have compassion, making a difference."*

Compassion should be the motive behind why you serve, tithe, witness, or do anything else for the Lord. Many think of compassion as simply feeling bad for someone. However, compassion is a much deeper character trait. Pity is when you feel bad, but compassion is when your heart moves you to act to make an impact when you see the need.

—— Today's Truth ——

Compassion is the key to making a difference. It is to be the "why" behind your service for the Lord and for people.

The Unveiling

Read Revelation 1–2

CHRISTMAS IS TIME for secrets. My wife and I reach the point each year where we say something like, "Don't look at my phone, my email, or my texts with family members." We don't want to spoil the surprise of each other's gifts, so we try (sometimes not as hard as we should) to keep it a secret. God is letting us in on a secret in the last book of the Bible. Revelation means an "unveiling or revealing" of something.

God's Word is given to us to provide clarity on God's plans for our lives and for the world. Revelation is an often debated book in the Bible. Ten different scholars can have ten different opinions on certain passages. It is often misunderstood, misrepresented, and misinterpreted. However, the book of Revelation is a wonderful book full of exciting truths. Many Christians are intimidated by it, but if it is a part of God's Word, then it was given for you to read and understand, and for your benefit.

What is the purpose of Revelation? Is it to embark on an exciting study of future events that mirror modern day science fiction movies? Is it to give us clues of the coming of Jesus so that we can predict when the rapture will take place? The purpose of the book is found in the first verse, in the first five words. Verse 1 says, *"The Revelation of Jesus Christ...."* God gave us this book to reveal things about the Lord and to draw men to Him. Never forget that the theme of the Bible has always been Jesus Christ. He is presented in many ways in Revelation, but He is the overwhelming theme of this book. That's why it has become a pet peeve of mine to hear people say "Revelations." It is not a plurality of revelations. It is the revealing of Jesus Christ. That is the purpose and what all of the Bible was given to guide us to.

———— Today's Truth ————

Jesus Christ reveals Himself to us by His Word. The last book of the Bible is no different in doing this, but it does so in a special way.

Autopsy of a Dead Church

Read Revelation 3–5

WE HAD TESTIMONY time one night in our church just months before I was to become the pastor. One of our dear ladies said, "When my husband and I moved to the area, we drove by this church all the time. To be honest, I didn't know people attended here. I thought it might have been abandoned." At that time, our church had a pastor who was near the end of his life who subsequently passed away. A retired pastor came to fill the pulpit in hopes that the church could survive. The incredible, faithful people of this church persevered through some trying times. When I became the pastor, that testimony stuck with me. I didn't want anyone to look at our church and wonder if we were in operation. I wanted people to see life, excitement, and the hand of God on our congregation.

When God gave His report on the church at Sardis, it was found to be a dead church. Revelation 3:1 says, *"I know thy works, that thou hast a name that thou livest, and art dead."* They were working, but they were still dead. Activity does not equal life. In other words, people in church can be spiritually dead. People who sing in choir can be spiritually dead. And if the servants of the church are spiritually dead, then the church is dead.

In God's report to each church, He also gives a challenge. Dead churches don't have to remain dead. Dead Christians don't have to stay dead. That which is dead can be brought to life by Jesus Christ. Their challenge was to watch, to work, and to wait. Does your Christian life need some life? Can your church use a Christian like you who has a real fire for the Lord? Our world needs churches that have life in them again. Don't ever let it be said of you that you are a dead Christian.

—— Today's Truth ——

Activity does not equal life. You are not alive because you are working, but because you are working God's way to fulfill His plan.

Who Is Worthy?

Read Revelation 6–8

Revelation 4:1 changes the tone in a way that helps us understand that there is a change in the era. The verse begins, *"After this...."* This is speaking of a time after the church age. This is also referring to a future event. Revelation 4:1 speaks of the rapture and makes it clear that John saw a vision where God's people will be with Christ in eternity. Christians will not endure the tribulation on earth, but will be with the Lord. Revelation 5 continues this heavenly vision, and before moving forward into the more bleak part of this book, we see a powerful passage in Revelation 5.

A scroll is presented. It is believed that this is the title deed to the world. John wept because no man was worthy to open the scroll. It was sealed, but it was out of man's reach. Most of the important things in life are out of man's reach. Try to accomplish it in your own strength, and you'll be sadly disappointed when you're reminded of your limitations.

The Saviour steps forward. He is presented as the Lion of Judah, the Root of David, and the Lamb. They rejoiced because of His redemption, which causes us to see this scroll as a work of redemption.

After Jesus opens the scroll, we see the saint's prayers, singing, and shouting. These things are eternal. Our prayers are not effortless. Singing is not just a temporal practice. Shouting and worship will be given in Heaven, because this is much of what we'll do in Heaven.

The details in this chapter have so much truth, but the focus on this passage reminds us that Jesus is worthy! No man can compare, no method can come close, and no adversary can touch His greatness. What we know now, we will realize in a greater light in eternity. Jesus is worthy of our prayers, our song, our shout, and all the glory that we can give to Him.

——Today's Truth——

In the end, Jesus will be the only one worthy to finish the work, and today He is worthy in your life and in our world as well.

Just Me and You

Read Revelation 9–11

I OFTEN HEAR people say, "It's getting bad." When you watch the news and see the events in America and around the world, the end is undoubtedly near. However, what is happening now is nothing compared to the horrors that will occur during the tribulation. Amidst all of the darkness and judgment that will come, God has His lights. In Revelation 11, God tells us about the two witnesses. They are alone in their work, but they have a great work to accomplish. They will preach for *"a thousand two hundred and threescore days"* (Revelation 11:3), which perfectly equals three and a half years. They will have power to perform miracles and protection against the wicked until their time is complete. Then they will be killed and left in the streets for three and a half days. The nations and people will rejoice, then God will resurrect them.

Application from passages that deal with the tribulation can be challenging, considering that Christians today will not be here during this time. I would have you think of our time. We are not in the tribulation, but there is great and exceeding wickedness in this world. There might not be judgment like there will be during the tribulation, but there is no question that God has judged nations and people in our world today. In the middle of all of this mess is a remnant of people. There are clearly more than two Christians in the world, and there are also clearly more than 144,000 Christians, too. Sometimes, it feels like it's just you and your spouse or friend against the world. Can I encourage you to see that as God gave power to His dynamic duo, God has also given you power to be a witness? You are not exempt from death, but until your determined days on earth are over, days that God has already determined, He will enable you to do a work for Him.

—— Today's Truth ——

Wherever God calls, God will enable. You are never alone if you're in the Lord's work. Numbers have never been on our side, but God is on our side.

The Mark of the Beast

Read Revelation 12–13

CHRISTIANS HAVE GENERALLY always been opposed to marking themselves. In recent years, we are seeing a growing tolerance for Christians to get tattoos—and if the tattoo is a Bible verse, that's even better! However, markings on the body have never been mentioned in a good light in Scripture—from tattoos or cutting to the mark of the beast. Few things have caused so much speculation and fear as this mark mentioned in Revelation 13, given to identify those who oppose God. Everyone alive will have to make a choice. If you want food, you have to get the mark. Christians today need not fear this choice, because we will not be present on earth at this time.

Speculation abounds regarding whether this mark will be a scannable computer chip, some kind of tattoo, a fingerprint or retina scan, a literal number, or something else entirely. Whatever it is, this mark, which is a symbol of idolatry, is received by those who have accepted the deceit of the world. The number 666 reflects this mark. It reflects man's system and falls short of God's perfection. Though the number 7 is seen many times throughout Revelation, man's number speaks of those who will oppose God and fall short of what God can do and give.

Some will reject this mark. Revelation 20:4 says, *"and I saw the souls of them that were beheaded for the witness of Jesus, and for the word of God, and which had not worshipped the beast, neither his image, neither had received his mark upon their foreheads, or in their hands."* A price will be exacted for refusing the mark of the beast. Living for God always has a price. When Jesus said to count the cost (Luke 14:28), He is telling His people that it won't always be easy to be a disciple and follow Christ.

——Today's Truth ——

Satan will use this mark to make a clear distinction between his followers and God's disciples. This is a battle in the future, but we face a similar battle today too.

Time for Harvest

Read Revelation 14–16

SEVERAL AGRICULTURAL ANALOGIES throughout the Bible give us an illustration of truth. John's vision speaks of grain and grapes—a reference to the Feast of Tabernacles. When God's people came together to celebrate His goodness and blessing, there would be grain and grapes. However, before this celebration can take place, the harvest must be taken. This will be the resurrection of tribulation saints.

In Matthew 13:24–30, Jesus gives a similar parable about the wheat and the tares. A *tare* is a bearded darnel. In its beginning stages, wheat and tares are indistinguishable from each other. They seem identical. However, as they grow, their differences begin to show. Wheat grows tall, and the weight of the grain bends the heads of the stalk. Tares grow straight and tall—a picture of humility and pride. Tares are poisonous to wheat. They will destroy the crop. When the harvest time comes, both must be harvested and then separated.

Jesus comes to bring in the harvest, and in doing so, will separate the tares from the wheat, which is the saved from the lost. I have no doubt that people in church will be separated, families will be separated, and those that thought they were saved will be revealed as tares who never received God's gift of salvation by faith alone. Matthew 7:22–23 tells of the surprise of many who are doing the works of the Lord without having their name in the Book of Life. The end will not be a pretty picture. This leads to the bloody event of the Battle of Armageddon. Revelation 14:20 tells us of the amount of blood that will span over 200 miles and fill the valley about 4 feet deep (up to a horse's bridle). This is a horrendous day, but it is a day of justice for those who have rejected Jesus.

—— Today's Truth ——

Jesus will separate the saved and the lost in the end. He will have the final word, and all will be revealed when He returns.

DECEMBER 29

Are You with Him or Against Him?

Read Revelation 17–18

The story of David and Goliath is commonly told among sports enthusiasts and even at other events to picture the ultimate underdog story. We know how the story concluded, but in the middle of the story, I'm sure that even good and faith-filled people wondered if David had lost his mind. David had courage because He had the Lord as his help. Had he not had the help from God to perfectly and precisely guide that stone to strike Goliath in the exact spot that would knock him down, David would have been ridiculed and then quickly killed. It's like the little child that weighs no more than fifty pounds who tries to fight a parent who at least triples their weight class.

The mother harlot, the antichrist, and the nations that rise up together will make war with the Lord in these times. Revelation 17:14 states, *"These shall make war with the Lamb, and the Lamb shall overcome them: for he is Lord of lords, and King of kings: and they that are with him are called, and chosen, and faithful."* They will fight an impossible battle, because they are fighting against the Almighty instead of fighting with Him. The *"called, and chosen, and faithful"* refer to Christians. When Jesus comes to earth, He calls us up to be with Him, but when He returns, He leads us back to reign with Him.

Are you fighting with Him or against Him? With Jesus, you can have great courage. The victory that will surely take place is the victory that God has promised to His people who stay close to Him. Victory is a great part of the Christian life, because the victory is possible because we reign with Jesus. Those who fight against Him are facing certain defeat. There are no exceptions. You can be sure that when you deny His Word and reject His way, destruction will be the result. This chapter speaks of a specific time, battle, and people, but this truth is the same for all generations.

—— Today's Truth ——

You're either with Jesus or fighting against Him. Both sides have a determined fate.

How It Starts Is How It Ends

Read Revelation 19–20

EVERY RACE HAS drama. Most games have drama. It may be short lived, but some of those events have drama that leads right up to the buzzer. I've played in games that felt like they were over after the first point was made. I'll admit I've been on both sides of that feeling. When it comes to the battle between the Lord and those who oppose Him, the fight was already over as soon as it began. There is no drama in this match. No bets should be made, because it's a done deal. The odds are as sure as anything else in the world.

The way that God defeats the enemy shows that God will destroy the world the same way that He started it. Revelation 19:21 says, *"And the remnant were slain with the sword of him that sat upon the horse, which sword proceeded out of his mouth: and all the fowls were filled with their flesh."* It was His Words that created the world, and it will be His Words that will have the final say. You cannot separate Jesus from His Words. The written Word that we hold today is a reflection of the Living Word that rules and reigns for all eternity. There is power in His Word.

This battle will not be drawn out. There will be no swords swinging for hours until fatigue plays a factor; the conclusion will be swift. When the Lord speaks, big things happen. In the Bible that you hold, God's Words hold great power. What He says has the power to create and destroy everything that you know. This power is what has been given into your possession. This is the voice that speaks to you. This is the Words of an Almighty God that has limitless ability.

—— Today's Truth ——

The power of God's Words will be evident in the end times, but that power is also evident in our world today. The Word that created the universe and the Word that will destroy the wicked in the last days is the Word that has been given to you.

I Come Quickly

Read Revelation 21–22

THIS STATEMENT IS repeated three times in the final chapter of Revelation that also concludes the written Word of God: *"I come quickly"* (Revelation 22:7, 12, 20). Jesus emphasizes this statement as His parting words. When someone is on their death bed and you have that final conversation with them, you hang on every word. A man's last words are always very serious and important.

I have thought of this statement many times and considered that the word "quickly" is a bit different to the Lord than my version of the word. When I tell my children to come quickly, I mean to come in a few seconds, not a few thousand years. Understanding a few things about the Lord helps us realize the statement is not invalidated.

God is not restricted by time. Also, His perception of time is very different than ours. It's like looking at a blade of grass from the perspective of an ant as compared to the perspective of a person flying in an airplane 30,000 feet in the sky. The blade of grass is the same, but the perspective is different.

When Jesus made this statement and repeated it for clear emphasis, it was given to create an excitement and urgency. We are to get busy for the work that God has commanded in our lives. If you believe that Jesus will come quickly, your actions will reveal what you believe. On several accounts in the Gospels, Jesus commanded the disciples to "watch." We are all watchmen in a sense. We are to be vigilantly standing on the wall with the spiritual view that God has given by His Word and by His Spirit, doing our part until the King returns. The great preacher F. B. Meyer once asked D. L. Moody, "What is the secret of your success?" Moody replied, "For many years I have never given an address without the consciousness that the Lord may come before I have finished."

—— Today's Truth ——

Jesus is coming back at any moment. This mindset should be the focus of every believer as we wait, watch, and work until He returns.

About the Author

PASTOR STEVEN BECKER IS the pastor of Regency Baptist Church in Loomis, California. He was called to the ministry at the age of sixteen at his home church and went to Golden State Baptist College, which he graduated from in 2013. Pastor Becker has been married to his wife, Alisha, since 2013, and they have four children (Jaxson, Kenlee, Juliet, and Hudson). Much of both of their family has the opportunity to serve together at the same church as they seek to impact the lives of others with the Gospel of Jesus Christ.

If you would like to contact Pastor Becker, you can reach the church office at (916) 652-6279, or you can reach him by email at pastor@rbcloomis.org.